# THE
# WAR STATE

## THE COLD WAR ORIGINS OF THE MILITARY-INDUSTRIAL COMPLEX AND THE POWER ELITE, 1945-1963

## BY MICHAEL SWANSON

Copyright © 2013 Michael Swanson
All rights reserved.

ISBN: 1484080769
ISBN 13: 9781484080764
Library of Congress Control Number: 2013907150
CreateSpace Independent Publishing Platform
North Charleston, South Carolina

"Were the Soviet Union to sink tomorrow under the waters of the ocean, the American military-industrial complex would have to remain, substantially unchanged, until some other adversary could be invented. Anything else would be an unacceptable shock to the American economy." - George Kennan, 1987[1]

---

1    George Kennan, *At Century's Ending: Reflections, 1982-1995* (New York: W.W. Norton & Company, 1996), 118.

# TABLE OF CONTENTS

Introduction ................................................................. i

Part I: The Emergence of the War State ..................... 1

    Chapter I - The Rise of the Military-Industrial
    Complex and the Power Elite ................................. 3

    Chapter II - The Atomic Bomb and
    the Cold War ........................................................... 37

    Chapter III - Capitalism's Invisible
    Army (CIA) and World Order ............................... 93

    Chapter IV - Constitutional Principles
    Displaced by Iron Triangles ................................ 143

Part II: The Permanent Government ...................... 197

    Chapter V - John F. Kennedy Faces the
    Permanent Government ...................................... 199

    Chapter VI - Targeting Everything Red ............. 259

    Chapter VII - Khrushchev, Kennedy,
    and the Killing Machines .................................... 317

Chapter VIII - Conclusion - A Twenty-First
Century Empire of Debt ...................................... 387

About the Author ....................................................... 411

# INTRODUCTION

This is not a book bashing military service. My grandfather fought in World War II as a sergeant under General Patton, and my father, Dennis R. Swanson, also served twenty years in the United States Army. At the start of his career, he interned as a doctor at Walter Reed, taking care of soldiers coming back from Vietnam. Then in the 1980s, toward the end of his career, he reached the rank of colonel and served as head of preventive medicine for the army and as an adviser to the army staff. In his last year in the military, he participated in many briefings with General Maxwell Thurman, who was the vice-chief of staff for the army from 1983 to 1987 and then went on to head the invasion of Panama for President Bush after my father retired.

I remember when I was a kid in 1989 watching my dad celebrate the televised fall of the Berlin Wall as he drank a few glasses of wine. He grew up as a child of the Cold War. As an adult, his whole life in the army was dedicated to opposing the Soviet Union. He worked on contingency plans to defend against Soviet chemical weapons attacks against American soldiers in Europe in case World War III broke out. He gave briefings at the Central Intelligence Agency's headquarters in Langley, Virginia, off the George Washington Memorial Parkway, and had an office in the Pentagon.

When he saw the Berlin Wall fall, he toasted to victory. Books came out saying how we were now approaching the "end of history," because the ideological battle against communism had been decisively won by the West and the United States. My dad knew he was reaching the twilight of his career, and I remember him marveling at the end of the Cold War. He wondered if in some way the US military would be out of a job. Without the Cold War spy conflict, he thought the Central Intelligence Agency no longer served any purpose, and he believed that without the threat of a war with the Soviet superpower, defense spending would shrink and the number of people serving in the military would too.

But none of this happened. Yes, there were force reductions and base closings during the presidency of Bill Clinton, but he did not reduce military spending in any big way. After George W. Bush succeeded him as president, shock from the 9/11 terrorist attacks in 2001 gripped the country and he announced a new "War on Terror" that proclaimed every nation in the world was now to be considered either friend or foe. He declared three of them—Iran, Iraq, and North Korea—part of an "Axis of Evil" even though they had nothing to do with the attacks of 9/11 and little to do with one another.

It was a good-and-evil dynamic similar to that of the Cold War. In the 1950s, during the first decade of the Cold War, Communist spy cells with more fictional substance to them than reality were all the fear of the age. In the years following 9/11, news of the capture of "sleeper cell" terrorists would repeat every few months on the television set, along with new terror alert codes of green, orange, and red; and once the terror danger level went above green, it never went below it again.

Military spending rose to record levels. The United States went to war in Afghanistan and Iraq and engaged in covert wars in the Horn of Africa, engaged in bombing campaigns in Libya, and in drone raids in Pakistan and Yemen. All too often, though, these wars seemed unwinnable or to only result in chaos and confusion in the nations where they took place. It seemed in many ways the United States had reverted to the ways of the Cold War, with big defense spending, bloated fiscal deficits, talk of nuclear attacks, fears of secret cells, and wars that seem to have no end, even though, if you step back and think about it, the number of real terrorists in the world probably only ever numbered one thousand people at the most. Why does the United States have a pattern of fighting so many winless wars?[2]

My dad and many others thought the end of the Cold War would bring a more peaceful world and change the place of the military in American society and in the federal government, but today the defense industry and the national security establishment are more powerful than ever, while the enemies of today are mere mites compared to the old Soviet threat. To really understand how we got to where we are today you must look back to the origins of the Cold War. The 9/11 attacks were not really the turning point people thought they were at the time. It takes some perspective to see this. You see, this is not your typical history book.

---

2   Carl Bialik, "Shadowy Figure: Al Qaeda's Size Is Hard to Figure," *Wall Street Journal*, September 9, 2011, accessed September, 12, 2012, http://online.wsj.com/article/SB10001424053111903285704576560593124523206.html.

What is this book about? If you consider the word history you will notice that the word story makes up half of it. Most historical works you pick up are narratives with a point to them. They may tell you the story of heroes of the past—presidents, soldiers, activists, or regular people—and the events that they were caught up in to give you a new respect for the people of history or to inspire you to believe in a certain way. This book is a little different. What I want you to do is to take a journey with me into the past to try to understand the forces behind events that still move headlines today. We are going to dig deep together and ask what is really behind the presidential decisions of war and peace?

History can tell us. This book focuses on the emergence of the United States as a global superpower after World War II and its Cold War with the Soviet Union. It looks at events familiar and unfamiliar to students of the era and looks deep into the complex political realities that drove them. It seeks to discover how the new post-World War II role of global supremacy changed the United States into a permanent big-government war state and to reveal the often hidden domestic power struggles at the top that took place inside the country as a result and have even put American democracy in peril.

This is a book ultimately about deep power and the processes of power often obscured behind the surface stories of history. To see this, one must look beyond single events and connect them together to understand the patterns of thought and action behind them. For example, in a typical history of war or foreign policy, one often thinks of countries as two forces against one another, such as the Axis versus the Allies during World War II or the free world, led by the United States, versus the Soviet Union and its satellite states behind the Iron Curtain during the Cold War. But to look at the real workings of power means looking beyond the external politics between nations and into the internal politics and bureaucratic infighting that often really drives a nation's foreign policy.

Looking deep into real history can be tough to do. One problem is what leaders say they are doing and what they are really doing are often two different things. As a result, to look deep at power can lead to shaking your own faith in one's leaders, something that can be too difficult for some to contemplate. It can also mean arguing against vested interests who seek to maintain their power by being as secretive as possible.

World War II was a turning point in the history of the United States as it came out of the war as the world's strongest power. We will examine how its new position in the world impacted its domestic politics and economy. We will look at the rise of the military-industrial complex and the national security state and how they transformed the federal government into a war state. We'll see how contemporaries tried to understand the huge shifts in power that were taking place inside the United States at the time and witness presidents try to deal with the new bureaucracies created as a result of the Cold War and the growth of the federal government and how they were often co-opted by them and at times tried to fight them.

You and I know that the president of the United States is the world's most visibly powerful person. But the president is not simply a free agent who can do anything he wants. Since the start of the Cold War, each successive president has inherited a far-flung military empire with bases all over the world and a national security state divided into various factions, each with its own different interests and competing priorities. The government the president oversees is not simply one big federal machine that bends to his will, but a complex organization made up of parts that often have minds of their own.

As chief executive of the United States, the president is in charge of a national security state made up of the Central Intelligence Agency, the State Department, and the military, itself divided into the army, the navy, the air force, and the marines. Each branch of the military has its own budget and is led by officers who have their own unique visions of what they think should be the nation's priorities for defending the country. These priorities are often at odds with what people in the State Department or intelligence agencies think, because all of them often have their own different vantage points from where they sit in the government. As a result, each time a president has had to make a national security decision, he often has received conflicting advice from the people who staffed each of the various security bureaucracies below him. Only the president and his immediate advisers have been in the position to make overall strategic decisions for the whole.

It is the nature of the bureaucracies that make up a larger organization to look after their own interests and exhibit rigid thinking. Every bureaucracy, no matter how large or small, is formed to serve a higher purpose, but almost all end up serving their own concerns above everything else. History proves that the people at the head of bureaucracies often come to confuse the narrow interests of their own group with those of the entire nation. They often believe that their role is the most important one that serves the good of everyone, when that is rarely the case.

Government bureaucracies are even more rigid and slow to adapt to change than a bureaucracy that is a division of a large private corporation is, because they are subject to severe budgetary constraints. A corporation's purpose is to increase profits, so if a corporate division is successful in helping to achieve this goal, it usually will have the benefit of an expanding budget, which it can use for new purposes. Government bureaucracies do not have the ability to grow their budget on their own, so they are dependent upon the president and Congress for their funds. If some big change in policy occurs, they may lose money while others gain at their expense.

As a result, government bureaucracies tend to simply do more of the same. Their own internal policies become rigid, doctrinaire, and self-perpetuating. In the national security state, only the president and his advisers have the ability to pronounce grand strategies and new policies that impact the whole, but such changes and even the threat of them can cause bureaucratic infighting and a need for each bureaucracy to impress upon the rest of the government, and sometimes even the public, its own unique importance.

All of this is critical to understanding how presidential power works, but it is rarely thought about in most works of presidential history, much less studies of foreign policy dominated by an us-versus-them dynamic.

In the United States, the president is in a unique position different than anyone else in the government. Elected by all of the people, his job is to represent the entire country even though not everyone voted for him.

The president acts as the figurehead of a national community and embodies the national will. While he is elected by a coalition of interests and groups, he has the ability to reach beyond them to build his own personal national constituency that does not necessarily share the interests of the groups that primarily got him into office. The best of presidents stir up various national interests in order to create their own personal national coalition and with its support announces new visions for the nation that successfully become new policies even on a global scale. They do it through ideology, the mantel of patriotism, and a charismatic relationship between themselves and the masses. They announce their own big initiatives, instead of speaking from scripts handed to them by others. Presidents who fail to do this fall captive to the mercy of special interests. Once this happens, his office then acts as if it is an appendage of the state bureaucracy, and to the nation as a whole he seems devoid of leadership abilities and his speeches turn into stale rhetoric.[3]

Since World War II, Presidents Ford, Carter, and Obama serve as the best examples of presidents who failed to battle against the interests, while Franklin Roosevelt and Richard Nixon are probably the only presidents who successfully fought in the realm of both domestic and foreign policy on their own terms in the last one hundred years. Reagan fought on the domestic front against Congress and the unions, but in the area of foreign policy, most of his initiatives in the first half of his presidency actually originated in the national security bureaucracies during the time of Ford and Carter, but then in the second half of his presidency, he changed course; while both of the Bushes virtually ignored domestic policy and focused solely on foreign policy, with only the latter Bush making decisions that required fighting against parts of the federal government—in his case career officers inside the Central Intelligence Agency and the State Department who were less than enthusiastic about his decision to conquer Iraq. Except for prosecuting gangsters, President Kennedy made no new grand

---

[3] Franz Schurmann, *The Logic of World Power* (New York: Pantheon Books, 1974), 17-30; Bruce Cumings, *The Origins of the Korean War, Volume II* (New Jersey: Princeton University Press, 1990), 20-23.

domestic policies of his own, but he fought against several of the national security bureaucracies until they devoured his plans after he died.

But what exactly is deep power that can go beyond the power of the president and Congress and isn't publicly visible in normal news accounts and books of history? What is the type of power that can put American democracy in peril? To answer that, you will have to turn the page and take a journey into this book.

# PART I:
# THE EMERGENCE OF THE WAR STATE

## PRESIDENT EISENHOWER'S DRAFT OF HIS FAREWELL ADDRESS

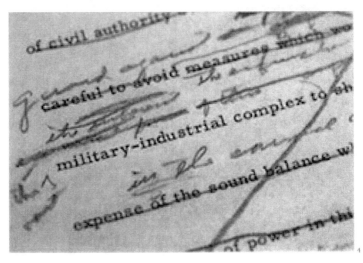

# CHAPTER I
# THE RISE OF THE MILITARY-INDUSTRIAL COMPLEX AND THE POWER ELITE

October 28, 1962 was the most dangerous day in the history of the world. If that day had ended differently, neither you nor I would be alive today. Do you know why? That date marked the high point of the Cuban Missile Crisis. Two weeks prior to that day, American U-2 spy planes discovered that Soviet Premier Nikita Khrushchev had secretly placed nuclear missiles in Cuba. The Soviet Union had fallen behind in the nuclear arms race, because at the time the Russians had only a few missiles powerful enough to reach the United States while America could strike the entire Soviet Union.

Khrushchev placed intermediate-range missiles in Cuba capable of destroying New York and Washington,

DC, in order to achieve strategic parity with the United States and discourage it from invading Cuba, which it attempted to do in the ill-fated Bay of Pigs invasion right after Kennedy got in office. After President Kennedy discovered what Khrushchev had done, he formed a group of twelve of his most important advisers to handle the crisis. The group, which he called EXCOMM, was made up of the Joint Chiefs of Staff, Secretary of Defense Robert McNamara, Central Intelligence Agency director John McCone, a few career diplomats, and his brother, Attorney General Robert Kennedy.

Almost all of his advisers advocated military action against Cuba, with the Joint Chiefs of Staff first recommending a full-scale invasion of the island as the only solution. After a long EXCOMM debate over the options, President Kennedy decided to blockade and quarantine Cuba in the hopes of pressuring Khrushchev into removing the missiles, and he announced his decision in a televised address to the world on October 22, 1962.

The Soviet Union had troops in Cuba defending the nuclear missile installations. As the crisis deepened, the Joint Chiefs of Staff placed American forces at the highest state of war readiness during the entire Cold War—DEFCON 2(with DEFCON 5 signaling peace and DEFCON 1 full-out nuclear war). B-52 bombers with cargos of hydrogen bombs were dispersed throughout the United States, ready to take off on fifteen minutes notice, while dozens of B-52s were sent to orbit points within attack distance of the Soviet Union. One-eighth of the air force's Strategic Air Command bombers were on airborne alert and some 145 intercontinental ballistic missiles sat on launch alert.

On October 27, Kennedy received news that a US U-2 spy plane had been shot down over Cuba. It had been US military policy to retaliate on installations that shot at its airplanes, and Kennedy came under pressure from his advisers to attack Cuba if another American plane or ship came under fire again. In the meantime, unknown to most of his advisers, Kennedy had been engaging in secret back-channel discussions with Khrushchev to resolve the crisis. But another spark could ignite a nuclear tinderbox.

The next day, Khrushchev woke up to a plethora of momentous news. He received a panic-stricken cable from Fidel Castro, the ruler of Cuba, saying that he expected the United States to start war and asking him to simply beat it to the punch, seemingly hinting that the Soviet Union should go ahead and launch a nuclear strike while it still could. Then he heard about the U-2 shooting and that Robert Kennedy had met with the Soviet ambassador to the United States, Anatoly

Dobrynin, in what seemed to be the last chance of diplomacy.

The ambassador informed Khrushchev that Robert Kennedy seemed "extremely agitated, the first time I had ever seen him in such a condition." The Kennedy brothers offered to remove nuclear missiles the United States had in Turkey and pledge not to invade Cuba if the Soviet Union would withdraw its missiles from the island. Robert Kennedy said he needed an answer within the next forty-eight hours.

Ambassador Dobrynin said that Kennedy told him "time was running out" and that he warned there were "hotheads among the generals, and in other places as well, who were spoiling for a fight." Khrushchev later recalled that Robert Kennedy had warned that "if this situation continues much longer, the President is not sure that the military will not overthrow him and seize power."

Khrushchev convened a meeting of the top Soviet leaders immediately. The atmosphere was tense, desperate, and in the words of one participant "highly electric." They debated whether they should allow the Soviet commander in Cuba to launch the nuclear weapons on his own initiative if he was attacked. Then the group read the report of Robert Kennedy's meeting with the ambassador and agreed to remove the missiles from the island nation. As one person recalled, "the entire tenor" of Robert Kennedy's words made it clear that "the time of reckoning had arrived" after which "it didn't take long to decide to accept President Kennedy's conditions."

With that, the Cuban Missile Crisis ended, but it could have easily gone the other way. If President Kennedy had blindly accepted the arguments of his generals and almost all of his other advisers, we probably would not be alive today. Another president may have done differently. At the time, it seemed to be a mystery why Khrushchev backed off, but we now know that he believed that if the crisis continued, war would have come, either under the command of Kennedy or after his overthrow by the military. That is what made him blink.[5]

Would the military really go so far as to overthrow a president of the United States? On the surface, that seems like a far-fetched notion, but you have to remember this was the height of the Cold War. In 1962 a best-selling book came out titled *Seven Days in May* that postulated just such a scenario. Kennedy read it,

---

5   William Taubman, *Khruschchev: The Man and His Era* (New York: W.W. Norton and Company, 2003), 573-575; Aleksandr Fursenko and Timothy Naftali, *"One Hell of a Gamble": Khruschchev, Castro, and Kennedy, 1958*-1963 (New York: W.W. Norton and Company, 1997), 280-285; *Michael Beschloss, The Crisis Years* (New York: Edward Burlingame Books, 1991), 530-540.

and when asked if it could happen, he replied, "It's possible, but the conditions would have to be just right. If the country had a young President, and he had a Bay of Pigs, there would be a certain uneasiness. Maybe the military would do a little criticizing behind his back. Then if there were another Bay of Pigs, the reaction of the country would be, 'Is he too young and inexperienced?' The military would almost feel that it was their patriotic obligation to stand ready to preserve the integrity of the nation and only God knows just what segment of Democracy they would be defending. Then if there were a third Bay of Pigs it could happen. It won't happen on my watch."[6]

Several members of the Joint Chiefs of Staff thought that Kennedy actually dropped the ball on the Cuban Missile Crisis. According to Daniel Ellsberg, who served in a working staff for the EXCOMM group under Secretary of Defense Robert McNamara, "after Khrushchev had agreed to remove the missiles, President Kennedy invited the Chiefs to the White House so that he could thank them for their support during the crisis, and there was one hell of a scene. LeMay (chief of staff of the air force) came out saying,

---

[6] Richard Reeves, *President Kennedy: Profile of Power* (New York: Simon & Schuster, 1993), 305-306.

'We lost! We ought to just go in there today and knock 'em off!'"[7]

John Frankenheimer adapted a Rod Serling, of *Twilight Zone* fame, script for *Seven Days of May* into a movie production. Kirk Douglas and Burt Lancaster played the leading roles. The military brass did not want the picture made and wouldn't allow the movie crew to go inside the Pentagon, but Kennedy was personally thrilled with the idea and left Washington one weekend for his home in Hyannis Port so that they could film in the White House. The movie ends with a speech by the president giving a defense of the US Constitution that today sounds overly sentimental, because most people do not have the faith and trust in the government that they did back then.

Of course the most famous warning about the power of the military came from Dwight D. Eisenhower, who commanded the Allied forces in Europe during World War II and went on to serve as president of the United States from 1953 to 1961. On his last day in office, he gave a televised farewell address to the nation in which he noted that "our military organization today bears little relation to that known of any of my predecessors in peacetime, or indeed, by the fighting men of World War II or Korea."

---

[7] Richard Rhodes, *Dark Sun: The Making of the Hydrogen Bomb* (New York: Simon & Schuster, 1995), 575.

He said, "Until the latest of our world conflicts, the United States had no armaments industry. American makers of plowshares could, with time and as required, make swords as well. But we can no longer risk emergency improvisation of national defense. We have been compelled to create a permanent armaments industry of vast proportions. Added to this, three and a half million men and women are directly engaged in the defense establishment. We annually spend on military security alone more than the net income of all United States corporations."

"Now this conjunction of an immense military establishment," Eisenhower continued, "and a large arms industry is new in the American experience. The total influence—economic, political, even spiritual—is felt in every city, every statehouse, every office of the federal government. We recognize the imperative need for this development. Yet, we must not fail to comprehend its grave implications. Our toil, resources, and livelihood are all involved."

"In the councils of government," the president warned," we must guard against the acquisition of unwarranted influence, whether sought or unsought, by the military-industrial complex. The potential for the disastrous rise of misplaced power exists and will persist. We must never let the weight of this combination endanger our liberties or democratic processes."[8]

What provoked President Eisenhower to issue this stern warning to the nation? Most historians even find the speech to be mysterious. We will look at this later in this book so you'll know the full story that only a few now know. First, though, we need to ask ourselves: What did Ike exactly mean by a "military-industrial complex?" He was the first person to ever use this term and it has stuck in the national consciousness ever since.

A key component of his speech is the word "new." Today we don't even think much about the fact that the United States has the most powerful military in the world, with bases spread across the planet and a large portion of its federal budget devoted to military spending. In 2010, at $687 billion, military spending made up 4.9 percent of the GDP of the United States. In comparison, Russia spent just over fifty billion dollars. But it's bigger than that. You see, the US military budget accounts for approximately 40 percent of total global arms spending and is over six times larger than the military budget of China, and is greater than the next twenty largest military spenders combined. Today

---

8   James Ledbetter, *Unwarranted Influence: Dwight D. Eisenhower and the Military-Industrial Complex* (New Haven: Yale University Press, 2011), 211-220.

over one million Americans serve in the armed forces. Perhaps these figures do not surprise you, because if you are like most readers of this book, huge military spending for the United States has always been a fact of life since the day you were born. That's why most don't even give it a second thought.

But this was not the case for President Eisenhower and the people of his generation. Before World War II, the United States never had a permanent arms industry. Yes, it fought big wars. The country came together out of the American Revolutionary War against England. It fought England again in the war of 1812. It mobilized the people and resources of the entire country to fight against itself in the Civil War. At the turn of the nineteenth century, it fought against Spain in the Spanish-American War, which led to over 120,000 American troops fighting in the Philippines. Then during World War I the United States sent over one million troops to Europe.

War has always been a part of the history of the United States and these are only a few of the wars that the nation became involved in before World War II. But after major wars, the country always demobilized its forces. That is, until World War II. To give you an idea of what peacetime was like in the United States, in the 1930s, before the start of World War II, the entire US Army consisted of only 140,000 soldiers. In 1934 the military budget for the war department was only $243 million and the whole army owned only eighty semiautomatic rifles, with most soldiers using out-of-date 1903 bolt-action Springfield rifles. Supplies were so low that in 1935 the army chief of staff, General Douglas MacArthur, set a "hopeful" goal of stockpiling enough ordnance for a thirty-day supply of ammunition. In 1940 the military had only eighty tanks and forty-nine bombers.[9]

By the end of the war, the United States produced over eighty-eight thousand tanks and self-propelled guns, 257,000 artillery pieces, two million machine guns, ninety-seven thousand bombers, ninety-nine thousand fighter aircraft, twenty-two aircraft carriers, eight battleships, and over four hundred destroyers and cruisers. The enormous war production created an economic boom for the United States that took the unemployment rate down from 14.6 percent in 1940 to 1.2 percent in 1944. At the end of the war, the United States had spent over $840 billion dollars in constant 1940 dollars or $13.59 trillion in inflation-adjusted 2012 dollars. Defense spending also reached 36 percent of GDP and 86 percent of all federal government spending by 1944. The huge military spending created a whole new class of corporate business

---

9   Burton Folsom Jr. and Anita Folsom, *FDR Goes to War* (New York: Threshold Editions, 2011), 10-12, 55, 68.

elite tied to the defense industry and dependent on government outlays.[10]

Have you ever heard the phrase "nothing is certain in life but death and taxes?" I suppose you can add military spending to the list too. But the funny thing is that just like military spending, taxes as you and I know them today really did not exist before World War II either. The Internal Revenue Service was not a part of most people's lives before the war.

You see, before the war only the wealthiest of Americans and corporations paid a dime of income tax. Between World War I and World War II the number of households paying income tax in any given year ranged from 1.25 to 2.5 percent. In 1939, 93 percent of the labor force paid no federal income tax at all. World War I was financed mostly through the sale of "war bonds" to the public. But World War II turned out to be ten times as expensive as its predecessor.

So the federal government needed more money to finance it and turned taxation from an affair for only

---

10   Robert Higgs, *Depression, War, and Cold War* (Oakland: The Independent Institute, 2006), 80-81; Mark Harrison, *The Economics of World War II: Six Great Powers in International Comparison* (Cambridge University Press); Alan Milward, *War, Economy, and Society, 1939-1945* (New York: Peter Smith Publishing, 1983); *Budget of the United States Government 2005*, accessed September 12, 2012, http://www.gpo.gov/fdsys/browse/collectionGPO.action?collectionCode=BUDGET.

the most wealthy to one that impacted everyone. By 1943 the government started to deduct money out of people's pay checks as practically everyone began to pay income taxes. In the last year of the war, personal income tax receipts surpassed corporate income tax as the largest source of revenue for the federal government for the first time. The size and power of the government grew as its revenue growth exploded by a factor of 8.8 from 1939 to 1945.

During the course of the next two decades, income taxes would come to gobble up 8 to 9 percent of personal income and take 10 to 11 percent of the nation's GNP. World War II marked the beginning of "big government." The saying "death and taxes" meant nothing to most people before the war, but today everyone instantly recognizes the phrase even though few realize when it started. The federal government gave birth to large military budgets and mass income taxes at the same time and both live on together today as twin siblings of the war state. Does this big-money spending lead to corruption?[11]

Well, World War II also brought a major change in the way military spending is allocated that remains to this day too. Before the war, President Roosevelt often

---

11   James Sparrow, *Warfare State: World War II Americans and the Age of Big Government* (New York: Oxford University Press, 2011), 122-159.

attacked businessmen when he gave speeches and addresses during the Great Depression. Once he needed businesses to produce for the war effort, though, he changed course from Dr. New Deal to Mr. Win the War and began alliances with favored corporations. Henry Stimson, who graduated from Yale as part of the elite blue-blood Skull and Bones fraternity and worked in the prestigious Wall Street firm Root and Clark before serving as secretary of war under president William Taft, and as secretary of state under president Herbert Hoover, explained, "If you are going to try to go to war, or prepare for war, in a capitalist country, you have to go let business make money out of the process or business won't work."

So to placate big business Roosevelt appointed ten thousand business executives to staff positions throughout various federal war agencies, many of which he created out of executive fiat. Some of his most important positions were Henry Stimson as secretary of war and Frank Knox, who had run against him in the presidential race of 1936 as the Republican Party's vice presidential candidate, for secretary of the navy. Below him, he then got James Forrestal, who had served as a Wall Street investment banker, to accept the position of undersecretary of the navy.[12]

---

12   Higgs, 23.

In January of 1942 FDR created the War Production Board to direct the economy for the rest of the war. The board had the power not only to decide on the allocation of war contracts but also to prohibit production that it deemed unessential to the war effort. It immediately issued decrees halting construction for various projects it decided weren't necessary and rationed gasoline, heating oil, metals, rubber, and plastic, thereby having an impact on the daily lives of every single American. It even regulated the amount of fabric that could be used to make clothes, one effect of this being that women's skirts had to be made shorter.

The president appointed Donald Nelson, vice-president of Sears, Roebuck & Co. to chair the board. Also serving on the board was Charles Wilson, president of General Electric, and T.S. Fitch, who was the CEO of the Washington Steel Corporation. Huge war contracts inevitably went to companies that the members of the war board had relationships with. "This defense program is big business," Charles Wilson declared, "we might just as well make up our minds to that. It is big business and it isn't going to be handled by thousands of small businesses alone. Small plants can't make tanks, airplanes, or other large complex armaments."[13]

---

13   Higgs, 64; Folsom, 121.

This wasn't entirely true, you see though, because before the war started there weren't a bunch of large plants owned by big companies just sitting around and waiting for orders. Big war production was a new thing and the federal government itself often paid for and built the factories used in the defense industry and then gave them to the companies for free once the war ended. Of the twenty-six billion dollars spent during the war to build plants, seventeen billion was financed by the government. Taxpayer money financed the growth of the private defense industry.

The government had always rewarded money to defense companies. What was really new, though, was that before World War II, the government accepted contracts from all companies and almost always gave them to the lowest bidder. Once the War Production Board was formed, within a few months 74 percent of the contracts were simply rewarded after negotiations and not through competitive bidding. Procurement officers started to award contracts based on a firm's ability to deliver the goods quickly and their research and development facilities, which made it so that the largest contractors rarely had to worry about submitting low bids to get the orders.

This meant cost-plus-fixed-fee contracts, which were contracts in which the government guaranteed to pay for the costs of fulfillment and then promised a fixed profit, usually around 9 or 10 percent above costs. But these contracts were created ahead of time and often the real costs turned out to be much lower than what was estimated, and if the costs were higher, then the government still would ensure a profit. Defense contracts are still made this way today. Yes, this all too often leads to corruption.

According to Harry Truman, who chaired the Senate Special Committee to Investigate the National Defense Program from 1941-1944, this meant that contracts were "offered by the government in much the same way Santa Clause passes out gifts at a church Christmas party...the fees allowed to contractors by the government sometimes made it possible for them to earn, on a three-month job at government risk, three or four times as much as they had formerly been able to make at their own risk in an entire year of work."

When it came to defense contracts, this system favored the largest and most politically connected corporations. By 1941 three-fourths of defense spending went to only fifty-six companies, and six companies had a third of the contracts, with Bethlehem Steel, General Motors, and Du Pont leading the way. Today even fewer companies dominate the defense industry thanks to corporate takeovers and consolidations that have taken place over the decades.

This combination of military contractors and decision makers at the top of the armed forces, the White House, and the Congress, which decides on where the money goes, make up what Eisenhower called the "military-industrial complex." This has created a unique and enormous area of the economy of the United States that does not operate like the rest of it. In a capitalist system the businessperson takes risks in starting a business, in producing goods, and in marketing and selling products and services to customers. If entrepreneurs make mistakes or misjudge opportunities, they can go out of business. No one guarantees them a profit.

However, the defense industry operates under a completely different set of rules with no-bid and cost-plus-fees contracts that guarantee military contractors a profit practically no matter what happens. All of a contractor's working capital is provided for by the federal government and payments are often made well in advance of final production. This makes for a form of corporate socialism in which all risks are placed on the shoulders of taxpayers while profits are given to privately owned and well-connected corporations.

According to the US Army's official history of the defense industry during World War II, "the relationship between the government and its contractors was gradually transformed from an 'arms length' relationship between two more or less equal parties in a business transaction into an undefined but intimate relationship—partly business, partly fiduciary, and partly unilateral—in which the financial, contractual, statutory, and other instruments and assumptions of economic activity were reshaped to meet the ultimate requirements of victory in war."[14]

Of course, this has led to scandals. In the 1980s, for example, Lockheed-Martin was caught selling $600 toilet seats and $7,662 coffeemakers to the air force. If that wasn't enough, they then sold mechanical aircraft clocks for $591 and cowling doors for $166,000 per unit. At the same time, the Gould Corporation was exposed for selling simple claw hammers to the navy at $435 a pop.[15]

Of course, the benefit went both ways. Some politicians with intimate connections to defense contractors rose in influence as the latter's profits swelled. For instance, Lyndon Johnson served as a congressman in Texas during World War II. He worked to steer defense funds to the construction company Brown & Root, which helped him get his start in politics with political money and loyally funded his campaigns from then

---

14  Higgs, 37-78.

15  William Hartung, *Prophets of War: Lockheed Martin and the Making of the Military-Industrial Complex* (New York: Nation Books, 2011), 137-139.

on. Johnson influenced Roosevelt to allow the company to build a large naval base at Corpus Christi, Texas. According to political operative Thomas Corcoran, "James Forrestal twisted a hell of a lot of tails to" keep the money flowing to "Lyndon's friends."[16]

Political scientists call this sort of relationship an "iron triangle." What they mean by this is a decision-making relationship between congressional committees, executive bureaucracies, and private interest groups with each one forming a side of the triangle and all linked together. When it comes to military spending, Congress is responsible for funding programs and then overseeing them. Lawmakers regulate or fail to regulate the industries impacted by their decisions that lobby and seek to benefit from them, while the Joint Chiefs of Staff and the Department of Defense push for larger military budgets and spending for new weapons. The "iron triangle" model can be used to describe the workings of many different segments of the economy that are closely linked to the government, but none of them compares in size and importance to that of the defense industry.

As World War II entered its final months, people connected to the defense industry decided that they did not want the nation to demobilize and return to a

---

16  Folsom, 45.

peaceful state as it had in all the wars before it, so they argued that the United States had to be placed on a permanent war footing. Charles Wilson, a member of the War Production Board, claimed that the country's security now required the ability to go to full war at a moment's notice. "What is more natural and logical," he said, "than that we should henceforth mount our national policy upon the solid fact of an industrial capacity for war, and a research capacity for war that is also 'in being'? It seems to me anything less is foolhardy." In Wilson's view, the industry would have to band together to prevent "political witch hunts" or to be "tagged with a 'merchants of death' label."

Some contemporary observers worried that such views would transform the United States into a "garrison state" in which the whole society would be organized around war and individual freedom and liberties would be curtailed as a result. The sociologist Harold Lasswell saw such a state as one in which "the specialists in violence are the most powerful group in society." He thought such a thing could happen in the United States if it developed into an empire, in which case "those standing at the top of the military pyramid will doubtless occupy high positions in the income pyramid." In 1950 Claude A. Putnam, the head of the National Association of Manufacturers, declared that indeed Americans were now "going to live in a garrison state for five, ten, or fifteen years."[17]

Writing in 1948, the historian Charles Beard worried that the war caused so much power to flow into the hands of the president that the system of government created by the Founding Fathers was being completely distorted and would eventually wreck the country. "The further away from its base on the American continent the government of the United States seeks to exert power over the affairs and relations of other countries the weaker its efficiency becomes," he wrote, "and the further it oversteps the limits of its strength the more likely it is to lead the nation into disaster—a terrible defeat in a war in Europe or Asia beyond the conquering power of its soldiers, sailors, and airmen. If wrecks of overextended empires scattered through the centuries offer any instruction to the living present, it is that a quest for absolute power not only corrupts, but in time destroys."[18]

Was the country changing for good? James Burnham, who went on to help found the magazine *National Review* along with William Buckley, wrote an influential book at the start of World War II titled *The Managerial Revolution* that promised to answer "what

---

17  Ledbetter, 32-39.

18  Charles Beard, *President Roosevelt and the Coming of the War, 1941: Appearances and Realities* (New Jersey, Transaction Publishers, 2003), 592-593.

is happening in the world." In it he argued that this revolution was a global trend in which private ownership and capitalism were being replaced by collectivism and central planning in "unlimited" states. He thought management elites had taken control of corporations, government bureaucracies, and the military and were now taking control of societies. He believed both Nazi Germany and Soviet Russia were variations of this formula while Franklin Roosevelt was moving the United States "in the same direction."

Burnham imagined a future after the war in which a small group of "super-states" would divide up the world. He thought there would probably be three of them, but whatever the case, once they consolidated their power, they would clash with one another but be unable to defeat each other. He thought this development was inevitable, because it was due to the rise of a new class of managerial elites who were indispensable to the functioning of modern economies and corporations. In Burnham's view they were now seizing power throughout the world.

Burnham's book became a best seller and was a huge influence on George Orwell as he wrote his classic novel *1984*. Orwell became inspired by Burnham's nightmare world divided among three perpetually warring superstates. However, there are some flaws to Burnham's thinking.

Of course, the world didn't exactly get divided up as he predicted after World War II. But more importantly, it wasn't managers who took control of Germany and the Soviet Union. It was the Nazi Party and the Communist Party that actually took power in both societies and then bent the state to their own purposes. Burnham made the mistake of obsessing over forms of organizations and not who controlled them and for what reasons.

Managers aren't free agents. They have to answer to those who pay them. It wasn't bureaucratic structures that were taking control of nations, but people using different organizations for their own ends. For example, the military-industrial complex was not a faceless bureaucracy that took power on its own, but something that developed inside of the United States and derived its power from the corporations that owned the industries that made it up and the politicians and leaders who set the policies that directed money toward it and set its objectives in a symbiotic iron-triangle relationship that transformed the federal government into a war state.[19]

Looking back from the vantage point of today, though, Burnham was prophetic in being one of the

---

19   James Burnham, *The Managerial Revolution* (Bloomington: Indiana University Press, 1960); Daniel Kelly, *James Burnham and the Struggle for the World: A Life* (Wilmington: Isi Books, 2002), 94-98; Daniel Geary, *Radical Ambition: C. Wright Mills, the Left, and American Social Thought* (Los Angeles: University of California Press, 2009), 54.

first voices to recognize that major changes were taking place in society that forever changed the flow of political power inside the United States. Burnham wrote his book in 1941. Maybe if he had written it ten years later, he would have painted a different picture of things. A book that is much more influential today and more accurate in its depiction of American society is the sociologist C. Wright Mills's work *The Power Elite* that came out in 1956 and is now considered a classic.

Have you ever heard of it? If you haven't, then you need to know about it, and if you already have, then you need to make sure you have a good grasp of its arguments in order to get a better understanding of how the real big decisions are truly made in this country when it comes to war, Wall Street bailouts, national security issues, and even the interest-rate policies that impacts your day-to-day life when it comes to things such as the price of oil, housing prices, and even the unemployment rate. These types of issues are not voted upon by Congress, hardly debated about in elections, and even more rarely decided upon by voters. The final decisions are made by a power elite, whose activities are barely understood by most but whose workings will be fully comprehended by you as you read this book.

Who makes up the power elite and how does it work? In Mills's view, the power elite consists of the most important men serving as the top executive officers of the nation's largest corporations, the nation's leading military leaders, and the executive branch of the government in what can best be described as a "permanent-war economy and a private-corporation economy." All three of these domains became increasingly centralized and powerful through the course of American history and in turn the consequences of their decisions have grown in importance.

At the time of the Founding Fathers and up until the Civil War, small farms and small factories with their own individual owners dominated the landscape of the American economy. Now, according to Mills, the economy "has become dominated by two or three hundred giant corporations, administratively and politically interrelated, which together hold the keys to economic decisions," while "the military order, once a slim establishment in a context of mistrust fed by state militia, has become the largest and most expensive feature of government."

In the past, Americans viewed their history as a "peaceful continuum interrupted by war." But now after World War II, in Mills's view, "the American elite does not have any real image of peace—other than as an uneasy interlude existing precariously by virtue of the balance of mutual fright. The only seriously accepted plan for 'peace' is the fully loaded pistol. In short, war or a high state of war preparedness is felt to be the normal and seemingly permanent condition of the United States."

It was World War II that brought a merger between corporate elites and the military. It is the war that created what Eisenhower called the military-industrial complex. The reason, as Mills noted, is that "unless the military sat in on corporate decisions, they could not be sure that their programs would be carried out; and unless the corporation chieftains knew something of the war plans, they could not plan war production." At the same time as the United States became more involved in the world, the executive branch of the government grew in power and more and more decisions that were once made in Congress came to be made there. The presidency of Franklin Roosevelt marked a tipping point in executive power.

Once military and political leaders retire, they often float into the corporate world by serving on the boards of corporations. At the same time, corporate leaders often drift in and out of positions in the private world and the executive branch of government. Representatives of the largest Wall Street banks and the nation's biggest companies serve on the Federal Reserve Board and the Treasury Department and in all sorts of positions in the executive branch of government, and at the highest levels of power they go back and forth between the public and private world. If you want, perhaps the best way to think of it is as a revolving door.

Of course there is also the Central Intelligence Agency, the State Department, and the dozens of other government bureaucracies besides simply the uniformed military that play a key role in national security. And all of these organizations are led by men who move from positions in the corporate world and in government too. At the very height of the power structure, as Mills writes, the "top positions are increasingly interchangeable."

These men, and they are still mostly men, do not meet and make decisions in one big grand conspiracy. They simply have similar views on the big issues. "They are more or less aware of themselves as a social class and they behave toward one another differently from the way they do towards members of other classes. They accept one another, understand one another, marry one another, tend to work and to think if not together at least alike," Mills said.

Do you know why they tend to think alike? They rise at the top of institutions and as Mills remarks, "although men sometimes shape institutions, institutions always select and form men." In order to be promoted they have to become useful to those above them. The ambitious bureaucrat learns to fit in and conform. And in time he comes to take the views of the organization as his own. He earns a reputation for having "sound" judgment and it is that reputation that serves as his key to advancement.

Now disagreements do come about within the power elite as a whole. Not all industries in the economy have the same exact interests as one another nor do all government bureaucracies. At times goals diverge. Cliques form. Competition can arise and sometimes disagreements create forces that make headlines or cause dark events to materialize.

But more often than not different interests and views simply work their way through the various government bureaucracies and end up being decided upon in the executive branch of the government by the president and his advisers—and all too often they simply ratify decisions brought to them. But it is inside the executive branch and its bureaucracies that disagreements occur and real politics plays out. Electoral politics means very little, because it is not in the political parties or in Congress that the truly big decisions are made. And if the president wants to embark on a bold new direction, he often must fight entrenched interests in his own bureaucracy allied with the power elite.

Now, yes, this is a view of government that is at odds with what you probably were taught in school about the workings of power in the United States, if you were taught anything at all. Political scientists often claim that democratic government in the country works through the competition of fairly equal and independent conflicting groups that lobby Congress with money and pressure groups. This theory is called pluralism. Its advocates claim that the competing interests in society balance themselves out so in the end decisions are made for the good of all.

However, this view is absurd when it comes to the big decisions of history. The pluralists don't stop to ask what did "small retailers or brick masons have to do with the sequence of decision and event that led to World War II," Mills writes, or "what did insurance agents or for that matter, the Congress, have to do with the decision to make or not to make, to drop or not to drop, the early model of the new weapon?" Matters of national security and grand economic policy are decided upon outside the domain of electoral politics and inside circles of the power elite.

Now, yes, there are decisions made in Congress and influenced by voters. To Mills this is the "middle level of power" made up of Congress and talked about in political campaigns. It is the decisions about social policy, taxation, and the spending of a portion of the federal budget that is openly talked about. Almost all of the political news reported about is simply gossip about the "middle level" issues and conflicts over them. Political scientists all too often relegate their focus and thought to this level of power, because it is only discussion of the "middle level" that can get them onto television as talking heads and grants from private foundations controlled by corporate money and corporate men.

Making up the "middle level" of power Mills placed the professional politicians in state governments and in the Congress and the leaders of pressure groups, as well as the upper classes of towns and cities. But all these men he saw as below the power elite. And below them he placed the general public, or what he called "the masses," nowadays captivated by the circus entertainment of television and celebrity culture typified by "reality" TV and online social networks where everyone can play a role, albeit a meaningless one when it comes to making a difference.

When it comes to politics, the masses turn their television sets to FOX News, CNN, and MSNBC, but only a small fraction of them even regularly watch these shows or keep up with the political news. Over the decades, the proportion of Americans who vote has dropped. It's not because they are dumb, but because they have come to realize that at the "middle level" of politics, where they can easily have the most impact, the decisions that are made are not of prime importance. Their congressional representative has no control at all over what the Federal Reserve may decide about interest rates and very little say over issues of "national security."

You and I may not like this situation, but members of the power elite view the situation as perfectly natural. As Mills writes, in their view "it is just that the people are of necessity confused and must, like trusting children, place all the new world of foreign policy and strategy and executive action in the hands of experts. It is just that everyone knows somebody has got to run the show, and that somebody usually does. Others do not really care anyway, and besides they do not know how."[20]

The problem is that the power elite has become a creature of bureaucratic processes and corporate groupthink. The world is changing and it has trouble adapting to a new world that is different from the one that it came out of. In the national security sphere, it tends to simply replicate old policies, while in the corporate world it tends to focus on short-term profits at the expense of even its own long-term health. It

---

20  C. Wright Mills, *The Power Elite* (New York: Oxford University Press, 1956), 7-8, 11, 96, 184, 212, 244, 276, 294.

doesn't make wise decisions. In fact many have been disastrous.

At the beginning of the twenty-first century, the result is a perpetual war on terror full of winless wars and a stagnant economy created by bloated government and flawed economic policies by the Federal Reserve. In the past few years, members of the power elite drove the nation's largest banks under due to their own lack of foresight and are sending the country on the path to bankruptcy. What is most troubling is that today's power elite has no solution to the problems they have created. We have now reached a point that only by exposing it can one hope for reform. You must learn and do your part. You must speak out.

The situation was entirely different just after World War II. As the war came to a close, the United States emerged onto the world stage as a global superpower. Henry Luce, the owner of *Life* magazine, boldly proclaimed it to be the start of the "American century." For a moment, the United States held sole possession of the atomic bomb and proved that it was capable of using it. Can you imagine a time in history when a single nation held so much power?

After the war ended, the Cold War began and the world divided into a "Communist bloc" led by the Soviet Union and China, and a "free world" led by the United States and its power elite. If the Cold War hadn't happened, the military-industrial complex probably would have quickly faded away after World War II. Instead it remains with us even today. How did the Cold War start and was it really necessary? There was something about the Cold War that was unique to all of human history.

# CHAPTER II
## THE ATOMIC BOMB AND THE COLD WAR

On August 6, 1945, a US B-29 bomber flew over the Japanese city of Hiroshima, with a population of about 340,000, and dropped an atomic bomb on to it. Seventy thousand people instantly vaporized. Another seventy thousand people caught on fire. Tokyo's railroad telegraph center noticed that the Hiroshima station went off the air. Reports from railway stops up to nine miles from the city reported of a massive explosion in its direction.

Military men in Tokyo were puzzled, because they had heard no reports of a large bomber raid on the city. So they ordered a young officer to fly to the area and see what had happened. He circled his plane over Hiroshima and radioed back in disbelief. He saw a great scar in the land and a huge cloud overhead. Two days later, US newspapers reported that Japanese radio broadcasts had described the city as a place where "practically all living things, human and animal, were literally seared to death." By the end of the year, an estimated 90,000 to 166,000 people would die from the effects of the atomic attack.

Three days after the atomic attack, the Soviet Union declared war on Japan and invaded territory Japan had conquered in Manchuria. The next day, the United States dropped another atomic bomb on the Japanese city of Nagasaki and wiped it out. On August 14, 1945, Emperor Hirohito broadcasted a surrender speech to the people of Japan and the world via radio.

By the end of the year, eighty thousand more people died from the effects of the atomic bombing of Nagasaki. How does the atomic bomb make you feel? The United States had successfully tested the bomb before it used it against Japan. After these tests, many people at the top of the military chain of command were uneasy about the weapon. When General Dwight Eisenhower, who commanded the Allied forces in Europe, was told of the bomb, he "expressed the hope we would never have to use such a thing against the enemy because I disliked seeing the United States take the lead in introducing into war something as horrible and destructive as this new weapon was described to be." The day after the bombing of Hiroshima, General Douglas MacArthur's pilot described him as being "appalled and depressed by this Frankenstein monster." Years later, MacArthur told President Richard Nixon that "he thought it a tragedy that the bomb was ever exploded."[21]

Of course, it was President Harry Truman, who became president of the United States after the death of Franklin Roosevelt in the final months of World War II, who made the ultimate decision to use the bomb. After the war, he explained that he believed that it sped up the end of the war and "saved millions of lives" by making an invasion of Japan unnecessary. There is some controversy over this as some, such as President Herbert Hoover, have argued that Japan was already beaten and would have surrendered anyway. He is not alone in this opinion. A month after the war ended, General Curtis LeMay who commanded the air wings that bombed Japan, stated that "the atomic bomb had nothing to do with the end of the war at all." Hap Arnold, his commanding officer and the man in charge of all American air forces at the time, wrote in his memoirs two years later, "it always appeared to us that, atomic bomb, or no atomic bomb, the Japanese were already on [the] verge of collapse."

In LeMay's view, though, what the bombs did was give "the Japanese an opportunity to surrender without

---

21  Gar Alperovitz, *The Decision to Use the Atomic Bomb and the Architecture of an American Myth* (New York: Alfred Knopf, 1995), 351-353.

losing too much face." Also, what if Japan didn't simply surrender? Then Truman still would have had to drop the bomb, and it's impossible to conceive of him not doing so in his position. If it came out that he had hesitated in using it, he would have faced political attack. But I want you to know that if the bomb troubles you, it troubled many of the men at the top of the US government who dealt with it too.[22]

Although Roosevelt and Truman had shared some of the technology behind the bomb with Great Britain and kept its leader Winston Churchill informed in regards to its development, they kept their ally the Soviet Union, ruled by Joseph Stalin, in the dark. Thanks to spies, though, the Soviet premier knew of it anyway and was working on a bomb of his own. But the Americans did not know that and the whole situation was a sign of mistrust.

After the United States dropped the bomb, Secretary of War Henry Stimson, who was personally in charge of the development of the weapon and answered only to the president, became deeply worried about it. He sent

---

22  Alperovitz, 517, 335-336; Herbert Hoover, *Freedom Betrayed* (Stanford: Stanford University Press, 560-565); for a good overview of the controversy surrounding the dropping of the atomic bomb, see J. Samuel Walker, *Prompt and Utter Destruction: Truman and the Use of the Atomic Bomb Against Japan* (Chapel Hill: University of North Carolina Press, 2004)

Truman a memo after its use in which he said that "in a world atmosphere already sensitive to power, the introduction of this weapon has profoundly affected political considerations in all sections of the globe." He didn't see this as merely another weapon of war, "but a first step in a new control of man over the forces of nature too revolutionary and dangerous to fit into the old concepts."

Now that the United States had discovered the bomb, and did not let all of its allies in on the decision to use it, Stimson argued that if it did not create some form of atomic cooperation with the Russians, it would "stimulate feverish activity on the part of the Soviet toward the development of this bomb" and create "a secret armament race of a rather desperate character." If Truman were to continue to simply deal with them "having this weapon rather ostentatiously on our hip, their suspicions and their distrust of our purposes and motives will increase."

Stimson pleaded with Truman to consider proposing to the Russians and the British that "we would stop work on the further improvement in, or manufacture of, the bomb as a military weapon, provided the Russians and the British would agree to do likewise. It might also provide that we would be willing to impound what bombs we now have in the United States provided the Russians and the British would agree with us that in no event will they or we use a bomb as an instrument of war unless all three governments agree to that use." If Truman did not create some mechanism for international control and cooperation over the atomic bomb, Stimson believed that a nuclear arms race that could destroy the world would be the result. The president ignored this advice.[23]

In reaction to the atomic attack, Stalin reportedly said, "Hiroshima has shaken the whole world. The balance has been destroyed." The bomb changed the course of human history by making total war obsolete. The twentieth century saw two great world wars. A third world war would mean the end of mankind. As Albert Einstein said, "I do not know with what weapons World War III will be fought, but World War IV will be fought with sticks and stones." Global war now meant world suicide. No longer could one nation attempt to invade and totally conquer another nation that had possession of the bomb without risking its own destruction, and even though the United States had sole possession of the bomb after World War II, the Soviet Union would successfully explode a bomb of its own in 1949.[24]

---

23   Alperovitz, 430-434.

24   Campbell Craig and Sergey Radchenko, *The Atomic Bomb and the Origins of the Cold War* (New Haven: Yale University Press, 2008), 94.

As Stimson understood things, the bomb posed an existential threat to the Soviet Union and sparked an arms race that divided the world into two factions—a "free" West and a "Communist" bloc led by the Soviet Union. By the 1980s, the Soviet Union and the United States each had over two thousand nuclear missiles and ten thousand nuclear warheads and their own military-industrial complexes that profited from the arms race and helped to keep the Cold War going. That's twenty thousand Hiroshimas and a capability to destroy the world over and over again. But the threat of nuclear destruction helped to make sure that the confrontation between the two world nuclear superpowers remained a "Cold War" and never became a true shooting war.

The dropping of the atomic bombs on Hiroshima and Nagasaki not only caused Japan to surrender, but it also should be seen as the first event of the Cold War. Looking at this history now, you may think that the confrontation was inevitable. Some in the United States felt so at the time. Although the Soviet Union, the United States, and Britain fought as allies against Nazi Germany and the Japanese during World War II, toward the end of the war a few believed that a war with the Soviet Union would be next.

Once Adolph Hitler gave up and shot himself, General Patton talked of combining American and

British forces with the defeated German army and attacking the Soviet Union. Of course, after several years of war, the American public would not be too supportive of starting a whole new one against the largest army in the world, much less turning against an ally. Nor could Patton's superior officers, much less the president, conceive of such a thing. James Burnham claimed that now that the United States had the atomic bomb, it must engage in an "offensive policy" against the Soviet Union before the latter started to build one of its own. In Burnham's view, the United States and Britain should combine together and use the advantage of sole possession of the new weapon to create a new "American empire" that would exercise "decisive world control."[25]

However, despite such ideas, the leaders of neither country had plans to set up a postwar world empire. Franklin Roosevelt, Winston Churchill, and Joseph Stalin met together repeatedly during the war in a spirit of cooperation and wrote letters back and forth in regards to the postwar order. Yes, they had their disagreements, but none of them meant Cold War.

---

25   Carlo D'Este, *Patton: A Genius for War* (New York: Harper Perennial, 1996), 735-757; Daniel Kelly, *James Burnham and the Struggle for the World*, (Wilmington: ISI Books, 2002), 121-130.

## Chapter Two

You may be wondering, then, what caused the Cold War? I've given you a hint to the answer by talking about the atomic bomb with you, but there is more to it than that. To really answer the question, we must first examine the goals and objectives of Roosevelt and Stalin. For decades, American scholars have based their conclusions on research done at presidential libraries and government archives in the United States and simply used educated guesswork when it came to Soviet intentions. But in the years after the fall of the Berlin Wall and the Soviet Union itself, old KGB and Soviet archives have opened up to scholars and we can now have a much more informed understanding of the past than was ever possible before.

It is clear that both leaders did not want a repeat of World War II. Germany invaded Russia in both wars and Stalin did not want it to happen again. Roosevelt likewise desired a peaceful postwar order and wanted the three major powers of the Soviet Union, Britain, and the United States, along with China, to work together to prevent new wars from breaking out while he and his presidential successors would work to create a world order based on law and the promotion of free trade and the encouragement of governments based on self-determination and democracy.

Such ideas were not new to the tradition of American foreign policy. They can be summed up in one world:

"internationalism." President Woodrow Wilson first tried to bring these ideals to the world after World War I with his League of Nations, but he could not get his European allies to go along with them nor the American people. In fact, the failure of the League of Nations and his own diplomacy is one of the many reasons for World War II.

The old European order had been based on imperial competition and balance-of-power alliances, with Great Britain being the nation most closely linked to the United States. The Germans tried to displace the Western-style democracies in two failed wars, while the Soviet Union created its own totalitarian alternative based on the ideology of communism. While the British, the Americans, and the Russians worked together to defeat the Germans and their allies, Roosevelt proved to be willing to compromise with both Churchill and Stalin at times to try to achieve his larger goals.

President Wilson simply did not have the leverage to force the Europeans to go along with his ideas. Roosevelt made sure that once World War II ended, the United States would be the most powerful nation in the world and would thereby be in a position to not only dictate terms to Germany and Japan but also to influence the Allied nations to become part of a new internationalist-style world order with the United States in the lead. As for the Soviets, he thought he could induce them to join this new world order and would be able to continue to work with them thanks to their shared interest in preventing any further European wars from breaking out and making sure the Germans in particular didn't start another war all over again.

For global security, Roosevelt created the United Nations with a Security Council that would be made up of several of the most powerful nations and have the power to create collective security pacts and declarations of war together and have veto power over the decisions of each other. He told Henry Wallace in 1942, "When there are four people sitting in a poker game and three of them are against the fourth it is a little hard on the fourth." And he explained his philosophy to the Soviet minister of foreign affairs Vyacheslav Molotov by telling him that "it would be necessary to create an international police force" to prevent new wars and that they'll have to disarm Germany and its satellite nations and remain armed together after the war. Stalin told Molotov to tell the president that he thought that he was "absolutely correct."[26]

---

26 Campbell Craig and Fredrik Logevall, *America's Cold War*, (Cambridge: The Belknap Press of Harvard University Press, 2009), 33-37; John Lewis Gaddis, *Strategies of Containment* (New York: Oxford University Press), 10; Vladislav Zubok, *A Failed Empire: The Soviet Union in the Cold War from Stalin to Gorbachev* (Chapel Hill: The University of North Carolina Press), 11.

Unlike Wilson, though, Roosevelt did not create a League of Nations and then try to get the United States to be a part of it, but instead he created a United Nations headquartered inside the United States and then invited the rest of the world to join it. But just as internationalism has a unique view of the world based on collective security, it also has a critical economic underpinning of free trade and seeks to create open markets everywhere.

So along with the United Nations, Roosevelt also created the Bretton Woods system to protect free trade with sound money. The world's currencies had been pegged to the price of gold before the Great Depression of the 1930s and World War II. Now Roosevelt pegged the dollar to the price of gold and turned it into the reserve currency of central banks and nations around the world, thereby putting the United States in a position of global advantage in the currency markets, a position that helped it borrow money from other countries after the war and finance its huge deficits of today.

Although these internationalist ideas had a long legacy in the United States, not everyone supported them. Still, they had their own unique but powerful constituency, and it was one that helped put Roosevelt in power behind the scenes. Who were these internationalists?

To answer that question, all you have to do is look at who benefits the most from free-trade internationalism and global currency markets. The answer is simple. Those who profit the most are Wall Street international bankers who loan money to nations around the world and facilitate global trade and large corporations that compete in the global marketplace with technological advantages and the efficiencies of vertical integration instead of trying to compete with cheaper third world labor costs.

Not all industries can do this. So, for example, a textile company in the United States in the 1940s that relied on the national market and whose biggest cost was the money it paid its workers may not have been too excited about lowering trade barriers and tariffs around the world, but many international oil companies were, and so were high-technology companies like International Business Machines. Some like to bash Franklin Roosevelt as an enemy of business, but in reality he became president thanks in part to money from some of the largest corporations in America.[27]

---

27 Bruce Cumings, *The Origins of the Korean War, Volume II* (New Jersey: Princeton University Press, 1990); Franz Schurmann, *The Logic of World Power* (New York: Pantheon Books, 1974), 48-72.

When Roosevelt first campaigned for president, he did attack "money changers" and financial elites, but in truth he was only attacking a small segment of them—those associated with the bank of JP Morgan and its holding companies who had agents in the Federal Reserve, which mismanaged interest rate policy during the 1920s, which in turn helped create the stock market bubble that crashed in 1929. Roosevelt had the support of the Rockefeller family, which owned Chase Bank, and the bank's managers, who were rivals of JP Morgan. He also got huge sums of money from industrialists, such as the owners of Standard Oil and Royal Dutch Shell, who did business on a global scale.[28]

Frank Vanderclip, the former president of National City Bank of New York, and James Rand of Remington Rand Company formed the Committee for the Nation to promote Roosevelt's inflationary monetary policies. General Robert Wood of Sears, Roebuck & Co. and Magnus Alexander of the National Industrial Board joined it, along with other executives of some of the

---

28 Thomas Ferguson, *Golden Rule: The Investment Theory of Party Competition and the Logic of Money-Driven Political Systems* (Chicago: The University of Chicago Press, 1995), 147-150; for Morgan interests and the Federal Reserve, see Murray Rothbard, *A History of Money and Banking in the United States: The Colonial Era to World War II* (Auburn: Ludwig von Mises Institute, 2002). 259-347.

nation's largest corporations. Roosevelt came into power thanks to a split within the power elite on the heels of the Great Depression.[29]

After World War II, people would call this internationalist corporate clique the "eastern establishment." If you listen to some of Richard Nixon's taped Oval Office recordings, you can hear him railing against it. Why was it called the "eastern establishment?" Well, most of its business support came from Wall Street banks and corporate conglomerates headquartered in New York City.

Its notions of international law, collective security, and global institutions also attracted liberal intellectuals, and many of its most important members came from Ivy League colleges. In the finance sector, many had an Anglophile affinity with Great Britain, whose largest banks historically had close connections with Wall Street banks. Their most important lobbying group was and still is the Council on Foreign Relations, and the quarterly publication *Foreign Affairs* is their journal.

Many of the men Roosevelt appointed to head the executive-branch bureaucracies shared his internationalist outlook and were themselves important members of the "eastern establishment." The best example

---

29   Murray Rothboard, *America's Great Depression* (Auburn: Ludwig von Mises Institute, 1963). 308-309.

is John McCloy, who served as assistant secretary of war from 1941 to 1945. Once the war ended, he was the US high commissioner to Germany and held this position until 1952. He then served as chairman of the Chase Manhattan Bank from 1953 to 1960, and as chairman of the Ford Foundation from 1958 to 1965. He was also a trustee of the Rockefeller Foundation from 1946 to 1949, and then again from 1953 to 1958, before he took up the position at Ford. From 1954 to 1970, he was chairman of the Council on Foreign Relations, to be succeeded by David Rockefeller, who had worked closely with him at Chase Bank. McCloy, in fact, had a long association with the Rockefeller family, going back to his early Harvard days, when he taught the young Rockefeller brothers how to sail. He was also a member of the Draper Committee, formed in 1958 by Eisenhower. He dedicated his life to liberal internationalism and to profits.

Joseph Stalin didn't care about global capitalism or about business profits. Liberal internationalism meant nothing to him. He didn't grow up at Groton or attend Harvard like Franklin Roosevelt. Nor did he come from a wealthy family of old money. Stalin was a brutal leader who worked beside Lenin in the violent Communist revolution in Russia and became the leader of the Soviet Union, maintaining his power through show trials and the forced liquidation of his enemies. Like all political ideologies, Russian communism professed to be a system for the good of all that would eventually bring a more peaceful and just world order, but in reality it operated as a totalitarian system with Stalin at its head.

Stalin and his Soviet comrades professed a desire for world revolution, but what he cared about more than anything else was to build the Soviet Union into a strong and secure state, and he would stop at nothing to do it. In the 1920s and 1930s, he forced Russia to industrialize. He also centralized agriculture and in the process sent millions of people he didn't think went along with his program to Siberia, where they died. After Adolph Hitler's Nazi Germany invaded his country, he demanded that any soldiers who retreated were to be shot. If they surrendered, he decreed that they were never to be forgiven and their wives were to be arrested. And he meant it. When Stalin found out that one of his own sons, who had been born to a deceased wife of his and raised by others, had been captured by the Germans, he refused to make a prisoner exchange for him and had his son's wife immediately arrested and sent to a work camp for two years.

When the Nazis invaded the Soviet Union, they didn't come to conquer, but they came to destroy. Hitler wanted to eliminate as many people as possible to provide new living space for Germans. As the

German army took Russian territory, it destroyed more than seventy thousand villages and 1,700 towns and left twenty-five million people homeless, sent five million to Nazi concentration camps, and simply shot seven million civilians. As for Russian soldiers, the Germans killed off about nine million of them.

The Soviet Union suffered more than any other country during World War II in terms of numbers. And it came close to losing the war. The Germans got within just a few miles of Moscow before their advance was finally stopped by what seemed by then to be an unlimited pool of Russian soldiers. Stalin gladly joined the Allies to help defeat the Germans and desired above any other goal to protect the Soviet state from another invasion after the war.

This meant, on one hand, cooperating with the United States and Great Britain to beat the Germans and their Axis allies. So, Stalin disbanded the Comintern, whose goal was to encourage communist revolutions in other nations to appease his allies. On the other hand, though, he sought to create a series of buffer states between the Soviet Union and Germany that would be under his thumb to protect Russia in a future war, which he thought was practically inescapable. The Soviet Union had already been invaded by Germany twice in his lifetime, and throughout its entire history, Russia had been invaded multiple times by European nations to its west. If cooperating with Roosevelt and Churchill after the war would help him bring more security to the Soviet Union, he would do it, and if it wouldn't, then he would act on his own.[30]

Once Stalin's army turned back the Nazis, he marched Soviet troops through Eastern Europe and into Estonia, Latvia, Lithuania, Poland, Bulgaria, Hungary, Romania, Czechoslovakia, and Albania on their way to Germany. He didn't simply march through these countries, though; he occupied them and installed puppet satellite governments in them. After the war ended, he created Soviet-style secret police systems in these nations to make sure they remained in his grip. Germany became a divided nation, with an eastern half subservient to the Soviet Union and a democratic government in the western part friendly to the United States. Inside East Germany, Berlin became an international city divided amongst the allies, with Russia holding the eastern half of the city and the western half of it divided into zones of control by England, France, and the United States.

Stalin, Churchill, and Roosevelt met together in Tehran and Yalta during World War II to make battle plans and to try to map out the postwar order. What

---

30  Melvyn Leffler, *For the Soul of Mankind: The United States, the Soviet Union, and the Cold War* (New York: Hill and Wang, 2007), 11-37.

Stalin sought was to separate Europe into spheres of influence and have his two allies recognize his control over Eastern Europe. They both saw him as a tough-as-nails, but pragmatic, negotiator.

Churchill met Stalin alone in Moscow and gave concessions in return for Stalin recognizing British dominion over Greece. "Let us settle about our affairs in the Balkans," the British leader told his Soviet counterpart, "your armies are in Rumania and Bulgaria. We have interests, missions, and agents there. Don't let us get at cross-purposes in small ways. So far as Britain and Russia are concerned, how would it do for you to have ninety per cent predominance in Rumania, for us to have ninety per cent of the say in Greece, and go fifty-fifty about Yugoslavia?" Stalin concurred.[31]

At Yalta, Stalin also agreed to enter the war with Japan three months after the defeat of Germany. In turn, the allies agreed to recognize the provisional government he installed in Poland while he agreed to hold elections in it and also allow the Soviet Union to redraw the border of Poland so that it took part of its eastern side and made up for it by giving land from Germany to it. The Soviets left the conference full of optimism for postwar cooperation. A memo of the meeting's results circulated by the Soviet foreign

---

31  Hoover, 428.

affairs office to Russian diplomats reported that "there was a palpable search for compromise on disputed issues. We assess the conference as a high positive fact, particularly on Polish and Yugoslav issues and on the issues of reparations."

Then on April 12, 1945, to Stalin's surprise, Franklin Roosevelt died and his vice president, Harry Truman, became president. Molotov appeared to be "deeply moved and disturbed" when he signed the condolences book at the American embassy in Moscow. A month later, the head of the Soviet intelligence station in New York warned that "economic circles" that had no influence over Roosevelt's foreign policy were now undertaking "an organized effort to bring about a change in the policy of the United States toward the USSR." These "reactionaries," he continued, "are setting particular hopes on the possibility of getting direction of the United States' foreign policy wholly into their hands, partly because Truman is notoriously untried and ill-informed on these matters." Was this an accurate assessment of the new president?[32]

Historians have rated Harry Truman as one of the better American presidents. Do you think of him as a basically decent and honest man? If you do, then you are right, because, yes, he was one. And, yes, he

---

32  Zubok, 14-15.

was humble too. President Roosevelt had not let him in on his decisions, so he didn't know everything that had been going on. Truman now had an awesome responsibility. He would need help and he knew it.

After being sworn in as president, Truman immediately held a cabinet meeting with Roosevelt's chief advisers and told them that he planned to continue his predecessor's policies. "They were all so broken up and upset that none of them did much talking," he remembered. Truman told them to feel free going forward to tell him when they thought he was wrong, but he made clear that the final decisions would be up to him. After the meeting, Henry Stimson stayed and told him about the development of the atomic bomb. Truman knew nothing about it. It had been kept secret even from him.[33]

Truman spent the bulk of the next day, his first full day as president, meeting with two men: Stimson and a man named James Byrnes, a figure not written about much in history books but who had grown to become one of the most powerful political operatives during World War II. Byrnes had been a senator from South Carolina from 1931 to 1941 and then Roosevelt picked him to be a Supreme Court justice. He got

---

33 Robert Moskin, *Mr. Truman's War: The Final Victories of World War II and the Birth of the Postwar World* (New York: Random House, 1996), 9.

bored with that job, so FDR made him the head of the Office of War Mobilization, which placed him right at the apex of the military-industrial complex and made him one of the most powerful men in the country. Reporters called him the "Assistant President for the home front." The President even gave Byrnes blank executive orders for him to do anything he thought necessary under the war powers act in case of an emergency when he was out of the country.

"Immediately upon becoming President," Truman wrote, "I sent for him because I wanted his assistance." The new president and Byrnes talked about "everything from Tehran to Yalta, law of the individual who had public office, and everything under the sun." According to the *New York Times*, Byrnes could now have "any job he wanted." The paper reported that he was "known to be one of President Truman's warmest friends in Washington." Indeed Truman and Byrnes went back to their days in Congress together. He quickly became his closest adviser when it came to foreign affairs and moved from being an informal confidant to becoming Truman's official secretary of state.[34]

After Germany surrendered, defeating Japan and dealing with the Soviet Union came to the top of their

---

34   Alperovitz, 198-207.

agenda. Harry Hopkins, one of Roosevelt's closest aides, advised Truman, "Stalin is a forthright, rough, tough Russian. He is a Russian partisan through and through, thinking always Russia first. But he can be talked to frankly." The Russian leader had promised to declare war on Japan three months after Germany gave up. Churchill, Truman, and Stalin were set to meet in Postdam, Germany.[35]

Byrnes convinced Truman to delay the meeting until they could test the atomic bomb. In his first meeting with the president, he told him that "the bomb might put us in a position to dictate our own terms at the end of the war." The United States was moving into a position so it would have much more power than any other nation on the planet by the end of the war. Its gross national product was three times larger than that of the Soviet Union and five times bigger than Great Britain's while it held two-thirds of the world's gold reserves, half of its shipping vessels, and half of its industry.[36]

President Truman and his advisers sought to create an internationalist world order just as Franklin Roosevelt promoted, but many inside the US government began to fear that the Soviet Union could

---

35  Moskin, 38.
36  Craig and Radchenko, 66; Leffler, 41.

become a threat to the United States. The Office of Strategic Services (OSS), the wartime US intelligence agency and precursor to the Central Intelligence Agency (CIA), warned that "in the easily foreseeable future, Russia may well outrank even the United States in military potential." Even though Stalin had agreed with Roosevelt and Churchill to create a "Government of National Unity" in Poland, the Soviet leader had maneuvered communists into power and was about to sign a Soviet-Polish treaty.

Harry Truman's advisers saw this as a dangerous sign. Averell Harriman, America's ambassador to the Soviet Union, rushed to the White House to tell Truman that in his view Stalin wanted to keep cooperating with the United States and Britain while at the same time creating his own sphere of domination in Eastern Europe. He advised Truman to stand tough against the Russians.

The next day, the president met with Soviet foreign minister Molotov and warned him that he expected Stalin to honor all of the Yalta agreements and allow the Eastern European nations to have democratic governments. If the Russians didn't let more men into the Polish government, he would consider Yalta done with. He said he wanted friendship with Stalin, but it couldn't be a "one-way street."

Molotov sat there stunned and said, "I have never been talked to like that in my life."

"Carry out your agreements and you won't get talked to like that," Truman replied.

Molotov stormed out of the room. Truman bragged to his advisers that "I gave it to him straight, one-two to the jaw." It seems almost as if the president put on a show to impress his men as much as he did to send a message to the Russians. But he indeed sent a message.

Stalin sent a note back claiming that "it is also necessary to take into account the fact that Poland borders on the Soviet Union, which cannot be said of Great Britain and the United States. The question of Poland has the same meaning for the security of the Soviet Union as the question of Belgium and Greece for the security of Great Britain."[37]

Relations between the two started to warm up again ahead of the Postdam meeting. The atomic bomb had not been successfully tested yet and Truman wanted to make sure Stalin would keep his pledge to join the war against Japan by keeping his promise to invade Manchuria. But he was nervous ahead of his meeting with the Soviet leader and traveled by ocean liner to prepare for it. "Now I'm on my way to the high

---

37  Moskin, 77-85; Craig and Logevall, 45.

executioner. Maybe I'll save my head," he wrote his wife. Between meetings with his advisers on the boat, he spent time relaxing by playing poker with some buddies he brought with him and drinking. Taking a shot or two of bourbon before going to bed at night was a normal part Truman's routine. So was exercising in the morning.

But once he met Stalin things went well and he felt good. "I told Stalin that I am no diplomat but usually said yes or no to questions after hearing all the arguments," he reported back to his wife, "it pleased him. I asked him if he had the agenda for the meeting. He said he had and that he had some more questions to present. I told him to fire away. He did and it is dynamite—but I have some dynamite too which I'm not exploding now...Most of the big points are settled. He'll be in the Jap War on August 15th. Fini Japs when that comes about... I can deal with Stalin. He is honest—but smart as hell."

The two could not agree, though, on the future of Eastern Europe. Stalin insisted that the countries of Eastern Europe were now to be considered in the sphere of influence of the Soviet Union. Truman insisted that the United States wouldn't recognize their governments unless they were established with democratic political systems. The two simply agreed to refer the matter to their foreign ministers to study and report back to them later. And of course they would never agree to anything either.[38]

During the conference, Truman received a report that an atomic bomb had successfully been detonated back at home and the explosion had been bigger than expected. Stimson saw the president all "pepped up" by the news. Truman recorded in his diary that he believed now the "Japs will fold up before Russia comes in. I am sure they will when Manhattan appears over their homeland."

Byrnes and Truman now no longer wanted Russia involved in the war against Japan. Accordingly, the United States issued a declaration of unconditional surrender against Japan, with Great Britain and China as signatories to it, but leaving the Soviet Union out of it. The United States had kept the atomic bomb secret from Russia. At the last Postdam meeting, Truman walked up to Stalin and simply told him that he had a "new weapon of unusual destructive force" he planned to use on Japan. Stalin simply nodded and said nothing.[39]

On August 6, 1945, the United States dropped its first atomic bomb on Japan and wiped out Hiroshima. The Soviet Union responded immediately by moving

---

38   Moskin, 198, 203, 291.
39   Craig and Radchenko, 78.

its planned invasion of Japan up by two weeks, marching troops into Manchuria. Truman then quickly bombed Nagasaki, and Japan surrendered a few days later. After destroying Hiroshima, he could have waited a few weeks before nuking another city to give the Japanese time to understand what had happened, but after the Soviets got into the game by attacking Japan too, Truman got into a panic to end the war as quickly as possible—as Stalin noted, the bomb changed the balance of global power. The Soviet Union did not have it and this instantly weakened its claims to superpower status.

Byrnes believed that the United States could use the fact that it had sole possession of the bomb as an intimidation factor against the Soviet Union to get concessions from it. It did strike fear into Russian leaders. Soviet nuclear physicist Yuli Khariton recalled that Moscow saw the bombing of Hiroshima and Nagasaki as "atomic blackmail against the USSR, as a threat to unleash a new, even more terrible and devastating war."

However, Stalin would not give in. He did just the opposite. Instead of cowering to the United States, he stiffened his backbone. He told Molotov to now "stand firm and make no concessions to the Allies." Stalin did not believe that the United States wanted to start another war. "We cannot achieve anything serious if we begin to give in to intimidation or betray uncertainty," he told his associates.[40]

The detonation of the atomic bomb on Japan marked the beginning of the Cold War, because it posed an existential threat to the Soviet Union. Secretary of War Stimson quickly grasped this. Truman later recalled that Stimson "seemed at least as much concerned with the role of the atomic bomb in the shaping of history as in its capacity to shorten this war."

About a month after Japan surrendered, Stimson retired from government service. At his last cabinet meeting as secretary of war, he made a plea for some sort of international control over atomic weapons with the Soviet Union. Truman made clear this could not happen, and perhaps he was right. "I don't think it would do any good to let them in on the know-how," he told reporters at a press conference. "Then, Mister President," one of them asked, "what it amounts to is this. That the armaments race is on, is that right?" Yes, and "we would stay ahead," Truman replied.[41]

The Cold War began. But Truman and his advisers knew that it would take several years before the Soviet Union would be able to successfully detonate an A-bomb of their own. With the war over, they were

---

40   Ibid, 97; Zubok, 27.
41   Alperovitz, 434-435, 539.

not fearful that the Soviet Union would launch an attack against the United States or its allies. The Soviets Union had lost millions of soldiers in the war against Germany, and most of its industry had been destroyed. British commander Bernard Montgomery visited the Soviet Union and found the Russians to be "very, very tired. Devastation in Russia is appalling and the country is in no fit to start a war."

US army intelligence figured that it would take the Russians fifteen years to overcome these manpower losses, five to ten years to build a viable air force that could compete with the United States, another fifteen to twenty-five years to build a navy, and ten years to rebuild its railway networks. It would be suicidal insanity for the Soviet Union to try to attack the United States or Western Europe in this condition and especially when it didn't have an atomic bomb against an enemy that not only showed that it had the bomb but also that it wouldn't hesitate to use it if necessary. And no one thought Stalin was crazy.[42]

In Molotov's view, "What does the cold war mean? We were simply on the offensive. They became angry at us, of course, but we had to consolidate what we conquered." Of course there was more to it than that.

---

42  Melyvn Leffler, *A Preponderance of Power: National Security, the Truman Administration, and the Cold War* (Stanford: Stanford University Press, 1992), 133, 149.

Truman and his advisers came to be deeply worried about the Soviet Union. But if it was in no position to wage war, then, you may wonder, what were they so worried about? What got the national security bureaucracy of the United States all worked up was the simple fact that the Soviet Union existed. It couldn't do anything now, but maybe it would cause trouble later. [43]

You see, all of Europe lay in a shambles after the war. John McCloy returned from a trip overseas and told Truman that "there is a complete economic, social and political collapse going on in Central Europe, the extent of which is unparalleled in history." The Undersecretary of State Dean Acheson reported that the "destruction is more complete, hunger more acute, exhaustion more widespread than anyone realized." In parts of Germany, people were down to food rations of one thousand calories a day. In Greece, inflation was soaring, with a dozen eggs costing people seventeen dollars and a pound of cheese eleven dollars. [44]

The hardships caused people to flock to the Communist Party. In France, Italy, and Finland, 20 percent of the people voted communist. In Greece,

---

43   Zubok, 49.
44   Leffler, *Preponderance*, 63-64, 74, 101.

there were seventeen thousand communist votes in parliamentary elections in 1935, and now seventy thousand voters went Red. In Belgium, Denmark, and Sweden, 10 percent of the people were voting for communists too. This disturbed Truman and his men. World War I brought the Soviet Revolution in Russia, and communists made inroads in Germany and other European nations after the war. The economic collapse of the Great Depression and the First World War brought fascist revolutions in Germany and Italy. The dire economic situation after World War II throughout Europe could bring more revolutions.[45]

US officials saw no evidence that the Soviet Union was encouraging communist activity in any of these nations. In fact, we now know that Stalin actually ordered Soviet agents not to agitate in France, Greece, and other Western nations because he did not want to provoke the United States. He was mainly obsessed with keeping Eastern Europe in his grip and still hoped to cooperate with his war allies. However, if any of these nations went communist, they most likely would align themselves with the Soviet Union. A red Europe would be a nightmare for the United States. By simply existing, the Soviet Union posed a potential threat to the "free world."

---

45  Ibid, 7.

General William Donovan, head of the OSS (the precursor to the CIA), sized up the situation in a long memo to Truman. The way he saw it, the Soviet Union would become a huge threat if she were to "succeed in uniting the resources of Europe and Asia under her sway. Within a generation Russia could probably then out build us in every phase of military production." His answer was to rebuild Western Europe and the Mediterranean countries such as Greece and Turkey and help Japan and Germany recover from the war in "our interest in developing a balance to Russia." This made sense to Truman.

Such ideas percolated throughout the national security bureaucracy thanks to a long telegram sent back from Russia by George Kennan, the charge d'affaires of the US embassy in Moscow. Kennan was one of the top experts on the Soviet Union. He sat down and wrote an eight-thousand-word analysis of US-Soviet relations. James Forrestal, who had succeeded Stimson as secretary of war, printed off hundreds of copies of it and sent it to his subordinates. It made its way throughout the State Department and into the White House.[46]

Kennan saw an emerging confrontation with the Soviet Union that would be more of an ideological

---

46   Ibid, 60-61, 109.

battle than a military one. He argued that the Soviet Union was an expansive state full of internal contradictions. The United States had to merely block its expansion and it eventually would turn inward and collapse on itself.

However, Kennan did not think it would be wise to try to resist communism everywhere and just anywhere lest the United States find itself overextended or go bankrupt trying to police the entire planet. If the country tried to do that, then "everybody in the world" would "start coming to you with his palm out and saying, 'we have some communists—now come across.'" The United States had to have priorities in the most vital areas where the great industrial centers lay in Japan and Western Europe. To one Pentagon audience, Kennan proclaimed that communism would eventually break up regardless of what the United States did. It was an inevitable trend. All they had to do was ride it.[47]

That trend took fifty years to play out. At the moment, Truman realized that "a chaotic and hungry Europe is not fertile ground in which stable, democratic and friendly governments can be reared." Over the next few years, the United States engaged in a successful policy of rebuilding Europe through economic

---

47   Gaddis, 24-52.

aid and blocking any attempts by the Soviet Union to expand outside of its sphere of influence in Eastern Europe. The program began with aid to Greece and Turkey and first became known as the "Truman Doctrine."[48]

Undersecretary of State Dean Acheson argued that if Greece turned communist, it would be "armageddon." It would be like "apples in a barrel infected by a rotten one" and probably lead to the loss of all of Europe. To get Congress to approve aid to Greece, though, Truman's team would have to really sell it as more than a giveaway program. Republican Senator Arthur Vandenberg told Truman he would have to "scare hell out of the American people" to get the congressional votes he needed for it.

President Truman gave a speech to a joint session of Congress on March 12, 1947, in which he laid out his "Truman Doctrine." He said that it would now be the policy of the United States to "support free peoples who are resisting attempted subjugation by armed minorities or by outside pressures...I believe that our help should be primarily through economic and financial aid...I believe that we must assist free people to work out their destinies in their own way." The bill passed the Senate by sixty-seven votes to twenty-three.

---

48  Moskin, 157.

The speech turned out to be very popular. In a forty-three page memo, presidential assistants Clark Clifford and James Rowe told Truman that the Soviet threat made for a great political issue for him. "There is considerable political advantage in the administration in its battle with the Kremlin," they wrote, "the worse matters get... the more is there a sense of crisis. In times of crisis, the American citizen tends to back up his President."[49]

Truman's aides told him that it would be best to keep things simple with the American people. "The people of the U.S. should be brought in and told—it is Communism or free enterprise," one said. According to Dean Acheson, "leadership requires understanding, responsibility, discipline. The flatulent bombast of our public utterances will lead no one but fools." In his Truman Doctrine speech and other statements of foreign policy, the president almost never went into detail on economic issues. He almost always focused on the threat of communism, but it was only one side of the coin.[50]

Truman replaced James Byrnes as secretary of state with George Marshall, who had become one of the most respected people in the United States thanks to

---

49  Craig and Logevall, 79-81.
50  Cumings, 39.

his role as army chief of staff during World War II. Why the change? First of all, Truman and Byrnes had something of a falling out. "After I got to be President," Truman said, "I knew every time Jimmy and I talked that he thought it ought to be the other way around. He ought to be sitting where I was sitting." One of Byrnes's assistants believed that "Byrnes had to spend so much of his time away from Washington, that he was unable to join the President at the end of the day at bullbat time for a drink of bourbon. This gave the Palace Guard, including Admiral Leahy, Harry Vaughan, Jim Vardaman and others of Truman's drinking and poker-playing coterie at the White House the opportunity to hammer away at Byrnes' independence."[51]

Secondly, George Marshall's move to secretary of state also allowed Truman to use his name in support of his policies. In 1948, the two announced the Marshall Plan, officially titled the European Recovery Program, which sent thirteen billion dollars worth of economic aid to Europe over the next four years. At the time, the size of the entire US GDP was $258 billion, so the Marshall Plan meant a huge economic commitment on the part of the nation. It wasn't easy for the president to get Congress to pass it, but with Marshall's help he did. Next he set up the NATO

---

51   Moskin, 139; Alperovitz, 201-202.

military alliance, which was really designed with the goal of integrating the countries of Western Europe together as much as it was aimed as a defensive alliance against the Soviet Union.

However, by rebuilding West Germany and integrating it with France and the rest of Europe, the United States made Stalin uneasy. The two sides had created what geopolitical strategists call a security dilemma. This occurs when defensive measures one nation takes to shore up its own security threaten another nation and cause it to carry out defensive measures of its own. Such patterns of behavior can lead to arms races and balance-of-power diplomacy. After World War II, neither the Soviet Union nor the United States sought to wage war against the other. Both sought security and did not want a repeat of World War II. The Soviets in particular did not want to see Germany ever to get in a position to start another war again.

The United States had to rebuild Western Europe. If it hadn't, then France, Germany, and the other nations of Europe may have gone communist and fallen into the orbit of the Soviet Union. But the Soviets took the rejuvenation of Western Europe as a potential threat to them, because it meant the potential revival of a hostile Germany and the possibility that its own Eastern European satellites could eventually break away and join Western Europe. In the 1970s,

Molotov looked back and claimed that the Americans were "trying to draw us into their company, but in the subordinate role. We would have got into the position of dependence, and still would not have obtained anything from them."

That is a position Stalin would never accept. So he reacted. The Cold War accelerated. He refused to join the Bretton Woods system. When Truman offered economic aid to Eastern European nations, Stalin forced them to reject it. He talked tough. At his first postwar "election," he gave a bellicose speech in which he said that the only way the Soviet Union could be secure is if it became a superpower in the next decade. In the Soviet newspaper *Pravda*, he called Winston Churchill "a warmonger."[52]

He then blockaded Berlin by stopping all ground transportation from West Germany to it. You see, Berlin lay in the middle of East Germany and was itself divided into a "free" western half and an eastern half controlled by the Soviets. The blockade served as a feeble attempt to get his old allies to abandon Berlin or negotiate to create a crippled Germany. And when the United States simply airlifted supplies to Berlin for almost a full year, Stalin gave up. It was a humiliating defeat for him.

---

52   Zubok, 52-53.

For all intents and purposes, by the spring of 1949, with Stalin's failed blockade, the United States and its allies had successfully contained the Soviet Union. Neither Stalin nor any of his predecessors would gain any influence over Western Europe. China went communist that year, but it had a very uneasy relationship with the Russians, and the two came to eventually view each other as rivals. Nonetheless, the US national security bureaucracy never felt secure and turned the Cold War from a containment operation against the Soviet Union in Europe into a struggle for world domination.

On August 29, 1949, the Soviets successfully exploded an atomic bomb of their own. The American people weren't alarmed. A poll taken five days later showed that only 5 percent thought that atomic weapons were the most important issue facing the country. But, nevertheless, Harry Truman ordered a reappraisal of national security policy. Completed on April 14, 1950, this report, titled National Security Council Report 68 (NSC-68), became one of the most important documents of the Cold War. It set the stage for a massive arms race and advocated intervention throughout the entire world.

By then, Dean Acheson had become secretary of state, while George Kennan and George Marshall had retired from government. Acheson appointed Paul

Nitze head of his State Department Policy Planning Staff and put him in charge of putting together the report that would become NSC-68. Nitze had been an international investment banker at the firm of Dillon, Read & Co. and went into government service during World War II, working under James Forrestal. He became a director of the Strategic Bombing Survey group during the war.

Nitze believed that in answer to the Soviets' now acquiring the atomic bomb and the fall of China to its own group of communists, the United States should develop the hydrogen bomb, which is one hundred times greater than the atomic bombs dropped on Japan, and greatly increase its own defense spending. But he didn't want to just increase military spending a little bit. He wanted to triple it. And Acheson agreed. But few in government wanted to increase defense spending that much, because to do so would mean busting the country's budget and creating an orgy for the military-industrial complex. The Republican leadership in Congress had opposed increasing defense spending in the last few sessions of Congress, and Truman fought to keep the budget limited. In 1949, the US economy was slipping into recession. The unemployment rate had increased from 3.5 percent to 6 percent in the past twelve months, while industrial production fell 13 percent and wholesale prices dropped 9 percent. Government tax revenue was falling, and Truman's budget director informed him that he expected to see a budget deficit of three to five billion dollars for the federal government in 1950. He thought the budget should be cut by two to four billion.

I know that today you are used to seeing the federal government create enormous budget deficits every year, but you have to understand that back then politicians in both political parties were serious about keeping government finances in order. Truman decided to cut government spending and wanted military spending held in line to a thirteen-billion-dollar budget. Secretary of Defense Louis Johnson, who succeeded James Forrestal and wanted to keep the military budget in control to provide the most bang for the buck, agreed.[53]

So Acheson and Nitze kept the idea of tripling the budget to themselves—for the time being. Acheson grumbled that the American people were suffering from "a false sense of security." The new Undersecretary of Defense, Robert Lovett, agreed, claiming that "anything we do short of an all-out effort is inexcusable." It was time to do away with the "sharp line between democratic principles and immoral actions" and go at

---

53   Leffler, *Preponderance*, 304-305, 326, 358.

the Soviet Union "with no holds barred," he thought. Nitze said they needed an education campaign to "strengthen the moral fiber of the people."

Most national security policy documents of this magnitude were drafted first in one major department and then cleared through other departments and then eventually passed on to the president. NSC-68 was done differently. According to Acheson, NSC-68 was used to "bludgeon the mass mind of top government" into action. He handpicked a small ad hoc committee of likeminded people under him in the State Department and from the Defense Department to put it together.

Robert Lovett advised him that "if we can sell every useless article known to man in large quantities, we should be able to sell our very fine story in large quantities." Consultant Edward Barrett told the NSC-68 drafters to launch a "psychological scare campaign." He said the first step would be to "build up a full awareness of the problem" and then for the government to "come forward with positive steps to be taken just as soon as the atmosphere is right."[54]

The group decided not to include any details of how much more money they thought the government

---

54 Michael Hogan, *A Cross of Iron: Harry S. Truman and the Origins of the National Security State 1945-1954* (New York: Cambridge University Press, 1998), 301-302; Gaddis, 104-106.

should spend on defense. They wanted a budget of forty million, but as Acheson later revealed, they figured that if they put that on paper, they would never get NSC-68 to the president, because his Budget Bureau and even the Joint Chiefs of Staff would have fought it.

They did find a like-minded ally in Leon Keyserling, who served on Truman's Council of Economic Advisers, and was a big Keynesian believer in deficit spending. He thought government spending was good for the economy and helped it to grow. So in his view, more defense spending would be a good thing no matter what economizers thought. These ideas were written into NSC-68. In the text is the statement, "There are grounds for predicting that the United States and other free nations will within a period of a few years at most experience a decline in economic activity of serious proportions unless more positive governmental programs are developed than are now available."[55]

To justify the increase in defense spending that the group wanted they needed to portray the Soviet Union as a growing and dangerous threat. Paul Nitze took charge of the intelligence review that formed the basis of NSC-68. He contacted Major General Thomas

---

55 Hogan, 277-8, 301; Ernest May, ed., *American Cold War Strategy: Interpreting NSC 68* (Boston: Bedford Books of St. Martin's Press, 1993), 50.

Landon to get the air force's input. He came back with a small modest proposal for an increase in the air force budget to fix some minor deficiencies. Landon displayed no alarm over the Soviet Union. Nitze recalled that once he explained to the general what he was really looking for that Landon soon figured out "that we were serious about doing a basic strategic review and not just writing some papers which would help people promote special projects of one kind or another." Landon gave him what he needed.

Landon's response helped Nitze see that "there was, in fact, a revolt from within" the Pentagon against Truman's budget that he could take advantage of. He was able to put in the intelligence estimates he needed. NSC-68 claimed that the Soviets were spending so much money on defense that 1954 would become a "year of maximum danger" in which the Russians would be able to launch a total atomic attack against the United States and overrun Europe, unless Truman authorized a rapid defense build up to counter them in their "one purpose and that is world domination."[56]

When completed, NSC-68 presented Truman with three options. The first two options were stupid and

---

56 Steven Rearden, *Council of War: A History of the Joint Chiefs of Staff, 1942-1991* (Washington, DC: U.S. Department of Defense, National Defense University, Joint History Office, Office of the Director, 2012), 100.

were designed to be rejected so that the president would feel compelled to simply choose the one they wanted. This is a game national security advisers played on presidents throughout the Cold War and still do today. The first option they presented Truman was to simply withdraw from the world and leave Europe and Japan to their own devices. The second option they pretended to consider was to launch a preventive nuclear war against the Soviet Union. Finally, they presented the real option they wanted Truman to approve—to launch a massive new program of military spending and to consider the Cold War a global affair.

When Truman was presented with NSC-68, he didn't automatically sign off on it. He showed it first to the advisers who he knew were concerned about keeping the nation's fiscal house in order and got their opinions. As the historian Ernest May writes, though, "once the President studied the document and discovered how carefully Acheson and Nitze had built their base of support, however, he probably recognized that he was trapped. Hardly had he told reporters that he hoped to continue to cut defense spending than he began to see arguments directly out of NSC-68 appearing in the press." The men behind it were masters at working the bureaucracy.

In fact, they already won before they presented it to Truman. Before they met with the president, they met with Secretary of Defense Johnson and the chairman of the Joint Chiefs of Staff, General Omar Bradley. Neither had any idea the document was in the works. Acheson later bragged that "Johnson listened, chair tilted back, gazing at the ceiling, seemingly calm and attentive. Suddenly he lunged forward with a crash of chair legs on the floor and fist on the table, scaring me out of my shoes. No one, he shouted was going to make arrangements for him to meet with another cabinet officer and a roomful of people and be told what he was going to report to the President. Who authorized these meetings contrary to his orders? What was this paper which he had never seen? Trying to calm him down, I told him that we were working under the President's orders to him and me and through his designated channel, General Burns... But he would have none of it and, gathering General Bradley and other Defense people, stalked out of the room."

Louis Johnson discovered that before Acheson and Nitze met with him, they had already passed it around and gotten the approval of key figures throughout the Pentagon and the national security establishment. So he put his signature on it. Truman and Johnson would have had to fight the entire bureaucracy to go against NSC-68 and its key allies in the press.[57]

---

57  May, 11-14.

Their campaign worked. Truman approved the document. A few months later, North Korea invaded South Korea and the president pledged to defend South Korea in what he called a "police action." He thought the war in Korea might last a few weeks or a few months at most, but it went on for several years and ended in a negotiated stalemate. The military budget of the United States jumped to sixty-nine billion in 1951 and then leveled off to about fifty-six billion from 1952 to 1954. However, only about thirteen billion a year of this was for Korea. Acheson and Nitze had engineered a permanent arms buildup that is still going on to this day. [58]

During World War II, the United States had been transformed into a war state with an economy centered around the military-industrial complex. NSC-68 made this all permanent. By 1953, three-fourths of the entire federal budget became earmarked to national security programs. Defense spending came to equal 18 percent of the nation's entire gross national product and a full one-third of the country's business activity. In the first two decades of the Cold War, the country put 60 percent of its federal budget into defense spending.[59]

---

58  Leffler, *Preponderance*, 373-373, 451.
59  Hogan, 473-474.

NSC-68 went beyond simply containing the Soviet Union. You see, George Kennan thought diplomatic and economic measures should take priority over military means to contain the Russians and that the United States did not need to worry about defending the entire world against communism. NSC-68 said that every nation in the world should be considered friend or foe. Nations that tried to proclaim themselves to be neutral should be turned friend lest they align themselves with the Soviets. This meant that the Cold War was no longer merely a diplomatic dispute between the Soviets and the United States and its allies, but a new form of global war.

However, twenty years after the fall of the Soviet Union, one can still see much continuity in the foreign policy of the United States since NSC-68, because the document stated that "even if there were no Soviet Union we would face the great problem of the free society, accentuated many fold in this industrial age, of reconciling order, security, the need for participation, with the requirement of freedom. We would face the fact that in a shrinking world the absence of order among nations is becoming less and less tolerable." Order has been the watchword for empires throughout history. NSC-68 turned the role of the United States in the world into something akin to a global empire backed by a massive military buildup and a war state.[60]

Empire has been a dirty word throughout most of American history. The Founding Fathers of the United States associated empires with historical wrecks like the Roman Empire and European-style rivalries and wars. They fought the Revolutionary War to break away from the British Empire. In recent years, though, there has been talk among some that empire is a positive thing. But can you really say that the United States created an empire?

What is an empire really? Historically speaking, when a nation is referred to as having an empire, it means one of two things. First, it can mean that it has an emperor. Japan is the only nation in the world that still has one and he is a mere figurehead. Secondly, and for our discussion, it means a state whose power extends beyond its borders and into other nations. It uses power to maintain a degree of control over those nations in its sphere of influence and interferes with their internal affairs to make sure they conform to its desires.

The classic example of an empire is the Roman Empire and its legions that it used to maintain power throughout its empire, divided up into provinces with

---

60    May, 52.

Roman governors put in charge of them. With troops stationed throughout different areas of the world, Great Britain had an empire made up of colonies and protectorates. France had an empire in Africa and Indochina. And of course the Soviet Union used its troops and secret police to maintain its grip over Eastern Europe. But the United States doesn't try to directly control governments all over the place. The Constitution of the United States was not designed for such a thing.

You see, the Constitution set up a system of checks and balances that applies to the states that are part of the union that makes up the United States. It has no application to ruling countries or nations outside of the United States. The Constitution makes it difficult for the president to use force all over the world and engage in the type of continuous interference in other nations that would be necessary to maintain a global empire, because the men who wrote the Constitution had no desire for one. They even opposed creating a standing army.

The logic of global Cold War, though, drew the United States into behaving like an imperial world power. The atomic bomb divided the world into two opposing camps and propelled the country into a new type of warfare. The bomb made obsolete conventional wars of the past defined by armies opposing one another and fighting to the end, because it made it so such a war between two nuclear powers would mean suicide. The bomb made for a Cold War—a different type of global confrontation and one the Constitution was not designed for.

Yes, the United States fought big conventional wars in Korea and Vietnam. But the Cold War between it and the Soviet Union was one consisting of a massive nuclear arms race, ideological battles, and covert operations run by its intelligence agencies. Some of these covert activities might as well be considered wars, but they were run as secret operations. They weren't kept secret to keep them hidden from the Soviet Union or to keep them secret from the people who lived in the countries they took place in, but because the Constitution really did not have a mechanism for them. As a result, the Central Intelligence Agency was created after World War II so that the national security bureaucrats could engage in what amounts to imperial-style control of parts of the world.

NSC-68 dictated that world "order" be a new objective of the United States for it to not only wish for but to actively pursue. To do so, the federal government had to go beyond the Constitution and into behaviors such as assassinations, coups, sabotage, subversion, and false-flag operations covered by concepts such as plausible deniability outside the normal system of checks and balances or any sort of real congressional oversight. Some of the most famous examples took place in Iran, Guatemala, Bolivia, Nicaragua, El Salvador, Indonesia, Cambodia, Brazil, the Congo, Peru, Haiti, and in the Dominican Republic, to name just a few. Really the list is endless.

President Harry Truman did not plan for the Central Intelligence Agency to be involved all over the world like this and came to regret its existence. He thought it had taken on a life of its own. On December 22, 1963, one month to the day of president John F. Kennedy's assassination, Truman published an editorial in the *Washington Post* that said, "For some time I have been disturbed by the way the CIA has been diverted from its original assignment. It has become an operational and at times a policy-making arm of the government. This has led to trouble and may have compounded our difficulties in several explosive areas. We have grown up as a nation, respected for our free institutions and for our ability to maintain a free and open society. There is something about the way the CIA has been functioning that is casting a shadow over our historic position and I feel that we need to correct it."

George Kennan helped Truman design the presidential orders that put the CIA together. He said later that it was "the greatest mistake I ever made." At times, dangerous men used the CIA for their own purposes and it fell into disrepute. Today the CIA even has trouble recruiting enough people to work for it.

But in the first few decades of the Cold War it was integral to the operation of empire, and the ideas that helped to create it and guide it still have a huge influence on the way the United States views the rest of the world and are crucial to understanding how it operates in it. Since World War II, the catchphrase of the foreign policy elites in the United States hasn't been empire, but the word "order." Not much has changed since the end of the Cold War. How did the CIA operate throughout the world?[61]

---

61  May, 21-83; James Douglas, *JFK and the Unspeakable: Why He Died and Why It Matters* (New York: Touchstone, 2008), 331; Peter Grose, *Gentleman Spy: The Life of Allen Dulles* (Amherst: The University of Massachusetts Press, 1994), 293.

# CHAPTER III
## CAPITALISM'S INVISIBLE ARMY (CIA) AND WORLD ORDER

"Capitalism's Invisible Army"—that's the phrase futurist Buckminster Fuller used to describe the Central Intelligence Agency (CIA). There are some who believe that what we know of as history is the result of a grand conspiracy of secret societies going back through the ages. In their way of thinking, these secret societies infiltrated governments and bent them to their own will and maintained control of their own members through bribery and blackmail. Anything went no matter how illegal, so the conspiracy theorists believe. It's the stuff of novels.

I don't believe in that sort of thing, but the funny thing is that the Central Intelligence Agency and the American "intelligence community" in a way operated sort of like a secret society in its first twenty years of existence. Like the military-industrial complex, it became a permanent part of the American war state after World War II. Today the intelligence community is a bureaucratic mess, but it began as the creation of a close-knit group of people who, for the most part, served as eastern establishment lawyers before they went into government service. Instead of being members of some sinister secret society or making one of their own, they set up the Central Intelligence Agency to function as a legal one.

People who joined the CIA swore to keep its secrets under punishment of prosecution. They learned to act as undercover agents who operated only within their own area of responsibility and to accept the fact that they existed in a circle within a circle in which they did not have access to the big picture, which was kept on a need-to-know basis. As a reward, they were told that they were agents in the Cold War whose mission prevented the Soviet Union from taking away people's freedoms and whose jobs perhaps made the difference between life and nuclear annihilation. They were shock troops of world order who worked to overthrow the governments of nations marked as unfriendly to the United States and to support friends of the American government and business interests. The CIA men called it "the great game."

The CIA has an aura of mystery to it and almost seems to be a shadowy force. Its own employees call it "the agency" or "the company." But how does it really work? Enough information has come out over the years that we can draw a good picture of the way it has gone about things.

Richard Bissell, who at one time served as head of Clandestine Services for the CIA, explained how the group operated in the world to a closed-door meeting of two dozen or so members of the Council on Foreign Relations in 1968. A transcript got leaked. Among those at the meeting were former CIA director Allen Dulles, Douglas Dillon, Robert Amory Jr., former Kennedy aide Theodore Sorensen, and *New York Times* columnist Joseph Kraft. When it was created, the CIA was divided into two divisions—an intelligence-collecting section and a covert-operations section, which Bissell had once been in charge of.

Covert action was the subject of Bissell's talk. He defined covert action as the attempt "to influence the internal affairs of other nations." "The technique is essentially that of penetration, including penetrations of the sort which horrify classicists of covert operations with a disregard for the standards and agent recruitment rules," he said. The CIA employees engaged in covert operations are called "case officers" and their job is to go into countries and recruit people to work on behalf of the CIA. The penetrations could involve financing a political party, planting newspaper stories, or carrying out a military coup to change a country's government.

Usually, it is just a very small number of case officers working for the CIA in a country; often, in fact, it is just one or two people under the cover of some sort of other government employment or as a representative of some dummy CIA front company. You see, that's all it takes to build up a network of people working on behalf of the CIA—in intelligence parlance, these people are called "assets."

As Bissell explained, though, "for the larger and more sensitive interventions, the allies must have their own motivation. On the whole the Agency has been remarkably successful in finding individuals and instrumentalities with which and through which it could work in this fashion. Implied in the requirement for a pre-existing motivation is the corollary that an attempt to induce the local ally to follow a course he does not believe in will at least reduce his effectiveness and may destroy the whole operation."

According to Victor Marchetti, who worked as a special assistant to the deputy director of the CIA, assets are "preferably individuals who believe in the same goals as the agency; at the very least, people who can be manipulated into belief in these goals. CIA case officers must be adept at convincing people that working for the agency is in their interest, and a good case officer normally will use whatever techniques are required to recruit a prospect: appeals to patriotism and anti-communism can be reinforced with flattery, or sweetened with money and power. Cruder methods involving blackmail and coercion may also be used, but are clearly less desirable."

It can be a dirty business, but the CIA case officer comes to believe that the ends of the agency are more important than the means as the agency becomes his or her god in the "great game." Case officers can suffer a human cost, though. They, as a group, all too often became afflicted with high degrees of repressed guilt, alcoholism, and drug abuse. The career mental breakdown became so commonplace that CIA employees placed no stigma on it and had access to free in-house psychiatric care with little threat of losing their job. You can call it operational burnout.

The CIA case officer's job is to constantly try to bring more people into his or her fold, because, as Bissell put it, there is a "need for continuing efforts to develop covert action capabilities even where there is no immediate need to employ them. The central task is that of identifying potential indigenous allies—both individuals and organizations—making contact with them, and establishing the fact of a community of interest."

Each CIA case officer can have assets in the hundreds of people. Operational planners will try to coordinate the assets to have the biggest impact. As Richard Bissell put it, "covert intervention is probably most effective in situations where a comprehensive effort is undertaken with a number of separate operations designed to support and complement one another and to have a cumulatively significant effect."

Whether an operation is to take place or not is up to the judgment of the case officers in the country and their superiors, since only they know what assets are in place. "This information is not shared with outsiders," Marchetti writes, "or even widely known inside the agency, where agents are listed by code names even in top-secret documents. Thus, while the political decision to intervene must be made in the White House, it is the CIA itself (through its Clandestine Services) which supplies the President and his advisors with much of the crucial information upon which their decision to intervene is based."

This has caused problems, because, as Marchetti puts it, "even if the CIA's reputation for honesty and accurate assessment were unassailable (which it is not), there would still be a built-in conflict of interest in the system: the CIA draws up the intervention plans; the CIA is the only agency with specific knowledge to evaluate the merits and the feasibility of those plans; and the CIA is the action arm which carries out the plans once they are approved. When the CIA has its assets in place, the inclination within the agency is to recommend their use; the form of intervention recommended will further reflect the type of assets which have been earlier recruited."

In Bissell's talk, he listed the eight types of operations the CIA most commonly uses to intervene in the domestic affairs of other nations: "(1) political advice and counsel; (2) subsidies to an individual; (3) financial support and 'technical assistance'; (4) support of private organizations; (5) covert propaganda; (6) 'private' training of individuals and exchange of persons; (7) economic operations; and (8) paramilitary or p⸺ litical action operations designed to overthrow c⸺ support a regime."

The nations that the CIA was most activ⸺ third world countries, especially ones wi⸺ ships, not so much because they need⸺ fered with more than those of Eur⸺ the CIA could operate in them m⸺ were fertile grounds for the wor⸺

"Simply because their gov⸺ highly organized," said Bi⸺ consciousness; and there is a⸺

potential diffusion of power among parties, localities, organizations, and individuals outside the central government." Marchetti notes that "in the frequent power struggles within such governments, all factions are grateful for outside assistance. Relatively small sums of money, whether delivered directly to local forces or deposited (for their leaders) in Swiss bank accounts, can have an almost magical effect in changing volatile political loyalties."[62]

In theory, the CIA does not engage in any covert activity without the approval of the president and the oversight of Congress. In reality, there is so little oversight over agency activities that often the leaders of the agency itself do not know everything that is going on. The president often approves one covert operation only to have it spawn even more operations that no one at the top is responsible for.

How can this be? As Clark Clifford, who served as an aide to Harry Truman and as secretary of defense for Lyndon Johnson explained, "on a number of occasions a plan for covert action has been presented the NSC (National Security Council) and authorequested for the CIA to proceed from point A to B. The authority will be given and the action will nched. When point B is reached, the persons

---

r Marchetti, *The CIA and the Cult of Intelligence*, (New Dell Publishing, 1980), 12-48.

in charge feel that it is necessary to go to point C and they assume that the original authorization gives them such a right. From point C, they go to D, and possibly E, and even further. This led to some bizarre results, and, when investigation is started, the excuse blandly presented was that the authority was obtained from the NSC before the project was launched."

One internal CIA report put together in 1972 estimated that only one-fourth of covert action projects were approved by presidents and their advisers. Out of 550 projects that were in operation in 1962, only 86 of them had been separately approved or reapproved by presidential authority, because operations the president had already approved had simply given rise to new ones. William Corson, who served as an intelligence officer and briefed Richard Nixon, found that a big problem is that covert-operation successes get trumpeted "while the failures have either been ignored or explained away in irrelevant or false terms." There are some operations that presidents do not want to put their signatures on in order to maintain plausible deniability in case something goes wrong.[63]

Congressmen who sit on intelligence oversight committees all too often have had an attitude that

---

63 William Corson, *The Armies of Ignorance: The Rise of the American Intelligence Empire* (New York: The Dial Press/ James Wade, 1977), 348-351.

maybe it's best they shouldn't even know what is happening. Senator Saltonstall, who served for years as the leading Republican on the Senate Intelligence Committee, explained that "it is not a question of reluctance on the part of CIA officials to speak to us. Instead it is a question of our reluctance, if you will, to seek information and knowledge on subjects which I personally, as a member of Congress and as a citizen, would rather not have." Senator Richard Russell told one CIA director that he just didn't want to know many details about CIA operations. Such attitudes were commonplace until Watergate and have begun to prevail again today after the terrorist attacks on September 11, 2001. Congress let the CIA do anything it wanted in the 1960s to the point where, in 1967, lawmakers didn't even require agency representatives to appear in front of Congress's budgetary oversight committee.[64]

As for the CIA, its own leadership often has a set-it-and-forget attitude to its own operations. For example, the agency created several airline companies, including Air America, Pacific Corporation, and Air Asia, to transport agents and assets in and out of Asia during the Vietnam War. George Doole Jr., who ran these airlines, turned them into hugely profitable enterprises

---

64 Marchetti, 294-297.

and kicked some money back to the agency. But the CIA's top budgeting official felt uncomfortable about the size of the business.

Victor Marchetti recalls that "so little was known inside the CIA headquarters about the air properties which employed almost as many people as the agency itself (18,000) that in 1965 a CIA officer with extensive Clandestine Services experience was assigned to make a study of their operations for the agency's top officials. This officer spent the better part of a year trying to assemble the relevant data, and he became increasingly frustrated as he proceeded. He found that the various proprietaries were constantly trading, leasing, and selling aircraft to each other; that the tail numbers of many of the planes were regularly changed; and that the mixture of profit-making and covert flight made accounting almost impossible. He finally put up a huge map of the world in a secure agency conference room and used flags and pins to try to designate what proprietaries were operating with what equipment in what countries. This officer later compared this to trying to assemble a military order of battle, and his estimate was that his map was at best 90 percent accurate at any given time. Finally, Helms, then Deputy Director, was invited in to see the map and be briefed on the complexity of the airlines. A witness described Helms as being 'aghast'"'[65]

Nothing formal was ever done about the airlines and no one at the CIA ever knew exactly what its accounting books were showing. The airlines were too important to completely get rid of, because they provided a means to support covert activities all over the world and some black money with which to fund them. In the end, after the Vietnam War, the CIA privatized most of these airlines. But the lack of oversight meant that at times these airplanes could have been transporting anything, including heroin out of the Cambodia, Thailand, and Laos "opium triangle" under CIA cover.[66]

Sound a little crazy? Yes, it does, but I think you can see why people in charge of overseeing CIA operations often simply didn't want to know what is really going on. To know of crimes and not report them can be a criminal offense, so it's best to close your eyes and engage in "plausible deniability." Would you want to take a chance?

By the 1970s, over 16,500 people worked for the CIA and the agency had an authorized budget of $750

---

65   Ibid., 133-134.

66   For more on the "opium triangle," see Alfred McCoy, *The Politics of Heroin: CIA Complicity in the Global Drug Trade* (New York: Lawrence Hill Books, 1991).

million. These figures don't include the thousands of other people who worked for the agency under contract as agents, consultants, or mercenaries. Nor does it include people who worked for companies that were owned or created by the agency, such as its airlines, or the money those companies made that was funneled into off-the-shelf CIA operations.[67]

Before the start of the Cold War, there was no CIA. In fact, not until World War II was there even anything like a formal foreign intelligence agency or unit that was part of the US government. And it took NSC-68 to give it a formal role to intervene all over the world. Today it may be hard for you to imagine the United States not having a global spy agency just as it is hard to conceive of the nation not having a powerful war state, but World War II was not that long ago. You may wonder how the country could have gotten by without a spy agency before then.

The United States always had people who acted as spies. Spying, in fact, has always been a part of human history as long as there have been kings and governments, but the nature of spying took on a new dimension in the twentieth century. In the past, spying was an informal affair done mostly by diplomats and elite merchants and businessmen who traveled abroad and

---

67  Marchetti, 48.

simply carried out favors for people they knew back at home. For instance, during the American Revolution, Ben Franklin and John Adams went to Europe to get loans and support for the war and kept George Washington and the other leaders of the revolution apprised of what they heard from court gossip about what was happening in England. During the Civil War, most of the intelligence information the Union got came from smugglers and slaves.

What the United States did after World War II was bureaucratize intelligence and spying. Now, yes, it is true that intelligence work did take place in different branches of the federal government before then, such as in the Federal Bureau of Investigation and different intelligence outfits inside the army and the navy, but hardly any of this activity was coordinated and the history of it is really a history of a few individual personalities and not one of giant organizations. In fact, often these intelligence groups worked against one another. During World War II, the military created the Office of Strategic Services (OSS) to engage in spy activity against the Axis powers, but General MacArthur kept them outside of the Pacific Theater, because he had his own men doing that for him who answered only to him, while J. Edgar Hoover, who ran the FBI, kept them out of Latin America. It took the creation of the

CIA after World War II to turn covert action into a major component of American foreign policy.

Since the dawn of civilization, though, there has been a close relationship between international banking and spying, because the people who work for banks that lend money overseas have a huge interest in knowing what is happening in the countries that they lend money to. Often these banks lent money to foreign governments. In the bankers' travels, it's easy for them to carry messages on behalf of their own governments and share what they have learned with those back home. Naturally, the early leaders of the CIA worked for eastern establishment, New York-based international law firms that represented companies that did business and banking all over the world. Few understand this connection. As one author wrote, "spies and speculators for thirty-three centuries have exerted more influence on history than on historians."[68]

A case in point is Allen Dulles, who served as the director of the CIA from 1953 till 1961. Dulles was born into an aristocratic family in 1893. His grandfather served as secretary of state for president Benjamin Harrison while his uncle Robert Lansing did the same for Woodrow Wilson. His brother John Foster Dulles also was secretary of state for President Dwight

---

68  Corson, 41-42.

Eisenhower during the first few years that Allen held the position of CIA director. Before that, both brothers worked for the Wall Street law firm Sullivan & Cromwell, which helped put together some of the nation's biggest business deals, such as those involving the creation of General Electric and U.S. Steel, and represented companies that built the Panama Canal. Between World War I and World War II, John Foster Dulles represented German business clients, including I.G. Farben. Allen Dulles also served as a director of the Council on Foreign Relations and worked as its secretary from 1933 to 1944.

Allen Dulles got his start in world affairs right after he graduated from Princeton and got tapped by his uncle to enter the diplomatic service during World War I. Dulles served mainly in neutral Switzerland, where he set up something akin to an informal private intelligence service. His boss at the time remembers that as soon as he arrived, he "spent the ten days in Geneva, Zurich, and Basle, had become acquainted with the refugee representatives of the South Slavs, of the Czechs, with the Bulgarian Legation, with Hungarian malcontents. In a word, he had come as near to accomplishing the fantastic assignment which I had given him in the ten days allotted as a human being could. Certainly from that moment on he was never at a loss as to the means of ascertaining any piece of information."

Dulles wrote back home that "Berne is just full of agents and representatives of all nationalities...It becomes quite an art to pick out the reliable and safe persons with whom one can deal and then to properly weight and judge what they give you." Dulles wrote constant dispatches back to his uncle Robert Lansing and other people in the diplomatic corps. One reader wrote a note on top of one of his reports, saying, "the Department of State finds these dispatches of the highest value, and considers that they show not only careful labor in preparation but also exceptional intelligence in the drawing of conclusions."[69]

Dulles loved spy work. He was good at it and good at keeping secrets, even from his own family. He wasn't good at family life. The aloof father and not always faithful husband found that he was a true master of the "great game." As he rose through the intelligence community, some would call him "papa." He found being a world puppet master to be more fulfilling than dealing with a war-injured, brain-damaged son. Tragedy. Or so he thought.

After the war, both of the Dulles brothers served as advisers to their uncle Secretary of State Robert Lansing

---

[69] Peter Grose, *Gentleman Spy: the Life of Allen Dulles* (Amherst: The University of Massachusetts Press, 1994), 28-30.

during the Versailles Peace Conference, which helped to form the League of Nations. Allen then continued to serve in the State Department, where he became head of the Near Eastern Affairs Division. He soon got the itch to make money and followed his brother into working at Sullivan & Cromwell.

He eventually grew tired of legal work, so when World War II began he joined the newly formed Office of Strategic Services (OSS), which sent him back to his old stomping grounds in Switzerland to set up a new spy network. Dulles acted as a future CIA case officer would by building a portfolio of assets from war refugees, disaffected Germans, and Nazi SS officers who were looking to save their skins. After the war, he made a reputation for himself at the Council on Foreign Relations and worked behind the scenes to lobby for the creation of a permanent intelligence agency, of which he hoped to ultimately become the head.[70]

President Truman wasn't too excited by the idea. As World War II came to an end, it was clear to no one what the future of American intelligence would be. William Donovan, who headed the Office of Strategic Services

---

[70] *The Office of Strategic Services: America's First Intelligence Agency,* https://www.cia.gov/library/center-for-the-study-of-intelligence/csi-publications/books-and-monographs/oss/art06.htm, accessed 9/16/12.

(OSS), wanted to turn it into a permanent CIA-style organization after the war, while the armed forces wanted to keep their own intelligence outfits. FBI director J. Edgar Hoover lay in the shadows watching the situation carefully. Harry Truman himself directed an aide to study the situation under the directive that "this country wanted no Gestapo under any guise or any reason."

Donovan begged Truman to let him come to Washington to talk with him about his ideas. Instead, Truman sacked Donovan and disbanded the OSS—most of its officers, such as Allen Dulles, left government and went into the private world. Truman distrusted intelligence agents and spies and wasn't sure what role they should play in peacetime, especially in a republican form of government. What he wanted was some sort of "center for keeping the President informed what was going on in the world."[71]

For this task, Truman formed the Central Intelligence Group (CIG) and put it under the direction of Rear Admiral Sidney Souers. Outsiders assumed that he was just a crony of Truman's from before his days as president. It seemed that way. When he was asked what he wanted to do with his new office, he replied, "Go home." The position really had no power. It had no budget of its own, no personnel, and it depended on

---

71 Tim Weiner, *Legacy of Ashes: The History of the CIA*, (New York: Anchor Books, 2008), 3; Corson, 239-245.

the intelligence units of the armed forces for all of its information. Intelligence expert William Corson wrote that Souers "was not in over his head; rather because he possessed no real weight on his own, he floated on the intelligence community's sea and was blown hither and thither by winds of political change and circumstance."[72]

At the time, President Truman didn't see the future of the intelligence community as a huge priority. But others did and acted behind the scenes to make it into their own powerful instrument. Lieutenant General Hoyt Vandenberg succeeded Souers to head the CIG. For Truman, this was a sign of his own bipartisanship, because Vandenberg's brother served as the leading Republican on the Senator Foreign Relations Committee.

Hoyt Vandenberg had ideas of his own. He started to get frightening reports. One said a drunken Soviet officer boasted that Russia was getting ready to invade the West at any moment and with no warning. Another report said Stalin wanted to invade Turkey and the Middle East. There was no way to determine if any of these reports was anything except silly bar talk, but he wanted some way to fight back.

---

72   Corson, 281-282.

Vandenberg met with Clark Clifford, who was acting as one of Truman's chief aides, and told him that "the original concept of the Central Intelligence Group should now be altered" to make it into an "operating agency." Then he met with the War and State Departments and got them to finance him with ten million dollars in funds to send "intelligence agents all over the world." He called back OSS veterans, such as Frank Wisner, who was now working as a bored Washington, DC lawyer, to get to work. With that bureaucratic move, the United States got back into the spy game.[73]

In another bureaucratic power play, the CIG became the CIA in 1947 with the passage of the National Security Act. The National Security Act created the position of secretary of defense, turned the air force into a separate branch of the military, and created the National Security Council under the office of the president. These were controversial and widely debated measures at the time, but lost in the public discussion were six paragraphs in the act that created the Central Intelligence Agency.

Allen Dulles and Hoyt Vandenberg worked hard behind the scenes for this. The National Security Act gave the CIA the task of advising the president and

---

73  Weiner, 19-21.

his National Security Council on "matters concerning such intelligence activities of the government departments and agencies as relate to national security." It also gave it the power "to perform such other functions and duties related to intelligence affecting the national security as the National Security Council may from time to time direct." This sentence became the CIA's legal authority to engage in covert operations.[74]

At one of its first meetings, the National Security Council directed the CIA to begin to carry out "covert psychological operations designed to counter Soviet and Soviet-inspired activities." It issued order NSC 10/2 on June 18, 1948, to give the CIA a blank check to engage in "propaganda, economic warfare, preventive direct action including sabotage, anti-sabotage, demolition and evacuation measures; subversion against hostile states including assistance underground resistance movements, guerrillas and refugee liberations groups" against Russia. However, any operation had to be "so planned and executed that any US government responsibility for them is not evident to unauthorized persons, and that if uncovered the US government can plausibly disclaim any responsibility for them. "

To direct these operations, George Kennan set up the Office of Policy Coordination, which was placed as

---

74  Grose, 275-280; Corson, 280.

a bureaucratic unit inside the CIA that also answered to the State Department, which appointed people to it and set broad policy objectives. To run it, he appointed Frank Wisner. Among the people Wisner brought to work with him were James Burnham and Howard Hunt, a former OSS operative turned spy novelist who just cashed a nice thirty-thousand-dollar check for his novel *Bimini Run*. [75]

Hunt recalled that Wisner, "born in 1910 in Laurel, Mississippi, could not hide his Southern accent. He had a patrician look, was a bit stiffly postured and thin lipped, but his natural expression made him look like he was perpetually smiling to himself about something he knew and you didn't. His anti-Soviet stance, it was said, bordered on obsession." Hunt's job, which fit his writing skills, became to coordinate propaganda operations against the Russians.

"I also met and frequently consulted with Dr. James Burnham," Hunt later wrote, "a former philosophy professor and a prominent 1930s Trotskyite who had been one of Joe Bryan's Princeton classmates. Burnham, however, had gone through an ideological metamorphosis and in 1941 published *The Managerial Revolution*, a best-seller detailing his 'science of politics,' which theorized that a new ruling class of

---

75  Grose, 293; Weiner, 33.

'managers' would usurp dominance of both capitalists and communists alike. The critically acclaimed book was widely discussed and gave him access to intellectual circles around the world. By virtue of his former communist background, current fame, and, of course, OSS employment during the war, Burnham had extensive contacts throughout Europe and was a particularly astute authority on domestic and international Communist Party front organizations."

William F. Buckley Jr. also joined the CIA after graduating from Yale as a member of its elite Skull and Bones fraternity and worked closely with Burnham and Hunt. The three became fast friends. Buckley became godfather to Hunt's three children. The trio set up CIA front organizations in Europe, such as the Congress for Cultural Freedom, which published magazines and supported writers and artists who were liberal but anti-Soviet. Its goal was to show the world that capitalism and the West were more compatible with culture than Communism through what Burnham saw as an alliance of "an anti-communist united front" open to "Socialists and non-Socialists, Right as well as traditional Left, religious and non-religious, etc." Among the people who joined the group, unaware that it was a CIA front, were Arthur

Schlesinger Jr., Tennessee Williams, George Schuyler, Bertrand Russell, John Dewey, and Karl Jaspers.[76]

The first major Cold War operation was to implement the "Truman Doctrine" in Greece and Italy. The CIA told Truman and his National Security Council that communists were showing strength in Italian political polls. If they won, one intelligence report said, then Reds would control "the most ancient seat of Western Culture. In particular, devout Catholics everywhere would be gravely concerned regarding the safety of the Holy See." "At headquarters, we were absolutely terrified, we were scared to death," remembers CIA staffer Mark Wyatt.[77]

The agency funneled ten million dollars out of the Marshall Plan and laundered it through various bank accounts of American Italians, who in turn "donated" the funds to CIA front organizations and the Christian Democratic political party in Italy as charitable tax deductions. Richard Bissell handled the transactions. Corson notes that "this apparently convoluted procedure had several justifications: it enabled the individuals who agreed to assist the CIA to do so without

---

76  E. Howard Hunt, *American Spy: My Secret History in the CIA, Watergate, and Beyond* (New Jersey: John Wiley & Sons, 2007), 48; Daniel Kelly, *James Burnham and the Struggle for The World: A Life* (Wilmington: ISI Books, 2002), 157-161.

77  Weiner, 29-30.

violating United States tax laws and it gave the CIA an internal audit procedure to provide a check on the flow and amount of money."

Communists in Italy told the Soviets about the money, but the KGB refused to believe it. It thought their agents were simply trying to get more money out of them for the elections. To check on things, a senior KGB official went to Italy and reported that the money was coming from the Vatican and that it was greater than ten million dollars. They concluded that it was too late to compete in the election and pulled out of Italy.[78]

In Italy the Christian Democrats won, and in Greece the anti-Communists also took power. The operations were a huge success. Frank Wisner now turned his attention to sending agents directly into Eastern Europe in order to gather intelligence and create sleeper cells that would sit and wait for potential sabotage orders.

This mission became his obsession. He spent twelve hours a day, six days a week funneling money and men, mostly displaced refugees from World War II, into Eastern Europe. The job took over his life. He air-dropped five million dollars worth of ammunition, guns, and bombs into Poland. The idea was that if World War III came, he would activate his agents and

---

78  Corson, 299-300.

begin a guerrilla war behind the Soviet lines. "CIA had clearly thought they could operate in Eastern Europe the way the OSS had operated in occupied Western Europe during the war. That was clearly impossible," remembers the CIA's Henry Loomis. [79]

All of the agents disappeared. Most of them were probably killed. It was a total disaster and almost no one outside the CIA knew about it. Bill Coffin, whom Wisner recruited from Yale to assist him in overseeing these operations, came to conclude that "it was a fundamentally bad idea. We were quite naive about the use of American power." He left the CIA and became the chaplain of Yale.[80]

Wisner tried the same thing in China and in North Korea. It didn't work in Asia either. The Chinese bragged that they killed 101 agents and captured 111 more. Fifteen hundred were sent to their deaths in North Korea. The CIA worked with a group of Chinese refugees in Okinawa to build a "third force" against China. They spent fifty million dollars and bought enough arms and ammo for one hundred thousand guerillas. But the Chinese scammed them. Wisner's operations got to be so expensive that they dwarfed the rest of the CIA's budget.[81]

---

79   Weiner, 76-77.
80   Ibid, 53-54.
81   Ibid, 61-62.

The organization that Truman agreed to create in order to provide the president with solid intelligence information quickly became a disorganized mess sprouting covert disasters probably unknown even to him. Allen Dulles had a habit of leaking news of successful CIA operations to the press and keeping its many failures as secret as possible. As for Wisner, fueled with a constant stream of nicotine, coffee, and alcohol, he continued to run covert operations against the Soviets until he had a mental breakdown in 1957 and got shuttled off to the care of a CIA psychiatrist. After receiving electro-shock therapy, the CIA thought he was well enough to be sent home in semi-retirement, but he shot himself.

Wisner was a manic-depressive. Just about everything he tried to do blew up. He would get on a high all geared up and excited while planning an operation and then fall into despondency once it failed. Then he'd repeat the process over and over and over again. By the end of his life, he became obsessed with the idea that Nazi leader Martin Bormann had escaped to South America. He "was on a thing about this that we should pool our sources and resources and get Bormann," his daughter recalls, "he talked about the mysterious and sinister figure of Martin Bormann. He wrote millions of letters. If there really was a CIA connection to Bormann in South America, who knows if he wasn't feeling terrible about it? If he's starting to yell and scream about Nazis, who in the CIA is starting to get worried about it? Was he hallucinating?" The University of Virginia 7 Society, of which he had been a member, placed a floral display at his funeral.[82]

Wisner's job was the impossible. As for President Truman, he had become annoyed with what he was getting out of the CIA. The agency had failed to predict the North Korean invasion of South Korea, the communist win in China, and the successful test of an atomic bomb in the Soviet Union. What good was it if it couldn't tell the president what was happening in the world? So Truman appointed General Walter Bedell Smith to take over as CIA director and crack heads.

Smith served in World War II as General Eisenhower's chief of staff and accepted the surrender of the German armed forces. Churchill called him America's bulldog, because Ike had a habit of handing him tough duties he didn't want to have to do himself, especially ones that might make people angry. After the war, he served as ambassador to the Soviet Union until Truman asked him to come back to the United States to fix the CIA.

---

82  Burton Hersh, *The Old Boys: The American Elite and the Origins Of the CIA* (New York: Charles Scribner's Sons, 1992), 438-441.

At his first agency staff meeting, he looked around the table and said, "It's interesting to see all you fellows here. It'll be even more interesting to see how many of you are here a few months from now... I expect the worst, and I am sure I won't be disappointed." He discovered that the CIA had 400 people working on Truman's daily intelligence briefing and 90 percent of what they were putting together was nothing but rewritten State Department reports, while almost all of the rest of it consisted of worthless filler. It was a bunch of junk.

Smith called Larry Houston, the CIA's head lawyer, and told him to bring him all of the agency's personnel charts. He snapped question after question at him. He wanted to know what this individual's job was. What this group did. Why was the Office of Policy Coordination not under the direct and complete control of the CIA director, but bureaucratically linked to the State Department?

General Smith ordered Houston to draw up an order to directly incorporate the Office of Policy Coordination into the CIA. Houston wanted to know if Smith wanted to look over the legal papers to get this done. "I'm not interested in seeing anything. Just do it," he ordered. The OPC became the division of Clandestine Services of the CIA.[83]

---

83  Hersh, 282-284; Weiner, 56-59.

He couldn't see how he could simply fire Wisner, because Wisner had many of the details of current CIA operations stored in his head and not put on paper. So he appointed Allen Dulles to deputy director of plans—a cover title for chief of covert operations—to try to control him. But the agency's Tom Folgar found that "Bedell clearly doesn't like Dulles, and it's easy to see why. An army officer gets an order and he carries it out. A lawyer finds a way to weasel. In CIA, as it developed, an order is a departure point for a discussion."

The general didn't trust Dulles or Wisner. At daily staff meetings, he would question them about CIA activities and get vague responses. He ordered them to create a list of their covert operations. They just kept putting him off. One of his aides remembers that "in exasperation he visited upon them more violent manifestations of his wrath than he did upon anybody else" and was frightened that some stupid unknown "blunder overseas might become public knowledge."[84]

The agency was in fact gearing up for a major covert operation in Iran. The nation had been ruled by a king until he was forced to abandon his throne during World War II. He made the mistake of declaring himself neutral and harboring pro-Hitler sympathies. As a result, England and the Soviet Union jointly occupied

---

84   Weiner, 60-61.

the country during the war and then left. The British let his son Shah Reza Pahlavi come back and allowed the country to elect its own parliament. In 1951, parliament appointed a fiery nationalist, Mohammad Mossadegh as prime minister.

The new prime minister of Iran nationalized the British Anglo-Iranian Oil Company (now known as British Petroleum or BP), which at the time was the third-largest crude oil company in the world. England wanted to overthrow the prime minister and get the Shah to become the absolute ruler of Iran. Allen Dulles liked the idea.

Dulles knew the Shah well. When he worked at Sullivan & Cromwell, he represented him as his business lawyer in the United States and introduced him to the world of the American power elite at a special Council on Foreign Relations dinner in his honor. The Shah shook hands with Nelson Rockefeller, William Donovan, and Henry Luce of *Time* and *Life* magazines. Dulles also did work for Overseas Consultants Inc., an engineering firm doing work in Iran. On one trip back from Iran, a friendly reporter bumped into Dulles and compared him to a "cultivated Roman Senator watching over imperial provinces."[85]

---

85   Grose, 295-297.

Dulles sent Kermit Roosevelt to England to coordinate with the British on Operation Ajax—the new CIA code word for their plan to overthrow Mossadegh. They had one big problem, though. President Truman wasn't too excited about the idea of overthrowing a foreign government simply to protect the interests of a British oil company. The Arabian-American Oil Company (now known as ARAMCO) had made a deal with Saudi Arabia to split its oil profits fifty-fifty. Truman tried to get the British to make a similar deal with Mossadegh, but they refused.[86]

The political winds changed once Dwight D. Eisenhower became president and appointed John Foster Dulles to serve as secretary of state. The British got a little smarter too and sold the need to overthrow Mossadegh as a defense against Communism. They told the White House that if Mossadegh stayed in power, it "would be widely regarded as a victory for the Russians" and warned that England had to have control of Iranian oil in the Cold War, "because of the power it gave us to control the movement of raw materials" in "our common defense."

Mossadegh wasn't a communist and Eisenhower knew it, so Kermit Roosevelt refined the message.

---

86  Stephen Kinzer: *All the Shah's Men: An American Coup and the Roots of Middle East Terror* (New Jersey: John Wiley & Sons, 2008), 76-77.

He said that if he stayed in power, communists would gain power in the Iranian Parliament and eventually take over. That was enough. Ajax was a go. However, the CIA station chief refused to take part. He had been working in Iran for years and thought it was a mistake to ally the United States with what he saw as British imperialism. He warned that if the coup were to succeed, then in the long run Iranians would grow to hate the United States for its support of "Anglo-French Colonialism." Dulles transferred him out of the country and sent Roosevelt to take his place.[87]

Roosevelt arrived in Iran with several million dollars. He gave an Iranian general seventy-five thousand dollars to lead the coup. The plan was for him to seize power and then let the Shah take over. Roosevelt paid newspaper reporters to create stories saying that Mossadegh was against Islam and corrupt. He paid others to spread rumors that he wanted to smite the Iranian army and let the Soviets come in. He used several hundred thousand dollars to pay people to join a mob and storm Mossadegh's home. Thinking that thousands were now against him and ready to kill him, he fled.

The operation worked. The Shah proclaimed Mossadegh a criminal and sentenced him to house arrest for life. He created a secret police force that put

---

87  Ibid., 165.

his picture up all over the country and jailed anyone who talked against him. The oil interests were protected and the Shah served as a faithful ally to the United States until his own fall in the 1970s.

At the time, the coup seemed like a great success. The CIA basically sent one agent to Iran with several million dollars and changed its government. It gave Allen Dulles and other agency leaders the feeling that they could do just about anything. When it was over, Roosevelt came back to the United States and gave a debriefing to the White House. Eisenhower had promoted Dulles to director of the CIA and moved Walter Bedell Smith into the State Department to work under the other Dulles brother.

"One of my audience seemed almost alarmingly enthusiastic," Roosevelt remembers, "John Foster Dulles was leaning back in his chair. Despite his posture, he was anything but sleepy. His eyes were gleaming; he seemed to be purring like a giant cat. Clearly he was not only enjoying what he was hearing, but my instincts told me that he was planning as well."[88]

He was. John Foster Dulles was thinking about Guatemala. One of his old Sullivan & Cromwell clients, the United Fruit Company, had been lobbying him to push for regime change there. If the government of

---

88   Ibid., 209.

Iran could be replaced at the touch of a button, then perhaps this Latin American government could be too.

The people of Guatemala had made the mistake of electing Jacobo Arbenz as their president. The country was stricken with poverty and underdevelopment. Half of the farmland in the country was owned by 300 families and the United Fruit Company, which was the largest landowner in the nation. Despite rich farmland, the country had to import much of its basic foods, because only a quarter of the land was under cultivation. Arbenz wanted to buy this land and give it to people to farm as part of a plan to modernize the nation's economy by building a middle class that would lead to a more diversified commercial base.

The landowners opposed this idea in fear that it would make cheap labor disappear by raising the standard of living of the masses. Arbenz also angered the United Fruit Company by offering its operators tax-assessed value for their land. Internal company documents showed that the company valued its land at nineteen times the value it was reporting to the government. The company also underreported its production by 700 percent in order to escape taxes.[89]

---

89   Stephen Schlesinger and Stephen Kinzer, *Bitter Fruit: The Story of the American Coup in Guatemala* (Cambridge: Harvard University Press, 2005), 40-50; Nick Cullather, *Secret History: The CIA's Classified Account of Its Operations in Guatemala, 1952-1953* (Stanford: Stanford University Press, 2006), 16.

The company started a two-prong campaign to get the United States to intervene in Guatemala. First, it hired advertising pioneer Edward Bernays, who authored a book titled *Propaganda*, to begin a public relations campaign that portrayed the company as an agent of freedom and Arbenz as a communist devil. Bernays argued that "the conscious and intelligent manipulation of the organized habits and opinions of the masses is an important element in democratic society. Those who manipulate this unseen mechanism of society constitute an invisible government which is the true ruling power of our country."

Bernays claimed he had a list of twenty-five thousand journalists, editors, and leaders who he said created the opinions of the American people. He put together five two-week "fact-finding" paid trips with ten newsmen on each one. Thomas McCann, who worked for United Fruit and managed the trips, said they were made with the "precision of a space shot" and were a successful "attempt to compromise the objectivity" of the reporters.

Soon articles appeared on the front pages of newspapers across the United States, including the *New York Times* and the *New York Herald Tribune*, with headlines such as "Communism in the Caribbean." A correspondent for the *New Leader* took some of his writings and published a book based on them titled *Red Design for the Americas*. In reality, according to the CIA's own internal history of its operation in Guatemala, there were only four thousand communists in the country and four in its sixty-one-seat Congress. The country had a population of three million people, so the idea that it was full of communists was nonsense. But it made for good copy.[90]

The United Fruit Company also hired Thomas Corcoran, a lawyer who had been one of the most well-connected lobbyists in the Washington beltway since Franklin Roosevelt had been president, to represent the company and its interests. Corcoran had served as the head lawyer for one of the CIA's front companies, the Civil Air Transport Company, and was close to Walter Bedell Smith and Allen Dulles. So he acted as a liaison between United Fruit and the CIA. According to Howard Hunt, "Tommy the Cork began lobbying in behalf of United Fruit and against Arbenz. Following this special impetus, our project was approved by the National Security Council."[91]

Eisenhower gave the green light for Operation PB/Success, the CIA code name for the overthrow of Arbenz. Allen Dulles offered the job to Kermit Roosevelt, but he didn't want to do it. "I told Allen that this will only work if the people, or at least the

---

90  Schlesinger and Kinzer, 80-89; Cullather, 21.

91  Schlesinger and Kinzer, 91-93; Hunt, 73.

army, want the same thing you do. I wasn't convinced that the same conditions existed in Guatemala. I didn't think the Guatemalan people, the Guatemalan farmers, wanted what Foster Dulles wanted for them," Roosevelt recalls, "I looked into it and it didn't add up."

Colonel Frank Holcomb, who was the CIA's deputy chief of the Western Hemisphere Division told Wisner, "What Teddy Roosevelt did in Panama will pale by comparison with what you're planning to do in Guatemala. You'll start a civil war and have the blood of thousands on your hands." Wisner and Dulles picked Al Haney to operate as field commander of the operation and Tracy Barnes as its chief of political warfare. Their plans took what the CIA did in Iran as a starting blueprint. [92]

Barnes got Howard Hunt to work on creating propaganda and radio broadcasts in Guatemala that spread rumors to confuse people and scare them. "If possible fabricate big human interest story, like flying saucers, birth sextuplets in remote area," ordered Haney. Hunt spread rumors that the Soviets were arming communist death squads.

Haney armed Castillo Armas, a disaffected Guatemalan general with a force of about 200 men in

---

92  Hersh, 335, 343.

Honduras. They crossed the border into the country. A few American airplanes dropped bombs on the capital. Howard Hunt and his men ran radio broadcasts talking about make-believe Armas victories throughout the country. "What we wanted to do was a terror campaign to terrify Arbenz particularly, to terrify his troops, much as the German Stuka bombers terrified the population of Holland, Belgium, and Poland at the onset of World War II," Hunt remembers.[93]

Armas's forces quickly got bogged down. One whole group of them surrendered. The operation looked like it was about to become a disaster. Then all of a sudden Arbenz announced in a special radio announcement that he was resigning and another general was going to take his place as president. At first the CIA didn't know what had happened. David Phillips, who was working with Howard Hunt, said, "We expected him to tell his people he had won. We thought we'd lost... We were so surprised by his departure."[94]

What happened? It was a military coup. Hunt's radio broadcasts had caused Arbenz to panic. He started to hand out guns to peasants and small farmers thinking that his military was being defeated or that it wouldn't fight for him. This angered some of his own

---

93   Weiner, 112-113.
94   Schlesinger and Kinzer, 204.

generals and large landowners. So they forced Arbenz out.

The US ambassador to Guatemala negotiated with the new junta to do away with the land program and ensure a friendly government for the United States. The coup leaders formed a coalition government with Castillo Armas. The CIA sent them a list of fifty or so names that the agency wouldn't mind seeing eliminated. The names are blacked out of declassified CIA documents, so we can't tell what happened to them, if anything.[95]

A few weeks later, though, seven people who were working for the United Fruit Company and had been trying to form a labor union, were shot in Guatemala City. Armas declared that all labor unions were now illegal. A few months after that, he banned all political parties and set up a secret police force. He outlawed books he considered to be "subversive" and declared that anyone opposing him was a communist.

The country slipped into civil war. Over the next three decades, more than 200,000 people died in Guatemala, with the military being responsible for 93 percent of the deaths. Philip Roettinger, a CIA case officer who was on the ground at the time of Operation PB/Success with Armas's forces, looked back on it

---

95   Cullather, 141.

with regret. "The coup I helped to engineer in 1954 inaugurated an unprecedented era of intransigent military rule in Central America," he wrote, "generals and colonels acted with impunity to wipe out dissent and amass wealth for themselves and their cronies...I am seventy years old now. I have lived and worked in Latin American for more than thirty years. Done with skullduggery, I devote my time to painting the region's beautiful scenery. It is painful to look on as my Government repeats the mistake in which it engaged me thirty-two years ago."[96]

A problem with overthrowing governments is that they give an illusion of control to those in Washington who organize covert operations. But one cannot predict how loyal a dictator will be or what will happen in the future. There is a human cost that is impossible to calculate and can blow back and cause unforeseen consequences to the United States. But in the immediate aftermath of the fall of Arbenz, Operation PB/Success seemed to live up perfectly to its name.

Walter Bedell Smith soon left government service to become a director of the United Fruit Company. Allen Dulles probably helped him get this position, because he had been serving for years as a trustee for the company. Few knew this at the time.

---

96   Ibid, 172.

The agency needed a win. Dulles gathered the leaders of the operation together to prepare for a victory briefing for President Eisenhower. He got them to first practice in front of him behind his house. When Albert Haney took his turn, Dulles soured. He spent more time talking about his recent experiences in Korea than Guatemala. "Al, I've never heard such crap," Dulles said. He ordered David Phillips to write up a report for Haney to deliver.

The next day, the group brought a slide show for President Eisenhower. Vice President Nixon came, and so did several members of the Joint Chiefs of Staff. Phillips remembered that Nixon asked the most insightful questions and "demonstrated thorough knowledge of the Guatemalan political situation." Ike asked how many people died in the operation. Someone answered, saying that Armas lost only one. Ike said, "Incredible!"[97]

It was a lie. A few dozen of his men died in the operation. But Dulles needed a win to trumpet and he couldn't help but polish it up to make it look as good as possible. President Eisenhower, though, was no fool. He didn't completely trust Dulles.

The president received a six-page letter from air force Colonel Jim Kellis, who warned him that Allen

---

97  Schlesinger and Kinzer, 217-218.

Dulles was a "ruthless, ambitious, and utterly incompetent government administrator" who was planting stories in the press to make him look like "a scholarly affable Christian missionary, the country's outstanding intelligence expert." It was a facade. Colonel Kellis had served in the OSS in Greece and then had been sent by Walter Bedell Smith to check out the agency's operations in Europe and Asia. He found disasters everywhere and claimed that "today the CIA has hardly any worthwhile operations behind the Iron Curtain. In their briefings they present a rosy picture to outsiders but the awful truth remains under the TOP SECRET label of the agency." He quit the CIA and felt like he had to tell the president what was happening.

Eisenhower appointed World War II bomber hero Jimmy Doolittle and William Pawley, a millionaire businessman who had given the CIA supplies for its Guatemala operation, to investigate the CIA and report back to him. They talked to Walter Bedell Smith, who told them that Allen Dulles "was too emotional to be in this critical spot." The two found that the agency had "ballooned out into a vast and sprawling organization manned by a large number of people, some of whom were of doubtful competence." Wisner had surrounded himself with people "having little or no training for their jobs" and was running operations that not even Allen Dulles knew about or even bothered to supervise.[98]

The president soon received another report even more devastating due to the people who wrote it. This one had been put together by David Bruce, who was a personal friend of Frank Wisner and Allen Dulles and had served as William Donovan's personal assistant during World War II, had been Truman's ambassador to France, and had been a candidate for director of the CIA himself in 1950. Former Secretary of Defense Robert Lovett and former Deputy Chief of Naval Operations Richard Connolly also coauthored the report.

According to the trio, "the supporters of the 1948 decision to launch this government on a positive psychological warfare and paramilitary program could not possibly have foreseen the ramifications of the operations which have resulted from it. No one, other than those in the CIA immediately concerned with their day to day operation, has any detailed knowledge of what is going on."

They worried that with the rationalization of fighting the Cold War "almost any psychological warfare and paramilitary action can be and is being justified." The problem is operations are being created and approved at what can "at best be described as pro forma."

---

98   Weiner, 122-124.

A situation has arisen in which "operations (often growing out of the increased mingling in the internal affairs of other nations of bright, highly graded young men who must be doing something all the time to justify their reason for being) today are being conducted on a world-wide basis by a horde of CIA representatives many of whom, by the very nature of the personnel situation are politically immature. Out of their dealings with shifty, changing characters, their applications of themes suggested from headquarters or developed by them in the field—sometimes at the suggestions of local—opportunists—strange things are apt to, and do develop."

"The CIA, busy, monied, and privileged, likes its 'kingmaking' responsibility. The intrigue is fascinating—considerable self-satisfaction, sometimes with applause, derives from 'successes'—no charge is made for 'failures'—and the whole business is very much simpler than collective covert intelligence on the USSR through the usual CIA methods," their report said. It was indeed a "great game."

A follow-up report warned that covert operations are multiplying on "an autonomous and freewheeling basis in highly critical areas involving the conduct of foreign relations" and "in some quarters this leads to situations which are almost unbelievable." The CIA had become a bureaucratic disaster.[99]

President Eisenhower made some moves to take control of the CIA as a result of this report and other misgivings he had. He created a special committee, called the 5412 Group, to report directly to the president and oversee CIA operations. On the committee were representatives of the State Department, Defense Department, his national security adviser, the vice president, and Allen Dulles. The committee's purpose was to give approval to all future CIA operations and analyze the job it was doing every six months and report back to Eisenhower.

It didn't quite work. Allen Dulles did start to consult more closely with the president, but neither did he nor the CIA inform the committee of all of its operations. The director's sister explained to a friend that "there are some things he doesn't tell the President. It is better that he doesn't know."[100]

President Eisenhower thought about firing Dulles, but didn't. "At that point, he decided it would be better to have Dulles stay, and keep the pressure on him," one of his aides remembers. Dick Lehman, a CIA analyst, said of his former boss, "He was, by that time, a

---

99   Weiner, 153-156; 667-671.
100  Weiner, 132.

tired old man" who "could be, and usually was, trying in the extreme."[101]

At President Eisenhower's last National Security Council meeting, Dulles said that over the past eight years at CIA "a great deal has been accomplished" and argued that without his leadership the entire intelligence community would be "a body floating in thin air." After he heard this, the president exploded in anger, saying that "the structure of our intelligence organization is faulty" and has been ever since Pearl Harbor. "I have suffered an eight-year defeat on this," and am leaving my successor a "legacy of ashes," Ike said.[102]

The problem wasn't simply Allen Dulles. The whole logic of total global Cold War led to an attempt at imperial world order through continuous covert operations. It was crazy, because it was impossible. The United States didn't have the ability then nor now to have a firm grip on every country in the world. It can't stop societies from changing and evolving. Bureaucratic logic meant the CIA kept looking for more reasons for more operations. It was its reason for being. It meant more madness. But Dulles and like-minded people saw it as a great game in which

---

101  Grose, 448; Weiner, 193.
102  Weiner, 193-194.

they could be global puppet masters. They loved power, but they were fools. Allen Dulles and the CIA were creatures of the war state.

When Eisenhower ran for president, a large faction of conservatives in the Republican Party questioned the logic of the Cold War. You probably have never heard of them, because few know of these men today, but their forgotten arguments provide a very important legacy for us even though they lost out. By the end of his presidency, Eisenhower himself began to worry not just about the CIA, but about the entire military-industrial complex and what it meant for the future of the country. The war state was hurling the nation toward what would be a total disaster.

# CHAPTER IV
## CONSTITUTIONAL PRINCIPLES DISPLACED BY IRON TRIANGLES

Ohio Republican Senator Robert Taft was the first powerful politician to warn about the coming war state and to try to stop it. Perhaps he was the only one who had a real chance. He was a man who had a reputation for great integrity, because he didn't blindly sign bills without reading them first and engaged in exhaustive personal studies before proposing new legislation of his own. A few years after he died, the Senate issued a proclamation honoring the men they considered to be among the five greatest senators in the entire history of the United States. They listed Taft as one of them. When John F. Kennedy wrote his book *Profiles in Courage,* he included an entire chapter about Taft in it. What made him so special? Robert

Taft's life lessons made him resist the centralization of power the war state demanded.

Robert Taft was born into the American power elite. His father, William Taft, served as president of the United States and as a justice of the Supreme Court. His great-grandfather had served as secretary of war and as the attorney general of the United States and even helped found the blue-blood Skull and Bones fraternity at Yale. So it was almost Robert Taft's destiny for him to leave his childhood home in Cincinnati and go to college at Yale too, graduate as a Bonesman, and enter a life of public service.

Fellow Bonesmen would be among Taft's closest friends and confidants for the rest of his life. "It is almost impossible to tell about adequately," he would write his wife later. When one of his sons went to Yale and entered the fraternity, he warned him not to give "more importance to it than it deserves," because "the effect in after life is negligible."

Robert Taft, much like the other members of his family, did not get ahead in life simply because of family connections. You see, the Tafts were geniuses. He graduated from Yale as the class valedictorian. His classmates voted him the "brightest" of their group and the fifth "most likely to succeed."[103]

---

103 James Patterson, *Mr. Republican: A Biography of Robert A. Taft* (Boston: Houghton Mifflin Company, 1972), 36-41.

After Yale, Taft went to Harvard and got a law degree. One of his classmates there wrote home and described Taft by saying, "He is very quiet, appears to not to be even the slightest swell-headed, yet seems not to care at all what people think or don't think, but does exactly as he pleases. He gives the appearance of a person with lofty ideals, and the courage of his convictions and to spare. He dressed in very plain and sober clothes, which strike me as being somewhat out of date. Finally he is a hard student, and an unusually intelligent one. I don't believe there is a brighter fellow... in our class... He is well built, but not very good looking."

Another classmate remembered seeing Taft studying at the law library for thirty days in a row. Just as he did at Yale, he didn't simply succeed, but he exceeded. He served as head editor of the Harvard Law Review in his senior year and graduated number one in the entire class. His father told a friend that his son "Bob has taken the highest marks that have been taken in Harvard in fifteen years, so we are going to let him take a run to Europe before he settles down."[104]

Robert Taft married Martha Bowers, who had attracted the attention of many other men while he courted her, including John Foster Dulles. Dulles

---

104   Ibid., 43-44.

actually proposed to her himself only to be turned down before Taft did. Despite that, Dulles and Taft became good personal friends. Unlike Dulles, though, Taft would not become a wild-eyed globalist captivated with exercising imperial power all over the world. Taft's views came from a tradition of American foreign policy that went back to the founders of the nation. These were principles he grew up on and tried to never deviate from.

You may think that with their similar elite backgrounds Taft would have come to think like the Dulles brothers did. What made the difference? After law school, his life took a different path than theirs did. Instead of moving to cosmopolitan New York City and becoming a corporate lawyer for Wall Street and giant US corporations, Taft moved back to Cincinnati. Right after law school, he had an opportunity to go to Washington, DC, and work as a law clerk for Supreme Court justice Oliver Wendell Holmes, but his father advised him to instead go back home and start a law practice.

The decision made it so that he could be his own man. Robert Taft didn't like the alternative of New York either. "Perhaps seeing so much of New York and Eastern people," he told a friend, "I have so long decided that New York was the last place, that I spend a great deal of time in argument, uselessly." His father believed that if Robert moved back to Ohio, he would be able to quickly rise in both law and politics and make a huge name for himself. Yes, he was right.[105]

As Taft moved back home, World War I began. He got bored with law and tried to join the military only to be rejected for poor eyesight. He then went into government service by becoming an assistant to Herbert Hoover, the future president of the United States who at that time was running the US Food Administration. As the war came to an end, the two went to Europe to coordinate food relief efforts. Taft and Hoover lived in the same house together as they served overseas, and his experiences in government service taught him to hate bureaucracy and all of its "red tape and delay and confusion."[106]

Taft learned a lot from Hoover about economics and politics, but as the two worked on the margins of the United States peace delegation to Paris and the making of the Versailles Peace Treaty, they did not like what they saw. Taft wrote back home complaining that the Europeans were not trying to create a just peace, because a "strong imperialist party" dominated each Allied government. "France wants at least the Saar

---

105  Ibid., 57.

106  Clarence Wunderlin, *Robert A. Taft: Ideas, Tradition, and Party in U.S. Foreign Policy* (New York: Rowman and Littlefield Publishers, 1995), 18.

valley and have a yearning for all of Germany west of the Rhine—they probably will get the Saar valley, although the population is German. Italy wants the whole Adriatic coast, & to hinder the Jugo-Slavs in every way," he wrote.

He repeatedly bumped into his friends the Dulles brothers and their uncle Robert Lansing, but he believed that "the American peace mission is hopeless, and the President is undoubtedly to blame." He thought Lansing's views were "as narrow and stupid as anything I know." In Taft's opinion, Wilson never outlined exactly what he wanted and his ideas were so full of mush that the "result is they all work along in the dark, afraid to call their soul their own... They have a corps of good experts, whose opinion seldom affects any decision." It seemed that George Washington was right to warn in his farewell address not to get involved in European alliance politics.[107]

Taft made it back home and got back into law, helping to found a legal firm that worked for some of the biggest businesses in Ohio and doing pro-bono work for people charged in criminal cases. His firm helped underwrite municipal bonds for the city of Cincinnati and helped his uncle Charles Taft, who had built up a business empire with interests all over the country. In

---

107  Ibid, 18-20.

1921, Robert Taft also got elected as a Republican to the Ohio state legislature.

There he rose to become Speaker of the House in 1926 and then became a state senator in 1930. His reputation as an independent politician who did what he thought was right even if it went against the prevailing winds of public opinion and even his own party began in the state house. As a state legislator, he supported a constitutional amendment banning child labor, a bill aimed at the Ku Klux Klan that would have forced it to give up its membership list to the state government, and opposed a bill that would have demanded that public school teachers read the bible every day to their students. He saw this latter bill as an infringement on individual liberty. It passed but was vetoed by the governor. Taft was elected to the US Senate in 1938.[108]

Over the next ten years, the press would come to call Robert Taft "Mr. Republican," as he became the country's biggest critic of Franklin Roosevelt's New Deal, and the Senate majority leader in 1953 when Dwight Eisenhower became president of the United States. Taft claimed that the New Deal was a huge deviation from the way the American government had operated since the ratification of the Constitution. He

---

108  Wunderlin, 21.

believed the founders had created a government system of checks and balances that kept the government out of people's lives and allowed them the freedom to take advantage of their own talents by providing equal justice under the law. To him this was what opportunity was about.

Taft explained that "the basis of the American business and constitutional system is political and economic liberty, with equal opportunity to improve one's condition by one's own effort. It is a system based on individual initiative, individual freedom to conduct agriculture, commerce, manufacture, in fact on rugged individualism. It attempts to reward by increase in material welfare those qualities of intelligence, ability, industry, and genius, which played such a great part in building up the nation as we see it today. Government is conceived as a keeper of the peace, a referee of controversies, and an adjustor of abuses; not as a regulator of the people, or the business and personal activities."

He claimed that Roosevelt and his New Deal defined opportunity differently by making it more about providing security than freedom. Taft thought what the New Deal offered was "a reasonable chance to improve your condition in life as you grow older; a practical assurance against want and suffering in your old age." It all sounded good, but it came with a hidden cost—a dangerous centralization of government and power.[109]

Taft did not deny that the Great Depression created a need for some government assistance for the economy, and he supported the few New Deal programs that made sense to him to restore business confidence. "Social conditions under some circumstances," he said, "demand government interference. We have not hesitated in the past to regulate or prohibit monopoly, to encourage trade unions, to encourage cooperative dealing by farmers and laborers, to tax wealth and income on a progressively higher rate, to regulate banking and currency."[110]

But Taft did not like it when the New Deal involved itself in the operation of businesses. "Planned economy has not produced any prosperity equal to that which existed before 1929," he said, "in spite of manipulation of the currency, in spite of devaluing the dollar, in spite of deficits amounting to $15 billion, and the pouring out of public funds, in spite of unlimited power given to regulate the farm industry, the coal industry, the utility industry, and the issue of securities, in spite of countless powers as great as could

---

109 Ibid., 26.
110 Russell Kirk and James McClellan, *The Political Principles of Robert A. Taft* (New Brunswick: Transaction Publishers, 2010), 13-19.

be granted within the constitution, we are faced today with complete failure."[111]

The senator had become even more alarmed about the growth of presidential power under Roosevelt. Taft said, "The founders of the Constitution knew that nearly every democracy in the history of the world had finally degenerated into a tyranny, an empire, or a kingdom. They knew that had happened because gradually all of the powers of the government were delegated by the people to one man or a small group of men. Delegated usually in an emergency, they were never surrendered. For that reason, they set up a written Constitution to be interpreted by independent courts. They retained vast powers in the hands of the states, and delegated only national powers to the federal government. Even these limited powers were divided between the Executive, Congress, and the courts and the courts were given the job of protecting individual freedom against the powers of government."

As for World War II, "there is no doubt in my mind," Taft said, "that many members of the administration have deliberately sought power much greater than required for the war for the purpose of extending the regulation of business and individuals with a view to the continuation of such regulation after the war.

---

111

Every law that has been written has requested wide-open power... Congress must have the independence when the end of the war has in fact occurred to declare the termination of these powers."

Taft deeply worried about those who claimed that the president had "inherent power" as the chief executive of the United States to be able to do what he thought was necessary to protect the country in the name of national security without the authorization of Congress. "The vague theory that the President has the inherent power by virtue of his office to meet a national emergency has no support in judicial decisions and runs counter to the sound and established principle that the President's authority comes simply from the provisions of the Constitution and the laws passed by Congress... The Constitution says nothing about national emergencies, and if the President could increase his powers by such a declaration, there would be nothing left to the limitations largely imposed by the Constitution," he said. [112]

When it came to foreign policy, Taft believed that the United States had to put its own national interest ahead of anything else. If the leaders of the nation did not do that and instead pursued ideological internationalism, then they could easily end stuck in military

---

112   Ibid., 91-93, 97.

and diplomatic disasters. These were the views that guided the country's Founding Fathers, and his experience in Europe after the First World War proved to him their validity. So it was logical for Taft to believe it to be best for the country not to get caught up in foreign alliances and European squabbles.[113]

Robert Taft called himself a "noninterventionist" before World War II. Before Japan bombed Pearl Harbor, the senator thought that the United States should pursue a foreign policy in which first "we should stay out of the war unless attacked; second, that we should build up our defense to meet any possible threat of attack; third, that we should aid Britain as much as possible, consistent with the policy of staying out of the war." He came to conclude that Roosevelt was moving the United States into war, while he wanted to avoid war if at all possible.[114]

Before the United States entered World War II, Taft promoted a "continentalist" foreign policy that made note of the fact that the nation was in a unique protective position, because unlike any other country in the world, it "was virtually self-sufficient and possessed such abundant resources as to make foreign trade and any other overseas interests very minor

---

113   Ibid., 162.
114   Wunderlin, 33.

and inconsequential national goals." The fact that it held complete mastery of North America and was surrounded by two massive oceans made it virtually certain that any enemy that "would be stupid enough to attack us by landing troops in the United States from across thousands of miles of ocean" would be crushed. All the United States had to do to protect itself was maintain a navy powerful enough to prevent any potential enemies from building strategic bases close enough to put together invasion forces.[115]

In other words, Taft did not see how Nazi Germany could possibly pose as an existential threat to the United States, because it was impossible to conceive of a situation in which it would be able to invade the country. He was very wary of supporting the Soviet Union in its fight against Germany, because he had an undying disgust for Communism. However, once the Japanese attacked Pearl Harbor and Hitler declared war on the United States, Taft fully supported the war effort.

He continued to ask questions, though, about the conduct of the war, the growth of executive power, and the future peace. Once the war ended, he became a cold warrior who saw the United States locked in a struggle with the Soviet Union and communism, but

---

115  Ibid., 57.

he did not believe in global Cold War and unlimited defense spending. He feared the growth of the war state. Writing in 1951, he claimed that "if the present trend continues it seems to me obvious that the President will become a complete dictator in the entire field of foreign policy and thereby acquire power to force upon Congress all kinds of domestic policies which must necessarily follow."

Taft had been disturbed that President Truman had gotten the country involved "in the Korean War without even telling Congress what he was doing for several weeks." The nation was now facing a dire issue. Eventually, if it did not limit the powers the office of the president was taking, then "if in the great field of foreign policy the President has the arbitrary and unlimited powers he now claims, then there is an end to freedom in the United States not only in the foreign field," but in domestic policy too; "one simple result is that war is more likely," he said.[116]

Another danger would be that the growth in executive power would cause the president to become some sort of emperor of the world sending armies all over the place and increasing defense spending so much that it would overtax the American people, cause rampant inflation, and turn the whole country

---

116 Robert A. Taft, *A Foreign Policy for Americans* (New York: Doubleday & Company, 1951), 21-23.

into a national security nightmare garrison state. The president, Taft wrote, "simply cannot send armies to block a communist advance in every far corner of the world. Consequently, we must consider the cost of the policies we adopt, both in men and money, and we are forced to be selective in determining the relative value and cost of each project."

Taft thought the country did have to build up its defenses against the Soviet Union, but it had to be careful, because doing so is also "in its extreme form the most disruptive to our national life, our freedom, our progress, and even our production." While NSC-68 advocated massive arms spending and placed the country on a total war footing, the senator argued that "the truth is that no nation can be constantly prepared to undertake a full-scale war at any moment and still hope to maintain any of the other purposes in which people are interested and for which nations are founded."

Taft warned that "an indefinite surrender of liberty such as would be required by an all-out war program in time of peace might mean the final and complete destruction of those liberties which it is the very purpose of the protection to protect." All the country had to do was to be prudent in its foreign policy and defense decisions and be economical in defense spending by sticking to a balanced budget.[117]

Such commonsense ideas would have stopped the growth of the war state in its tracks. Unlike NSC-68, which advocated global Cold War, Robert Taft saw foreign policy as having two simple goals—to protect the liberty of the people in the United States and to do what is possible to maintain the peace, because "the results of war may be almost as bad as the destruction of liberty, and, in fact, may lead, even if the war is won, to something very close to the destruction of liberty at home."

Taft claimed that the Founding Fathers got it right. "Our traditional policy of neutrality and non-interference with other nations was based on the principle that this policy was the best way to avoid disputes with other nations and to maintain the liberty of this country without war. From the days of George Washington that has been the policy of the United States," Taft wrote. Of course NSC-68 did away with over 150 years of tradition by declaring it the policy to intervene in the entire world to prevent any nation from becoming allied with the Soviet Union or even declaring itself to be neutral.[118]

---

117  Ibid., 64-71.
118  Ibid., 11-12.

However, the Cold War now required the United States to work with other nations. Instead of NSC-68, what Taft advocated was selective containment. He desired to provide aid to those countries that were critical to the United States with a "kind of Monroe Doctrine for Europe." However, the senator did not believe the United States should send hundreds of thousands of Americans over to Europe for NATO, because "the Russians are not going to be deterred by land armies until such armies are built up to a strong defensive force able to stop them and they can always attack before that point is reached." The Soviet Union had a huge advantage in Europe in conventional forces. But Taft had an answer to this problem.

Instead of unlimited military spending in an arms race, Taft thought that it would make more sense for the United States to simply build up its air force to seventy wings armed with an atomic arsenal. A big enough air force combined with a strong navy, in his view, would recreate a "continentalist" strategy by making it impossible for the Soviet Union to attack the United States without itself being destroyed. It could also be done on the cheap and wouldn't require the country to have hundreds of thousands of troops spread out all over the world or to just keep spending itself into oblivion. He wanted a defensive strategy that would work with a limited budget.

He thought all the United States had to do to stop the spread of communism was to protect key "centers of strength" in the world and stand as an example to all. Such a strategy would keep the peace long enough for people to abandon communism for the superior system. He put a price tag on it of thirty billion dollars, with a cap of seventy-five billion on all federal spending.[119]

Taft almost put those principles into action by coming inches to becoming president of the United States. He ran for the Republican nomination for president three times and came close to winning it the last time he ran. At the time, the Republican Party was split into two groups. One group was a more liberal wing with most of its support coming from New York City and backed by Wall Street interests, and a conservative wing whose base of support came from the midwestern states and farmers and small businessmen.

The historian Lynn Eden described this conservative faction as being made up of "business nationalists." Through a careful analysis of US senators, their votes, and their sources of support, she identified twenty senators who fit this category during the Truman administration. All but three came from states in the midwest or in the western mountains. They had

---

119  Ibid, 19, 77; Wunderlin, 123; Patterson, 436.

very little interest in the internationalist issues of free trade, global alliances, foreign aid programs such as the Marshall Plan, and they opposed big-government, New Deal-style programs.

These views matched the financial interests of many of the people who gave them money and votes. Eden notes that at the time "the economy of the midwest and mountain regions contained a number of regional economies, generally non-export oriented, in which major economic interests looked to the home market for prosperity, felt that government regulation of business frequently worked against their interests, saw United States agricultural and industrial exports exacerbating shortages at home, and in some cases the wool industry being the most notable example, saw themselves threatened by foreign imports." Many were involved in mining, retail, farming, and light-goods manufacturing.[120]

The liberal wing dominated the national Republican Party until the party nominated the more conservative Barry Goldwater as its presidential candidate over Nelson Rockefeller in 1964. In 1940, it helped to get the New York corporate lawyer Wendell Wilkie nominated as the Republican candidate for president, and

---

120 Lynn Rachele Eden, *The Diplomacy of Force: Interests, the State, and the Making of American Military Policy in 1948*, (PhD dissertation, University of Michigan, 1985), 176-186.

New York Governor Thomas Dewey in 1944 and 1948. After Wilkie got crushed by Roosevelt, losing 82 to 449 electoral votes, he published a book titled *One World* in which he advocated for world government.

While Robert Taft was the leader of the conservative wing of the Republican Party, Thomas Dewey led the liberal wing. Dewey called himself a "New Deal Republican" and claimed that President Roosevelt was so popular that in order to win elections the Republican Party couldn't oppose the New Deal, but instead should promise to run government programs more efficiently than the Democratic Party did.

Dewey and his campaign staff used membership in New York society clubs, such as the Recess Club, Tavern Club, and Downtown Club, to create a network of Wall Street supporters and raise money. He had so much campaign cash that he was able to offer visiting Republican activists limousine rides, World Series tickets, and boxing seats. Allen Dulles served on Dewey's "entertainment committee" along with Winthrop Aldrich, who was the head of the Chase National Bank.[121]

---

121 Michael Bowen, *The Roots of Modern Conservatism: Dewey, Taft, and the Battle for the Soul of the Republican Party* (Chapel Hill: The University of North Carolina Press, 2011), 21, 59, 215.

Dewey ran in the 1948 presidential election against Truman and lost. He tried to run as a nonpartisan by mouthing platitudes, such as "you know the future is ahead of you," instead of criticizing New Deal-style programs that Truman was creating. He avoided talking about issues and thought if he could run on his force of personality he could win. He was wrong.

Thomas Dewey had ran as the Republican candidate for president twice and failed to win both times. That opened the door for a new candidate in the 1952 election. Robert Taft walked into that door and became the front-runner for the Republican nomination. Whoever the Republicans nominated looked to be a likely winner, because Truman had decided to retire and the Democrats nominated Adlai Stevenson as their candidate for the Oval Office. He seemed to be a weak candidate destined to lose.

Taft had strong support for the Republican nomination, but if he won, Dewey and the men around him would lose their hold on the party, so they began to search for a candidate of their own. They found one in General Dwight Eisenhower, who at the time was serving in Europe as the commander of NATO. They began a draft-Eisenhower movement and spread articles in the press attacking Taft as an "isolationist." Taft complained to a friend that "the main Eisenhower men seem to be the international bankers, the Dewey organization allied with them, Republican New Dealers, and even President Truman. Apparently they want to be sure that no matter which party wins, they win."

The Dewey forces helped to plant editorials in the *New York Times* with headlines such as "MR. TAFT CAN'T WIN." They couldn't say he was corrupt or attack his record, so they simply smeared him. They said he couldn't talk well and wasn't as good-looking as most politicians. They said he was too shy and abrupt with people to be president and claimed that only Eisenhower could win as a Republican. Then they called him names. The *Nation* smeared Taft as a "neofascist," while the *Progressive* declared him to be "the last of the old breed... already he begins to take on the slight glazed look of the high button shoes and nickel beer era." [122]

Dewey personally directed the campaign to nominate Eisenhower. He held secret talks with the former Minnesota governor Harold Stassen to get him to run for president in the primaries to keep Taft from collecting uncontested delegates to use at the Republican convention. Dewey thought this way he could get "some opposition to be artificially stimulated" against Taft and get Stassen to lose on purpose

---

122 Patterson, 530, 536.

in landslides against Eisenhower in a few primaries to make Ike look strong. Stassen hated Taft's fiscal views and wanted more military spending and a more internationalist foreign policy, so he agreed. Dewey and Stassen put a snow job on the voters, but it helped Eisenhower win the nomination.[123]

Taft saw that he lost the nomination for two reasons. First, there was "the power of the New York financial interests and a large number of businessmen subject to New York influence who had selected General Eisenhower as their candidate at least a year ago," he wrote. Secondly, "four-fifths of the influential newspapers," he continued, "were opposed to me continuously and vociferously and many turned themselves into propaganda sheets for my opponent."[124]

Eisenhower became president after he beat Stevenson in a landslide. As Senate majority leader, Robert Taft met with the new president frequently and the two had a good working relationship. Then Taft died of cancer in 1953, just a little over a year after his campaign for the presidential nomination. Taft's campaign for president has become forgotten history to most people, but it was one of the most important campaigns in the United States since the

---

123 Bowen, 114-116, 119.
124 Patterson, 571.

end of World War II, because it changed the face of the Republican Party. After he died, the Dewey forces launched a purge of small-government conservatives in the Republican Party, and all of their major candidates for president ever since have been closely allied with the defense industry. If Eisenhower hadn't ran, Taft probably would have become president of the United States and altered the direction of US foreign policy.

What about Eisenhower? Today most historians think of him as a bipartisan moderate Republican. During the years of his presidency and immediately after, though, they thought he was an uninvolved chairman who let cabinet members run his administration for him. One described him as "a genial, indolent man of pied syntax and platitudinous conviction, fleeing from public policy to bridge, golf, and westerns." Some portrayed him as being politically naive and almost stupid. Most historians tend to be politically liberal, so at the time they liked to contrast his intelligence with the egghead Stevenson and his age with the youth of John F. Kennedy.

It is evident now that this was a vastly mistaken view of Eisenhower. Once his presidential archives opened up in the 1970s, it became clear that he was much more of a hands-on president than people realized. The papers forced the historian Arthur Schlesinger

Jr., who had served as an adviser to John F. Kennedy, to reappraise his own opinion of Eisenhower. He said that they "showed that the mask of genial affability Ike wore in the White House concealed an astute, crafty, confident, and purposeful leader." The journalist Theodore White came to conclude that his public appearances obscured the real Eisenhower. "The rosy private smile could give way, in private, to furious outbursts of temper; that the tangled rambling rhetoric of his off-the-record remarks could, when he wished, be disciplined by his own pencil into clean hard prose," White wrote.[125]

As president, Eisenhower posed as a nonpartisan and distanced himself from the more controversial policies of his own administration by using cabinet members to promote them. He worked to avoid personal fights and controversies with other politicians and rarely used his office as a podium to advance his policies. As a result, one author has called his leadership in the Oval Office a "hidden-hand Presidency." Richard Nixon, who served as his vice president, noted that Ike "always applied two, three, or four lines of reasoning to a single problem and he usually preferred

---

125 Brian Jones, *Abolishing the Taboo: Dwight D. Eisenhower and American Nuclear Doctrine 1945-1961* (Dorchester: Helion & Company, 1995), 12-17; Fred Greenstein, *The Hidden-Hand Presidency: Eisenhower as Leader* (Baltimore: The Johns Hopkins University Press, 1994), 16.

the indirect approach where it would serve him better than the direct attack on the problem."

Ike's longtime aide General Andrew Goodpaster sized up his thinking processes by saying, "Anything that's based on the theory of games, or a doctrine or technique that conforms to that fits well... into the way that General Eisenhower's mind works. He's a great poker player, and extremely good bridge player. He plays bridge very much in poker style and he's a tremendous man for analyzing the other fellow's mind, what options are open to the other fellow, and what line he can best take to capitalize or exploit the possibilities, having figured the options open to the other man." [126]

President Eisenhower actually attended more National Security Council meetings than any other president. On many domestic issues, he was hands-off, but he practically created his own defense policy. He may have given the CIA a free reign to do whatever it wanted in the third world, but when it came to the military budget and defense strategy, he may have been the most involved president there has been since World War II.

His chief of staff Sherman Adams noted that Ike "knew more about the intricacies of high government

---

[126] Greenstein, 9, 126.

than many professional politicians." He graduated at the US Army Command and General Staff college at the top of the class and then served as an assistant to General Douglas MacArthur in the Philippines in the 1930s. After Pearl Harbor, he served on the strategic planning staff of General George Marshall, the army chief of staff, and then took command of the allied forces in Europe, where he led campaigns in North Africa, Italy, and on to the beaches of Normandy. After the war, he took Marshall's place as the head of the US Army and resigned in 1948 to become president of Columbia University. While at Columbia, he became a personal adviser to President Harry Truman and then became commander of NATO during the Korean War.[127]

Eisenhower was more prepared than any other president since World War II before he got into office thanks to his long life of service in the military. After his first day in the Oval Office, he wrote in his diary that he was now facing "plenty of worries and difficult problems. But such has been my portion for a long time—the result is that this just seems today like

---

[127] Jones, 18.

a continuation of all I've been doing since July 1941—even before that."[128]

This was a man who had a deep understanding of politics and bureaucracy. As head of the European Theater during World War II, he had to get not only the military forces of different countries to work together as a team but also the separate branches of the US armed forces, and the generals, many of whom had their own egos and personalities that needed to be massaged. He came to believe that a clear-cut, unified command structure worked best and tried to promote the unification of the armed forces after the war, but that idea got shot down.

The problem with the armed forces was that after the war it was divided up into separate branches with an army, navy, air force, and marines, each of which had its own agenda and appetite for money and resources. The result was a redundancy in missions and wasteful spending. One branch would often see another as a threat to its own interests. For example, in the 1950s the navy claimed that the Strategic Air Command of the US Air Force wasn't good enough to attack the Soviet Union by itself so it should have its

---

128 William McClenahan Jr. & William Becker, *Eisenhower and the Cold War Economy* (Baltimore: The Johns Hopkins University Press, 2011), 20.

own fleet of atomic-bomb-armed aircraft just so that it could get into the nuclear defense business too.[129]

It became clear that each branch of the military would not support any doctrine that clashed with its own priorities or limited its ability to get as much of the defense budget as it could. Just like any other government bureaucracy, each division of the armed forces tended to define its own success in terms of its own growing importance. That meant enhancing the missions they are involved in and growing their budgets as much as possible. Of course this meant more personal power for the generals and admirals at the top. It's human nature to always want more, but all of this also encouraged policies that led to waste and an eye toward self-preservation. As Eisenhower put it, no one at the Pentagon ever told him, "Let's get rid of something... it took the army fifty years to get rid of horses after they became obsolete."[130]

As Ike entered the White House, he had two main goals. First, he wanted to end the Korean War and much like Robert Taft he wanted to get defense spending under control. He believed that the Truman administration had increased the defense budget

---

[129] Gerard Clarfield, *Security with Solvency: Dwight D. Eisenhower and the Shaping of the American Military-Establishment* (Connecticut: Praeger, 1999), 35-58.

[130] McClenahan and Becker, 37.

so much that the government was now sending the country "straight toward inflation of an uncontrollable character." He thought that the military should be "ruthlessly pulled apart and examined in order to get down to the country's requirements," because, "if we don't have the objective, industry-government-professional examination that will show us where and how to proceed in this armament business we will go broke and still have inefficient defenses." He wanted "security with solvency."[131]

The federal government was now spending over fifty-five billion dollars on defense, foreign aid, and nuclear programs, making up 70 percent of its entire budget. As a result, Eisenhower began his first year in the Oval Office facing a projected ten-billion-dollar budget deficit. He agreed with the overall philosophy of NSC-68 but disagreed with its alarmist nature. Ike wanted to launch more CIA operations in nations all over the world in order to try to control it as much as possible, but he did not think the Soviet Union posed an imminent threat.

The only way he could see justifying current defense spending levels was if one believed in "an immediate prospect for war," but he did not think the Soviet Union wanted to start one. "Any person," Eisenhower

---

131  Clarfield, 92.

thought, "who doesn't clearly understand that national security and national solvency are mutually dependent, and that permanent maintenance of a crushing weight of military power would eventually create dictatorship, should not be entrusted with any kind of responsibility in our country."[132]

President Eisenhower told one delegation of Republican congressmen who came to the White House, "I'm damn tired of Air Force sales programs. In 1946 they argued that if we can have seventy groups we'll guarantee security forever and ever and ever. Now they have a trick figure of 141. They sell it. Then you have to abide by it or you're treasonous." He told them he'd no longer "tolerate anyone in Defense who wants to sell the idea of a larger and larger force in being, because that results in too much obsolescence and waste."[133]

Eisenhower proposed a defense budget to Congress that cut military spending by five billion dollars to thirty-six billion, with further cuts to come until an annual figure of thirty-three billion would be achieved in 1957. By the time he left office, he had put his hands on military spending so that it made up 60 percent of the federal budget instead of 70 percent and put the

---

132    McClenahan and Becker, 19; Clarfield, 92.
133    Clarfield, 111.

budget in the black. His first budget came with a force reduction of 250,000 military personnel. But people in the military and defense industry tried to stop it.

High-ranking officers made leaks to the press. One air force general said, "You can't make across the board cuts without hurting the whole armed forces." Defense reporter Ann McCormick editorialized that "the talk of slow-downs and cut backs reported from Washington is the height of folly. More, it is dangerous and irresponsible beyond belief."

Charles Wilson, Eisenhower's secretary of defense, went to Congress and said that there was something much bigger than simply the budget at stake. He reminded them that under the Constitution the "authority, direction, and control" of the military was in civilian hands and that those in the armed forces arguing against the budget were threatening that principle.

Eisenhower went on the radio and directly appealed to the American people as only the president can, telling them that it was time to stop the deficits and end "the indefinite continuance of a needlessly high rate of federal spending" and eliminate the "penny–wise, pound-foolish policy that could, through lack of needed strength, cripple the cause of freedom." The Soviet Union, he claimed, "hoped to force upon America and the free world an unbearable security burden leading to economic disaster." He would not let that happen.

His talk worked. Politicians responded. Les Arends, the Republican House whip, reminded his colleagues that Eisenhower, "by the very nature and background of his experience is better equipped than any member of the Joint Chiefs of Staff, individually or collectively, to decide just how much of what... we need for our security." It was time to ignore the annual "Air Force drive for a larger budget," which, he said, "used to be accompanied by air shows, remarkable higher speed or long distance flights, and suddenly uncovered enemy threats to our nation."[134]

The budget passed, but to make it work President Eisenhower had to come up with a new defense doctrine that would work within the budget and protect the United States and its allies at the same time. He was "convinced that a freer and a more normal economy would in the long run provide the nation with greater economic strength" and told his advisers that their goal was "to achieve adequate military strength within the limits of endurable strain upon our economy." Ike announced that the treasury secretary would

---

134  Ibid., 110-114; Dwight D. Eisenhower: "Radio Address to the American People on the National Security and Its Costs," May 19, 1953. Online by Gerhard Peters and John T. Woolley, *The American Presidency Project*, http://www.presidency.ucsb.edu/ws/?pid=9854, accessed 5/8/2013.

attend all National Security Council meetings to make sure economics would be factored into all future policy considerations.[135]

President Eisenhower created Project Solarium, a formal meeting of military and foreign policy advisers named after the Solarium room in the White House where they met and divided into three separate task forces to create a new national security policy. The result was NSC 162/2, a policy statement that put Ike's directives onto paper. Outside the White House, his policies became known as the "New Look." It placed an emphasis on using nuclear weapons and air power to deter war by threatening to inflict "massive damage on the USSR" if it started one. It called for using nuclear weapons "whenever the employment of atomic weapons would be militarily advantageous" and the creation of a mobile combat reserve to be stationed inside the United States but ready to be deployed anywhere in the world if needed.

Eisenhower's new strategic policy enabled him to save money on defense spending by placing a priority over using nuclear weapons as a strategic deterrence rather than relying on conventional forces stationed all over the world. As a result, NSC 162/2 planned to reduce military personnel by 600,000 and required

---

135 Jones, 44.

the army to make a one-third cut in its manpower. Of course many in the military were not pleased. Army chief of staff General Matthew Ridgway claimed that the cuts would "so weaken the Army that it could no longer carry out its missions." To no surprise, though, air force chief of staff Nathan Twining supported the policies, because they seemed to favor the air force over the army.[136]

In order for Ike's new strategic plan to be credible, the Soviet Union and the rest of the world had to be convinced that the United States would be willing to use nuclear weapons if necessary. NSC 162/2 stated that "the United States will consider nuclear weapons to be as available for use as other munitions." President Eisenhower was now playing a game of nuclear poker. Some would call it brinksmanship. At the time, the United States had way more weapons than the Soviet Union had, but once they reached parity with each other, nuclear policy became known as "mutually assured destruction."[137]

Did Eisenhower's strategic policies work? His first test was in Korea. The United States had been fighting Chinese and North Korean forces over Korea for three years by the time he got into the White House. The war

---

136  Clarfield, 139-142.
137  Jones, 46-47.

seemed to have become an unwinnable stalemate and Eisenhower wanted to end it. He even promised the American people when he ran for president that he would go to Korea to do something about it. He kept that pledge by going on a personal fact-finding tour a few weeks after winning the election. A few talks to end the war occurred, but they kept going nowhere.

General Douglas MacArthur, who had been relieved of his Korean command by President Truman, sent Eisenhower a memo on how to end the war. He claimed that Ike should try to bring a close to the entire Cold War by proposing to the Soviet Union to allow both Korea and Germany to reunite their halves with elections and to remove all troops from both of them and from Japan. If the Soviets agreed, then the Cold War would be over. If not, then they should be told that the United States would begin the "atomic bombing of enemy military concentrations and installations in North Korea and the sowing of fields of suitable radio-active materials" and would "neutralize Red China's capability to wage modern war."[138]

The president must have thought that was a little too crazy, because he did not respond to this memo. What he did, though, was let the Soviet Union know that he wanted better relations with them, but it could

---

138 Jim Newton, *Eisenhower: The White House Years* (New York: Doubleday, 2011), 84.

not happen without an armistice in Korea first. He also wanted them to believe that he might use nuclear weapons in the war if the situation did not improve. He had John Foster Dulles send a message to the prime minister of India that "the grim logic of the situation would finally compel the United States to seek to win by new offensives" with the expectation that he would pass it on to the Soviet Union. And he sent a warning to China through Taiwan that it would "remove the restrictions of area and weapons."

North Korea and China agreed to end the war and the parties partitioned Korea near the 38th parallel. President Eisenhower believed his nuclear card forced them to fold, although today historians cannot find hard evidence to back up this conclusion. The timing of the armistice may have been a coincidence, because all sides were being exhausted by the war and the prime minister of India claims he never passed on Eisenhower's message. South Korea remains to this day a key ally of the United States.[139]

Whatever the case, President Eisenhower played another hand of nuclear poker against China in order to guarantee the safety of Taiwan. In the 1940s, Chiang Kai-shek and his nationalist army lost his civil

---

[139] William Stueck, *The Korean War: An International History* (Princeton: Princeton University Press, 1995), 329; Jones, 53.

war against Chinese Communists and fled to the islands of Taiwan and established a new government on them. China began to organize an invasion force on its shores near the small desolate islands of Quemoy and Matsu that were part of Taiwan and began to shell them with artillery. They hoped to force Taiwan to give them up for peace.

Eisenhower privately joked that he wished "the damn little offshore islands" would sink, but he publicly argued that if Chiang were forced to surrender the islands, it could lead to the fall of Taiwan and would cause the allies of the United States to wonder if he would fail to protect them from bullying too. A strong stand would send a message to the world. So he pledged to defend the islands and stated that he would use atomic weapons "just exactly as we would use a bullet or anything else." The threats worked and China backed down.[140]

You may wonder if Eisenhower would have really used atomic bombs? His aide General Andrew Goodpaster remembered that "he ultimately never told anybody whether he would or not, not even within the administration." "He did think of things in poker terms," he recalled, "he put on a mask of ambiguity

---

140 Campbell Craig and Fredrick Logevall, *America's Cold War: The Politics of Insecurity* (Cambridge: The Belknap Press of Harvard University Press, 2009), 151-153.

in the sense that you did not show your hand to the other fellow. One of the things he always talked about was getting inside the other man's head." The truth was that Eisenhower had nuclear weapons and China didn't, so there wasn't much the Chinese could do. He forced them to fold their hand to stay in the game.

President Eisenhower well understood, though, what a nuclear war with the Soviet Union could mean. First, if the use of nuclear weapons began, it would mean that the country would have to use them all in the hopes of a total victory, because those not used would become vulnerable to attack. Secondly, such a war had to be avoided. "Even assuming that we would emerge from a global war today as the acknowledged victor," Eisenhower said, "there would be a destruction in this country that there could be no possibility of our exercising a representative free government for, I would say, two decades at the minimum" and "we would have to run this country as one big camp."[141]

One government study predicted that in a nuclear war, between 15 and 30 percent of Americans would be killed. That would be twenty-five to fifty million people just in the United States. The Department of Defense put together *The Emergency Plans Book*, which assumed that the Soviet Union would attack the United States

---

141 Jones, 53, 66.

with submarine-launched nuclear missiles and strategic bombers to kill twenty-five million people from the blast and radiation of the attack in the first week. After that, another twenty-five million casualties would linger on, with one in five of all Americans ending up dead. The federal government would become paralyzed and perhaps fatally crippled.

Eisenhower came to conclude that "we are in fact talking about something the results of which are almost impossible to conceive of." In fact it is "unthinkable" and would be an "unmitigated disaster." He thought it could even mean the end of human civilization, because "there was obviously a limit—a human limit—to the devastation human beings could endure." At the Republican National Convention of 1956 he said, "With such weapons, war has become, not just tragic, but preposterous. With such weapons, there can be no victory for anyone." However, the Cold War confrontation made keeping the threat of massive retaliation and mutual destruction alive the logical thing to do.[142]

Although President Eisenhower's "New Look" strategic doctrines allowed him to keep the United States from fighting any wars during his administration, it created a torrent of critics from the military and the defense industry. They were not upset over the

---

142  Jones, 64-68.

dangers of world destruction but were angry because Eisenhower's emphasis on using nuclear weapons as a strategic deterrent made conventional forces less important and helped to put a lid on defense spending. It was hard to imagine what role the US Army could now play in Europe or elsewhere in a total nuclear war. What could destroyers do in an atomic attack? Why make any more of them?

Some of those who saw Eisenhower's "New Look" as a threat to themselves fought back. Army chief of staff Matthew Ridgway testified to the congressional Appropriations and Armed Services Committees and claimed that the defense cuts were going to put the nation in danger, because the Soviets were "increasing the combat effectiveness, the training level, and equipment of its ground forces." Democrats took his testimony and ran with it. Senator Richard Russell said that "this is no time to engage in any wishful thinking about Communist intentions," while Stuart Symington argued that "these heavy cuts in our Armed Forces are not justified from the standpoint of national security."

At a press conference, President Eisenhower defended himself by saying that Ridgway's views were "parochial." He told a group of Republican congressmen that the army general was just like any other service chief. "They simply want additional manpower and always will," he said, while as president he had to weigh "the very delicate balance between the national debt, taxes, and expenditures." The president decided not to reappoint Ridgway for another two-year term as head of the army. He resigned and attacked Ike's policies in the *New York Times*.

Eisenhower promoted General Maxwell Taylor, who was serving in Tokyo as commander of the US forces in the Far East, to take Ridgway's place. Before Taylor took the position, he first had an interview with the secretary of defense, who, he recalls, "began to cross-examine me on my readiness to carry out civilian orders even when contrary to my own views. After thirty-seven years of service without evidence of insubordination I had no difficulty of conscience in reassuring him, but I must say that I was surprised to be put through a loyalty test." The president then met with him and went over the same ground.[143]

Air force General Curtis LeMay and several congressmen connected to the defense industry used congressional hearings for the 1957 defense budget to scare the country into believing in a "bomber gap." LeMay told Congress that the Russians were now building so many bombers that "we will be inferior in striking power to the Soviet long-range air force by 1958-60." He offered a "guess" that in three years the

---

143  Clarfield, 159-163.

Russians would be able to launch a surprise knockout attack on the United States. He thought danger could be averted if Congress allowed him to increase his forces to 1,800 B-52s and give him an extra $3.8 billion annually. He said the current 137-wing air force had to be increased.

Eisenhower's intelligence data told him that no such "bomber gap" existed or was going to exist. But Congress added a billion more to the air force budget than he wanted. The move made him furious. He told his secretary of defense he never wanted to see something like it happen again. When the defense secretary told him that each branch of the military seemed to have its own spending program, Ike told him from now on he would have to "put every single person on the spot to justify every single nickel." "You people never seem to learn whom you are supposed to be protecting. Not the generals, but the American people," Ike said, "you've got to be willing to be the most unpopular man in government."[144]

The next year, Trevor Gardner, the assistant secretary of the air force for research and development, resigned and charged the Eisenhower administration with not giving him enough funds for missile research and development. He said the Soviet Union was about

---

144  Ibid., 180-181.

to develop the first ballistic missile and would use it to threaten the whole world.

Henry Jackson, a Democratic senator from Washington, charged that if the Russians test-fired a ballistic missile, the effects "would be so devastating that Western Europe's public opinion would force its leaders, no matter what their inclinations, to withdraw at least into neutrality if not out-and-out collaboration with communism." The Soviets would "very likely take over Europe without firing a shot," he claimed. Now there was a supposed "missile gap."

Jackson's state was home to Boeing and its massive airplane factory right outside Seattle that produced the B-52. In fact, Jackson received so many campaign contributions from the company that, yes, you could consider him as Boeing's own senator in the Congress. He claimed that the number of bombers being built was "just a small trickle of what it should be" and charged that the air force was over "90% manned by obsolescent if not obsolete planes."

Of course the "missile gap" was just as imaginary as the "bomber gap." Eisenhower told legislators that twenty-five thousand people, including ten thousand scientists, were working in the missile field, with fifty thousand hours of overtime being worked. The simple truth, he said, was that "we are already employing so many of the nation's scientists and research facilities that even the expenditure of a vastly greater amount could scarcely produce any additional results." He authorized an extra $1.2 billion for missiles in 1957 anyway. The armed services were working on a total of six different missile programs, when three—Titan, Minuteman, and Polaris—would have been enough. Herbert York, who was the director of Defense Research and Engineering, said, "As a result we spent about twice as much money and employed about twice as many people on these development programs as we should have."[145]

Nonetheless, criticism of President Eisenhower's defense policies continued. The army in particular felt threatened by the strategic doctrine of massive retaliation and the growing importance of the air force. *Army*, the monthly publication of the Association of the United States Army, ran an editorial attacking "the confused thinking" that had "obscured defense matters since World War II" that sought to rely on one single service or weapon to win wars. It argued that the United States had to be prepared to fight not only big wars but small nuclear and conventional wars too, so it needed an army with "sizeable forces in being, ready to move by land, sea, or air and fight any time, any place."

---

145   Ibid., 170-173; 231.

General Maxwell Taylor claimed that those planning for a full-scale nuclear exchange with the Soviet Union were not looking at things right. "Personally," he said, "I rate this concept of war as only one of the forms, and not necessarily the most likely, which war may take." He thought it "increasingly improbable that an aggressor would intentionally embark on the gamble of atomic world war." Only the army existed as the branch of the military with the "unique ability to proportion punishment to fit the crime of aggression," he said, and with "versatile and flexible military forces."[146]

Taylor called for a new strategic doctrine of "flexible response." Several army generals through leaks to friendly reporters and politicians worked to make it an election issue in the presidential race between the Democrat John F. Kennedy and Eisenhower's vice president, Richard Nixon. In reality, "flexible response" made very little sense when applied to the Soviet Union and the United States, because in order for it to work any war between the two nations would have to remain limited. But any escalation would quickly lead to a nuclear exchange, and when it came to nuclear war the logic was use all of the weapons or lose them. Democrats saw "flexible response" as a way

---

146  Clarfield, 181-183.

to contrast themselves with the Eisenhower administration and pose as being tough on national security while those congressmen of both parties tied to the defense industry used it as a way to lobby for more defense spending.

To try to appease critics, or at least to give them a place to keep them busy and vent their views inside his administration instead of publicly, President Eisenhower commissioned a top-secret study on the ability of the United States to withstand a nuclear attack and what to do about it. The report was titled "Deterrence and Survival in the Nuclear Age," but it was nicknamed the Gaither Report, because a man named Rowan Gaither, who was a founder of the RAND Corporation and chairman of the Ford Foundation, headed the committee that put it together. Paul Nitze, who drafted most of NSC-68, served on the committee and wrote most of its final report.

The report claimed that the Soviets had 1,500 nuclear weapons, 4,500 bombers, and 300 submarines pointed at the United States. It said that the Soviet Union was growing stronger every year and "the evidence clearly indicates an increasing threat which may become critical in 1959 or 1960." Nitze claimed the Russians were now building so many weapons that "by 1959 the USSR may be able to launch an attack with ICBM's carrying megaton warheads against which

SAC will be almost completely vulnerable under present programs."

"If we fail to act at once, the risk, in our opinion will be unacceptable," the report said. Its recommendations were to increase defense spending by forty-four billion dollars over five years, and in repudiation of Eisenhower's "New Look" strategy, it advocated spending not only on more nuclear weapons but more conventional forces too in order to "enable us to deter or promptly suppress small wars which must not be allowed to grow into big ones." The report claimed that the Soviets now "maintained and largely reequipped their army of 175 line divisions"—a wildly exaggerated number—in Europe and hinted that they were making such "spectacular" progress with their missiles that the United States was about to become "completely vulnerable" unless defense spending was increased.

The committee members did not use hard intelligence data to back up their claims. Much of it came simply from their imagination. In a writing draft of the report, next to one paragraph, Nitze wrote, "Is this right?" and farther below wrote, "I doubt anyone knows." Perhaps he believed what he wanted to believe. Eisenhower, though, did know. The CIA was running U-2 spy plane flights all over the Soviet Union and giving him intelligence reports on their nuclear capabilities. By 1960, the Soviet Union did not have the hundreds of intercontinental missiles that the Gaither Report predicted it would have. It had four.[147]

Nitze expected the Eisenhower administration to accept the Gaither Report's recommendations when the report was presented to the president's national security team. Instead Ike angrily told them he was not going to turn the United States into a "garrison state." Nitze said, "Someone had advised him recently not to say this is a problem that will last forty years, but simply to call for a spurt of activity now. He thought this was inaccurate, and besides we must bring ourselves to carry the load until the Soviets change internally."[148]

A few days later, Nitze wrote a letter to Secretary of State John Foster Dulles telling him that the administration's policies were leading the country to "default on our obligations to ourselves, to all who have gone before us, and to generations yet to come." He hinted that Dulles was a coward and told him to resign. Someone on the committee, probably Nitze himself, leaked the Gaither Report to the *Washington Post*,

---

147 David Callahan, *Dangerous Capabilities: Paul Nitze and the Cold War* (New York: Harper Collins, 1990), 169-175; Nicholas Thompson, *The Hawk and the Dove: Paul Nitze, George Kennan, and the History of the Cold War* (New York: Picador, 2009), 164; Tim Weiner, *Legacy of Ashes: The History of the CIA* (New York: Anchor Books, 2008), 183.

148 Stephen Ambrose, *Eisenhower: Volume Two, The President* (New York: Simon and Schuster, 1984), 435.

which said that it "portrays the United States in the gravest danger in its history."[149]

By the time he left office, Eisenhower had increased the size of the nation's nuclear arsenal to 18,638 warheads, an increase of 2,000 percent from the day he became president. He kept the United States out of war and the whole time faced continuous attacks from Congress for being soft on defense and constant demands from the military for more money. In one of his final cabinet meetings, he said that the country now faced two grave problems. He asked, "Can free government, faced by the threat of a singly-controlled economy [the USSR's], continue to exist? And can free government overcome the many demands made by special interests and the indulgence of selfish motives?"

Would all of the energy of the United States be channeled into the war state and would freedom become curtailed in its name? Eisenhower came to conclude that more government spending meant more concentrated power in the hands of the executive branch. Congress could not exercise enough restraint over spending on new programs to control the situation, because politicians had to answer to the demands

---

149 Thompson, 165.

of special interests and elections. Only the president could provide the necessary restraining hand.

But thanks to the growth of the war state, government bureaucracies tied to the defense industry and the military had become the most powerful special interest group in the country. Eisenhower feared that it could all lead to "heavy spending leading in the direction of authoritarian government." The president decided to warn the country about his concerns in his final farewell address to the nation in which he talked about the "military-industrial complex."

Most ignored his speech. John F. Kennedy became president on a cold-warrior campaign platform advocating "flexible response" and promising to bridge the "missile gap" while attacking the Eisenhower administration as being "soft" on defense. William Buckley and James Burnham hated the farewell address. Their *National Review* magazine editorialized that Eisenhower may have been trusted by the American people, but "yet it must be said, what a miserable President he was."[150]

The constitutional conservatism of Robert Taft faded away from the Republican Party, and the wise example of Eisenhower when it came to government spending was forgotten. In the decades that followed, most

---

150  William McClenahan and Becker, 226-233.

Republicans gave lip service to reducing government spending but ignored concerns that big government could grow out of an iron-triangle alliance among the defense industry, Congress, and the Pentagon. They treated big government as if it were only caused by domestic social programs and ignored the reality that the United States had become a bloated war state.

So-called "neoconservatism" now dominates the Republican Party, but politicians of both parties cater to the war state and benefit from it. As Richard Nixon supposedly said, "we are all Keynesians now." To believe in the goodness of the war state meant to accept endless deficit spending. Today the country's debts are on a path to becoming so large over the next decade that massive inflation or a debt crisis lies in the future. Only by tackling the size of the military-industrial complex can this be averted.

World War II gave birth to today's military-industrial complex. Yes, the United States had mobilized to fight in several major wars in its prior history, such as the Civil War and World War I, but after all of them, the country reduced its military industry to nothing. With President Truman's approval of NSC-68, a permanent war industry became established in the country. With each passing year, its influence grew. By the end of Eisenhower's presidency, it became the most powerful special interest group in the nation, with powerful tentacles reaching into the economy, the defense bureaucracies, and dozens of congressmen. It transformed the federal government of the United States into a war state. President Kennedy would discover how entrenched and dangerous it had become.

# PART II:
# THE PERMANENT GOVERNMENT

## PRESIDENT JOHN F. KENNEDY SIGNING THE ATOMIC TEST BAN TREATY - OCTOBER 7, 1963

---

151 Wikimedia Commons, http://commons.wikimedia.org/wiki/File:President_Kennedy_signs_Nuclear_Test_Ban_Treaty,_07_October_1963.jpg, accessed 9/16/12

# CHAPTER V
## JOHN F. KENNEDY FACES THE PERMANENT GOVERNMENT

John F. Kennedy became president of the United States on January 20, 1961. He came from an Irish-Catholic family of great wealth and privilege. His father, Joseph Kennedy Sr. made a fortune in banking, real estate, stock market, and bootlegging operations in the 1920s. He became a person of influence. Before World War II, President Franklin Roosevelt tapped him to become ambassador to Great Britain. He pushed his children to do great things and encouraged them to get into politics.

John F. Kennedy seems to have been shadowed by death throughout his life. He grew up as a sickly child and suffered from back pain and ailments resulting from Addison's disease, a chronic condition of the adrenal glands that produces fatigue, muscle weakness, diarrhea, and darkened skin pigmentation, until the day he was killed. He liked to sit in a rocking chair to ease the pains in his back. His brother Joseph Kennedy Jr. died in a plane crash during World War II. At one point, while Kennedy was a young man, doctors thought he was going to die and he received the last rites. Senator George Smathers, who spent a lot of time with him, recalled that "twenty times or more" Kennedy asked him what would be the best way to die and wondered whether one would "think about all the good things that had happened to you, or regret all the things you hadn't done."

The idea of being courageous captivated John Kennedy. He tested himself by commanding a PT Boat during World War II and wrote a Pulitzer Prize-winning book whose theme was "political courage in the face of constituent pressures." According to his brother Robert Kennedy, "he sought out those people who had demonstrated in some way, whether it was on a battlefield or a baseball diamond, in a speech or fighting for a cause, that they had courage, that they would stand up, that they could be counted on."[152]

---

152   Michael Beschloss, *The Crisis Years: Kennedy and Khrushchev 1960-1963* (New York: Harper Collins, 1991), 10; James Douglas, *JFK and the Unspeakable: Why He Died and Why It Matters* (New York: Touchstone, 2008), 135-136; for a recent overview of the Kennedy presidency, see Alan Brinkley, *John F. Kennedy* (New York: Times Book, 2012).

## Chapter Five

President Eisenhower, though, did not think too much of him at first. He thought Kennedy was too young and inexperienced to be a good president, too liberal, and Ike did not appreciate the political criticisms against him that emanated from the Kennedy campaign to win the presidency. Whenever a new man gets elected to the White House, there is a presidential transition period between the time he wins the election and the time he takes the oath of office. The new president uses this time to choose his advisers and catch up to speed as much as possible on the challenges that he will face. Most of the time, he meets with the outgoing president right before he takes his oath.

President Eisenhower thought he would have a little fun with Kennedy. The two had a private meeting in the Oval Office the day before Kennedy's inauguration. Eisenhower talked to him about what it meant to be president. He started by showing him a black briefcase, called "the Football," inside of which were codes for launching the country's nuclear missiles. He handed Kennedy a laminated plastic card which he said was used to identify himself to the electronic systems that controlled the nuclear weapons and could be used to choose among the various strike options contained in a stack of thirty pages of attack plans inside the briefcase. He explained how in minutes he could relay launch orders to men in nuclear missile silos in the midwest, submarine commanders, and SAC bomber crews and begin Armageddon.

"Watch this," Eisenhower said as he walked to the presidential desk. He picked up a telephone and yelled "Opal! Drill Three!" Within minutes a Marine helicopter landed on the lawn outside the Oval Office. The helicopter could take them away to a secure location in the event the nuclear attack orders had been given.

Eisenhower walked Kennedy into the Cabinet Room and announced, "I've shown my friend here how to get out in a hurry." Sitting at the giant briefing table in the center of the room were the old and new secretaries of state, defense, and the treasury. Kennedy had requested a formal discussion for "(1) Trouble Spots - Berlin, Far East, Cuba; (2) The National Security Set-up—including how the Pentagon is working; (3) Organization of the White House; (4) President's Confidential Comments regarding Macmillan, de Gaulle, Adenauer," who were the leaders of England, France, and Germany.

Eisenhower told Kennedy to consider Laos as the big hot spot. The United States might have to send troops and go to war there he told him. Laos? The country lay in Southeast Asia and sat between Vietnam and Thailand. "This is the cork in the bottle of the Far East," Ike said, "if Laos is lost to the free world, in the long run we will lose all of Southeast Asia... You are going to have to put troops in Laos. With other nations if possible—but alone if necessary."

"What about China?" Kennedy asked. Would China join such a war in opposition to the United States as they did in the Korean War? Could that lead to the Soviets moving on West Berlin or even a nuclear confrontation?

"It's a high-stakes poker game," Eisenhower said, "there's no easy solution." Kennedy got the impression that Ike liked talking like this.

The new president had heard of CIA plans to overthrow Fidel Castro, the new dictator of Cuba. "Should we support guerrilla operations in Cuba?" he asked.

"To the utmost," Ike said, "we can't let the present government there go on." Eisenhower's treasury secretary explained that "large amounts of United States capital now planned for investment in Latin America are waiting to see whether or not we can cope with the Cuban situation."

As the meeting broke up, Eisenhower got Kennedy alone again and told him that the missile gap he talked about during his campaign didn't exist. He didn't care what he may have heard, "you have an invulnerable asset in Polaris," the nuclear-armed submarines surrounding the coasts of the Soviet Union, "it is invulnerable."

"I'm going to try to support you every way I can on foreign policy," the outgoing president told his successor, "but there is one point on which I would oppose you strongly—the seating of Communist China in the U.N. and bilateral recognition."

After the meeting, Kennedy met with his brother and some of his closest associates to go over the discussion he had just had with Ike. He said he was amazed at how calm Eisenhower seemed as he talked about nuclear war. He thought there was almost something frightening about it.[153]

Kennedy himself was scared of nuclear war and worried over the possibility that one could start due to a miscalculation on the part of the Soviet Union or the United States. The new president would soon recommend to some of his advisers that they read the bestselling Barbara Tuchman book *The Guns of August* that chronicled the beginning of World War I. It described the start of that war as an almost automatic process in which once one switch was triggered, the war could not be stopped. In talks with people, Kennedy would recall a passage from the book in which two German leaders talked about the war: "How did it all happen?"

---

153   Richard Reeves, *President Kennedy: Profile of Power* (New York: Simon & Schuster, 1993), 31-33; Jim Rasenberger, *The Brilliant Disaster: JFK, Castro, and America's Doomed Invasion of Cuba's Bay of Pigs* (New York: Scribner, 2011), 108-109.

one asked. The other answered, "Ah, if one only knew." Now an accidental war or one sparked by some crazy incident could mean the end of life as we know it. Kennedy had the book placed in every single Officers' Club on US military bases all over the world.[154]

However, Kennedy was a confident man who had been preparing to take the oath of office for the past several months. He had put a lot of thought into how he wanted to manage his presidency and decided that he did not exactly want to do it the same way Eisenhower did. Ike had run a formal executive branch full of national security and cabinet meetings. Kennedy thought this made it so that many of the real decisions were made before they ever reached him. As a new president, he wanted to rely more on a few trusted personal advisers who would be able to reach into the bureaucracy for him.

Eisenhower created the position of chief of staff during his term, and the position has come to be a key cog in just about every presidency since then. Kennedy, though, didn't use it. Instead he brought several well-trusted aides with him into the White House, including Kenneth O'Donnell and Theodore Sorensen, both of whom he had known for years, and Arthur Schlesinger Jr., a historian who had written

---

154  Reeves, 305-306.

best-selling histories of presidents Andrew Jackson and Franklin Roosevelt. When he asked Schlesinger to be on his team, he didn't even tell him what his role or title would be. He just used him as a trouble-fixer. Dave Powers, who was one of Kennedy's best friends, also joined the White House as "Special Assistant and Assistant Appointments Secretary," but he had no real official duties. Kennedy simply wanted him around. The press jokingly dubbed his closest advisers the "Irish mafia."

Washington insider Clark Clifford, who helped Kennedy manage his transition into the White House, told him that by having three or four key aides instead of a "number-one boy" he would "be your own chief." Instead of having his name penciled in the box at the top of a typical organization flow chart, Kennedy wanted to be at the center of all of the action. Kennedy's organization style would turn out to exhibit some serious strengths and weaknesses.

One wonders if it didn't appeal to him from hearing stories from his father about business operations on the edges of the criminal underworld and stock market pools where informal one-on-one interactions with trusted associates are key. Or perhaps it came from the camaraderie he experienced in World War II or a simple desire to be a hands-on president. Whatever the case, loyalty and trust were important to him and he had many loyal men around him who loved him. He would not be alone in the White House.[155]

Right after he got elected, Kennedy picked up the phone and called Allen Dulles and told him he wanted him to remain as CIA director. He then let J. Edgar Hoover know that he was staying on as the director of the FBI too. Kennedy's aides were hoping he would let them both go, but as Arthur Schlesinger explained, "this was part of his strategy of reassurance. Hoover and Dulles were still national icons in 1960. Since the political cost of discharging them would have been considerable, reappointment enabled Kennedy to get full credit with their admirers for something he had no real choice but to do anyway." Ecstatic with the decision, the now elderly Dulles let the new president know that he planned to retire in a few years and was grooming Richard Bissell, who had succeeded Frank Wisner as covert operations chief, as his successor.[156]

As for picking his cabinet members, Kennedy had a problem in that he really did not personally know many qualified people that would be acceptable to the power elite. He knew few corporate leaders, university

---

[155] Reeves, 23; Arthur Schlesinger Jr., *A Thousand Days: John F. Kennedy in The White House* (New York: Fawcett Premier, 1965), 119-121.

[156] Schlesinger, 122; Peter Grose, *Gentleman Spy: The Life Of Allen Dulles* (Amherst: The University of Massachusetts Press, 1994), 511.

presidents, and foundation heads, who typically are used to staff the executive branch. "In particular," Schlesinger wrote, "he was little acquainted in the New York financial and legal community—that arsenal of talent which had so long furnished a steady supply of always orthodox and often able people to Democratic as well as Republican administrations. This community was the heart of the American establishment.... Roosevelt and Truman had drawn freely upon them, partly to avail themselves of establishment competence, partly to win protective coloration for policies which, with liberals in front would have provoked conservative opposition. It was never clear who was using whom; but since it was never clear, each side continued to find advantages in this arrangement."

This "eastern establishment," as Richard Nixon called it, looked on Kennedy with suspicion. "This was mostly because of his father, whom it had long since blackballed as a maverick in finance and an isolationist in foreign policy," Schlesinger recalled. Kennedy also provoked their wrath several years ago when he was a senator by supporting the independence of Algeria from France, which led to editorials attacking him in *Foreign Affairs* and the *New York Times*.[157]

---

157 Schlesinger, 125; Caroline Kennedy and Michael Beschloss, *Jacqueline Kennedy: Historic Conversations on Life with John Kennedy* (New York: Hyperion, 2011), 65.

Kennedy wanted his brother Robert to become a key part of his administration, so he got him to agree to become the attorney general and then tapped into the establishment by picking men such as Dean Rusk, the head of the Rockefeller Foundation, for secretary of state, and Douglas Dillon as treasury secretary. He also got Robert McNamara, who was the president of Ford Motor Company, to accept an appointment to become the secretary of defense.

McNamara and Kennedy didn't know each other before that. The president's wife, Jacqueline Kennedy, remembers, "They came in for their little conference in our tiny Georgetown house, and the first thing McNamara asked him was, 'Did you really write *Profiles in Courage?*' and Jack said he had.... And then McNamara really had this worship for Jack, and then he said, well fine, that he'd love to be it."[158]

Kennedy also chose McGeorge Bundy to become his national security adviser. Bundy's brother William, who had served as a CIA analyst, also became a part of the executive *bureaucracy* as a deputy to Paul Nitze, who drafted NSC-68 and came back into government as assistant secretary of defense for international security affairs, which made him a senior staffer for McNamara. The two Bundy brothers were born into

---

158 Ibid., 114.

the power elite. Their father, Harvey Bundy, graduated from Yale as a member of the Skulls and Bones fraternity, went to Harvard Law School, and then worked as a clerk for Supreme Court justice Oliver Wendell Holmes Jr.

McGeorge Bundy also went to Yale and was a Bonesman. He even kept a ceramic skull and bones propped up on the desk of his study and kept in touch with his fellow fraternity members his entire life. He received letters from them addressed to "Odin," Bundy's initiation nickname. Bundy graduated from Yale at the top of his class, and when he applied to the college he had three perfect test scores on his college entrance exams, a feat that had never been achieved before.

During World War II, Bundy's father served as an assistant to Secretary of War Henry Stimson and became one of the few people involved in the development of the atomic bomb. After the war, McGeorge Bundy helped Stimson compose his memoirs and then became a foreign policy adviser to failed Republican presidential candidate Tom Dewey where his boss was Allen Dulles, who at that time was working in the Dewey campaign. After that he went back to Harvard and became a professor of government and dean of the Harvard faculty. Bundy wrote a book titled *The Pattern of Responsibility in 1951*, an anthology of speeches and statements by Secretary of State Dean Acheson, who happened to be the father-in-law of his brother Bill Bundy. At one point, Kennedy considered Arthur Schlesinger for national security adviser, but instead he chose McGeorge Bundy, who, looking back later, thought the president was looking for someone he felt comfortable with and would be more "acceptable to what was then called the establishment."[159]

Two weeks after the election, Bundy presented Kennedy with his first major foreign policy decision—what to do about the CIA plans to topple Fidel Castro from power in Cuba that he had talked briefly about with Eisenhower. The Cuban dictator came into power by defeating the US-friendly and mafia-owned dictator Fulgencio *Batista* and had begun to align himself with the Soviet Union. The CIA plans had started as simple small-scale infiltration and sabotage operations inside Cuba and had grown to an amphibious invasion of the island with an army of 1,500 Cuban refugees. They would face Castro's army of 25,000 soldiers and 250,000 militiamen who could mobilize in a day's time. The idea was that the 1,500 CIA-backed Cubans would be able to establish a beachhead on the island

---

[159] Gordon Goldstein, *Lessons In Disaster: McGeorge Bundy and the Path to War In Vietnam* (New York: Henry Holt and Company, 2008), 8-14, 35.

and spark a mass uprising against Castro. Bundy gave Kennedy two papers about the proposed invasion.

One of the papers was written by Richard Bissell, who was the CIA director of covert operations and in charge of the invasion plans, and the other was written by Thomas Mann, who had served as assistant secretary of state for inter-American affairs. While Bissell's memo was all for the invasion and outlined how he thought it would succeed, Mann thought the idea of invading Cuba was crazy. He didn't think such a small force would be able to survive and doubted that it would inspire Cubans to fight against Castro. Castro himself had known that the CIA was training an army against him and had arrested hundreds of suspected "counterrevolutionists."

Richard Goodwin, one of Kennedy's aides, told Bundy he thought the operation would put Kennedy into a trap. "Even if the landings are successful and a revolutionary government is set up," Goodwin wrote him, "they'll have to ask for our help. And if we agree, it'll be a massacre... We'll have to fight house-to-house in Havana." A few people told Kennedy that if the United States flat out invaded Cuba, it might harm the nation's image throughout the rest of Latin American and may tempt the Soviets into responding by invading West Berlin. So the anti-Castro Cubans would have to succeed first before the United States would be able to get overtly involved.

"I am against it," Arthur Schlesinger told Kennedy. In his view, the whole idea rested on two implausible ideas. First, "that, if only Cubans took part, the United States could dissociate itself from the consequences; and that, if the beachhead could be held for a few days and enlarged, there would be defections from the militia and uprisings behind the lines," he told the president in a memo. No matter how much the United States tries to make "Cuban" the equipment and personnel, it "will be held accountable for the operation" and "since the Castro regime," he warned, "is presumably too strong to be toppled by a single landing, the operation will turn into a protracted civil conflict" at best. He thought that if that happened, Congress would demand that Kennedy "send in the Marines."[160]

McGeorge Bundy knew Richard Bissell well. Bissell had a reputation as a CIA genius for creating its U-2 spy plane program. Robert Amory Jr., the CIA's deputy director of intelligence, called him a "human computer." Bissell floated around Georgetown cocktail parties and grew up as best friends with Joseph Alsop, the

---

160 Peter Wyden, *Bay of Pigs: The Untold Story* (New York: Simon & Schuster, 1979), 108; Goldstein, 36-37; Schlesinger, p237-238.

powerful Washington reporter, so everyone important in Washington knew of him. Before World War II, he worked in the Truman administration as "the real mental center and engine room of the Marshall Plan," according to William Bundy. Then he took a job as an economics professor at Yale, where both of the Bundy brothers studied with him. McGeorge Bundy's deputy Walter Rostow did too.[161]

Bundy recommended to Kennedy that he approve the plan, because "Defense and CIA now feel quite enthusiastic about the invasion. At the worst, they think the invaders would get into the mountains, and at the best, they think they might get a full-fledged civil war in which we could back the anti-Castro forces openly." The men were being trained in small bases in Florida and Louisiana, and in a large base in Guatemala.

Bundy remembers that Kennedy "was informed that the force must leave Guatemala within a limited time, and that it could not be held together in the United States for a long period. It would begin to deteriorate; its existence could not be kept quiet; and if it were disbanded within the United States the results would be damaging." He would come under political attack. In Allen Dulles's view, that "would have meant

---

161 Wyden, 12-18.

that we were not behind these people who were trying to over-throw Castro."[162]

The operation had taken on a life of its own. Although Eisenhower had first approved the operations against Castro when he was president, he never had given his go-ahead for invasion planning. "At no time did I put before anybody anything that could be called a plan," he wrote. Yes, he approved a CIA project to overthrow Castro, officially titled "A Program of Covert Action Against the Castro Regime" on March 17, 1960. According to the document he signed, the purpose was to remove Castro "in such a manner as to avoid any appearance of U.S intervention." What it called for was to develop a political opposition government, to spread anti-Castro propaganda, to create a covert guerilla force to run intelligence and sabotage missions inside Cuba, and to train "an adequate paramilitary force outside of Cuba for future guerilla action." Nowhere did the plan call for an invasion of Cuba, and it asked for a budget of only $4.4 million.[163]

Many of the men who were involved in PB/Success, the CIA's overthrow of Jacobo Arbenz of Guatemala in 1954, joined the Cuba operation. Howard Hunt worked to form a political refugee group that could act as a

---

162  Goldstein, 36; Grose, 516.
163  Wyden, 25; Rasenberger, 55, 386.

government-in-exile, while David Phillips set up Radio Swan off the coast of Honduras to broadcast radio messages into Cuba. The CIA eventually set up a base for anti-Castro operations it code-named JM/Wave in a group of buildings at the University of Miami.

On August 18, 1960, Allen Dulles and Bissell met with President Eisenhower and got him to approve an additional $10.75 million to train 500 Cubans in Guatemala. He agreed, but only "so long as the Joint Chiefs, Defense, State, and CIA think we have a good chance of being successful." He did not want to make "false moves" or to be "starting something before we are ready," he told them.[164]

The CIA tried to use this force to support anti-Castro forces in Cuba. On September 28, a CIA plane took off from Guatemala and dropped a pallet of machine guns and rifles good enough to supply one hundred men. Castro's men took the supplies and captured the Cuban CIA asset who was waiting for them and shot him on the spot. The pilot of the plane got lost and landed in Mexico, where he was arrested. The CIA flew thirty missions like this and all but three failed.

"We had made a major effort at infiltration and resupply, and those efforts had been unsuccessful," Bissell said. So now he thought "what was needed was

---

164 Tim Weiner, *The Legacy of Ashes: The History of the CIA* (New York: Random House, 2008), 187.

a shock operation." During the presidential transition period between the election of Kennedy and his taking the oath of office, Bissell made the decision to formally change the plans against Castro from one of infiltration to a full invasion. He now hoped that a direct invasion of the island could establish a beachhead and spark a mass revolt against Castro. Neither he nor Allen Dulles ever asked for Eisenhower's approval to do this. Nor did they bring the changes to the attention of the National Security Council or the president's Special Group to oversee covert operations. In Bissell's words, the decision was "internal really to the people involved in the operation."[165]

He ordered CIA operative Jake Esterline, who was in charge of the forces in Guatemala, to get more men and put marine Colonel Jack Hawkins in charge of their training. Most of the men they recruited came from the one hundred thousand Cubans who had fled Castro and gone to Florida. They were told that thousands of men were joining the new exile army in Guatemala. "When I got there," Maximo Cruz remembers, "I realized they did not have thousands of people. There were probably three or four hundred." Over a thousand more would join, though.[166]

---

165 Ibid., 187-191; Wyden, 69.

166 Rasenberger, 85; Schlesinger, 234.

How could Richard Bissell believe that these men could defeat Castro? He thought he could repeat in Cuba what the CIA had done in Guatemala. But some in the CIA doubted it. One intelligence memo Bissell received argued that in Guatemala, Arbenz had very little popular support and was not fully backed by his own military, whereas Castro was in full control of Cuba and was seen as a hero by most Cubans. What is more, the whole Guatemala thing had worked due to a "unique coincidence of favorable factors" and "unbelievable luck" that probably would not happen again, the memo argued. [167]

Some high up in the CIA hierarchy distanced themselves from the operation. Richard Helms, at the time one of the assistant operations directors, attended several of the early planning meetings for the Cuba operation. He sat in them and hardly said a word. David Phillips thought it "incredible" that he wasn't asking any questions. Helms stopped coming to the meetings. Bissell started to think that he didn't "want to be connected" with it.[168]

Jake Esterline heard rumors from his recruits about conditions in Cuba. He started to think the invasion would be impossible. "Our original concept is now

---

167 Rasenberger, 66.
168 Wyden, 33-34.

seen to be unachievable in the face of the controls Castro has instituted," he warned Bissell in a memo, "there will not be the internal unrest earlier believed possible nor will the defenses permit the type of strike first planned. Our second concept (1,500 - 3,000 man force to secure a beach with airstrip) is now also seen as unachievable, except as a joint Agency/DOD action." It would need the full force of the US military to succeed.[169]

Neither Bissell nor Dulles passed these doubts on to the president. Two hundred and fifty of the Cubans being trained in Guatemala resigned. The CIA put a dozen of the men in a stockade to prevent them from leaving. They told the White House that morale was high.[170]

The CIA needed the assistance of the US military to help with the invasion. They got a dozen B-26 two-engine bombers for the Cubans to fly. But they found people in the Pentagon very reluctant to get involved. Stanley Beerli, who was in charge of the CIA's planes, said they put him "in a begging position" where "he had to fight for every damn airplane, everything we wanted, every bit of the way."

---

169   Weiner, 191.
170   Schlesinger, 222.

Beerli called Fletcher Prouty, an air force colonel working in the defense secretary's office as the liaison officer with the CIA, only to be treated with suspicion. "He would try to pry information" from him and ask questions such as "Why do you want this?" or "What are you going to do with that?" Beerli recalls. Like a good employee of the CIA, though, he wouldn't answer Prouty's questions. "They were very concerned, and the less they became involved, the less the blame would be on them," he concluded.[171]

Kennedy asked the Joint Chiefs of Staff to evaluate the CIA's plans. General Wheeler, who was the director of the chief's planning staff, ordered General Gordon Gray to form a committee with four other officers and go meet with the CIA people planning the invasion and write a report. Gray and his men met with six CIA officers. He paid no attention to their names, because he assumed they were "pseudonyms." He "expected to be handed a plan thick with documents and appendices," but he was "surprised and shocked" when he got nothing but a "verbal rundown," he said.

They spent an afternoon sitting around a big conference table with a map of Cuba on it. The CIA men explained that they planned to land the brigade of Cubans at a beach near the small town of Trinidad,

---

171   Wyden, 71.

a shore city on the southern coast Cuba. They expected that the brigade would double in size in four days thanks to locals joining in and that anti-Castro guerilla forces supplied by the CIA in the Escambray Mountains would join in the fight. In reality, there were no such forces waiting in the mountains.

Gray's group left the meeting, headed to the Pentagon, and from memory quickly wrote up a twenty-five-page doubled-spaced report on what they just heard. They thought the CIA Cuban brigade would be able to survive on its own for four days given complete air supremacy. After that, ultimate success would depend on mass uprisings and the mountain fighters.

Gray called General Wheeler and told him that he thought the plan had a "fair" chance of success. Wheeler asked him what he meant by "fair." Do you mean something like "thirty in favor and seventy against?" Wheeler asked.

"Yes," Gray said.

The Joint Chiefs sent a report to the White House and the CIA carefully worded to appear to support the plan, but to express doubts at the same time. It didn't include the thirty-to-seventy odds of success, but instead said "this plan has a fair chance of ultimate success, and even if it does not achieve immediately the full results desired, could contribute to the eventual overthrow of the Castro regime."

But the chiefs warned that their "assessment of the combat worth of assault forces is based upon second and third-hand reports, and certain logistic aspects of the plan are highly complex and critical to the initial success. For these reasons, an independent evaluation of the combat effectiveness of the invasion forces and detailed analysis of logistics plans should be made by a team of army, naval, and air force officers."

General David Shoup, the commander of the Marine Corps, said, "No military man would ever think that this force could overthrow Castro without support. They could not expect anything but annihilation." Someone from the CIA told him that the invasion force was going to bring thirty thousand rifles with them because people in Cuba were there waiting for the arms. That changed his mind.

The president received a briefing by Richard Bissell on the military's appraisal of the plan. General Lemnitzer, the chairman of the Joint Chiefs, thought it "very peculiar." Bissell never broke the plan down into specifics. "He never walked through it step by step," Lemnitzer said. People in the room thought that the argument that moved Kennedy the most was that the rebels would be able to "fade" into the Escambray Mountains if they got into trouble.

Allen Dulles said, "Don't forget that we have a disposal problem. If we have to take these men out of

Guatemala, we will have to transfer them to the United States and we can't have them wandering around the country telling everyone what they have been doing."

According to Robert McNamara, "we were led to believe that the cost of failure would be small," but the president didn't seem to be enthused by the plan either. As the meeting ended, Kennedy said, "Dick, remember I reserve the right to cancel this right to the end." General Gray thought the Joint Chiefs now took their attention away from the operation. It no longer seemed to be a pressing issue.[172]

Bissell's assistant Tracy Barnes wrote him, "There is no doubt in my mind that our only chance is to be very firm in our position and be very strong in urging the need for the proposed action. This means, as I see it, persuading the Boss that this must be done." Kennedy told Bissell that the whole thing seemed "too spectacular" and that "it sounds like D-Day. You have to reduce the noise level of this thing." Secretary of State Dean Rusk suggested finding an area that had a landing strip on it so that they could fly the B-26s to it and claim that the bombers were really Castro defectors.

The CIA moved the landing site to a beach area called the Bay of Pigs. It was in a deep narrow bay surrounded by swampland and home to an airstrip. Also,

---

172 Wyden, 86-92; Schlesinger, 227; Rasenberger, 137-138.

few people lived in the area, so they figured the landing would be quieter than Trinidad. The Joint Chiefs approved the change. Dulles and Bissell told Kennedy that they had 2,500 people organized inside Cuba in resistance groups and that those men had twenty thousand sympathizers. They said the brigade could get the support of up to a quarter of the Cuban people. The men behind the operation were judging its viability.

However, there were some new problems. David Phillips looked at a map of the new plan and quickly noticed that the landing site was too far from the Escambray Mountains for them to serve as an escape hatch. Bissell realized this too, but he decided to keep that information to himself. "It must be admitted that we either encouraged or allowed the president and his advisers to believe that in the event of uncontainable pressure at the beachhead the brigade could retire and thereby protect the guerilla operation," Bissell later wrote.[173]

General Gray studied U-2 photos of the new landing area and noticed a dark mass in the water right off the shore. He thought they were coral reefs. A CIA photo interpreter told him not to worry—it's just seaweed. He was wrong. In Guatemala, one of the Cuban

---

173  Schlesinger, 232; Rasenberger, 139-141.

brigade leaders looked at the pictures too and saw the reefs. "It is going to be stupid to try to get landing barges in there, because you won't have more than two or three feet of water over those coral heads, and that's going to stop you," he told one of the CIA camp commanders. Don't worry, "those are clouds," the CIA man reassured him. Who were they to question headquarters? The CIA men told the Cubans that they would have the full force of the US military behind them. They had high hopes of returning to their homeland.[174]

McGeorge Bundy wrote Kennedy that Bissell and the CIA "have done a remarkable job of reframing the plan so as to make it unspectacular and quiet, and plausibly Cuban in its essentials. I have been a skeptic about Bissell's operation, but now I think we are on the edge of a good answer."[175]

A few still doubted the wisdom of the invasion. Undersecretary of State Chester Bowles had gotten wind of the details of the plan and sent a memo to his superior, Dean Rusk, telling him that he thought the whole scheme was "crazy." "I think you can kill this thing if you can take a firm stand on it," he wrote, "but if you can't I want to see the President." Rusk simply

---

174  Wyden, 136-137; Schlesinger, 234.
175  Rasenberger, 140.

put his initials on the memo to show that he had read it and sent it back to Bowles. Rusk did recommend to Kennedy that perhaps someone other than him should make the final decision to go ahead so that person could take the blame and be sacrificed in case the whole thing failed.[176]

Kennedy flew down to Florida on Air Force One with William Fulbright, the head of the Senate Foreign Affairs Committee. Fulbright handed him a memo expressing his doubts about the Cuba operation. He had only heard rumors about it. But he said it was "an open secret" and that an invasion of Cuba would violate international law. "To give this activity even covert support," he wrote, "is of a piece with the hypocrisy and cynicism for which the United States is constantly denouncing the Soviet Union in the United Nations and elsewhere. The point will not be lost on the rest of the world—nor on our consciences." He warned that if the enterprise got into trouble he would come under pressure for "the use of armed force; and if we came to that, even under the paper cover of legitimacy, we would have undone the work of thirty years in trying to live down earlier interventions. We would also have assumed the responsibility for public order in Cuba, and in the circumstances this would unquestionably

---

176   Wyden, 121; Rasenberger, 150; Schlesinger, 239.

be an endless can of worms." "The Castro regime is a thorn in the flesh, but not a dagger in the heart," he concluded.

Kennedy quickly read the memo, but he didn't express any reaction to it. Fulbright decided that he didn't want to be rude, so he didn't press the issue. He had given his opinion. Fulbright didn't know that inside Kennedy's briefcase were unprocessed CIA reports that claimed Cuba was ripe for invasion—"Anti-Castro terrorists are exploding bombs daily in Havana—twelve in a single day, according to one report... Armed dissidents are said to be active in Pinar del Rio and Las Villas provinces..Sugar cane fires—allegedly set by saboteurs—may be increasing." None of this was real.

Kennedy invited Fulbright to fly back home with him. On the trip back, he told the senator he was going to hold a meeting about Cuba at the State Department and he'd like for him to attend.

Fulbright was surprised when he found himself seated next to the president in the White House Cabinet Room in a full conference with over a dozen men, including senior cabinet members. He was "taken aback by the size and formality" of the meeting. Richard Bissell stood up and gave an updated briefing on the invasion plans. Fulbright had no idea the plans were so advanced nor that the operation was so large.

Schlesinger was in the room and realized that this was a "climactic" decision meeting they were holding.[177]

"Kennedy started asking people around the table what they thought," Schlesinger remembers, "Fulbright, speaking in an emphatic and incredulous way, denounced the whole idea. The operation, he said, was wildly out of proportion to the threat. It would compromise our moral position in the world and make it impossible for us to protest treaty violations by the Communists. He gave a brave, old-fashioned American speech, honorable, sensible and strong; and he left everyone in the room, except me and perhaps the President, wholly unmoved."[178]

Fulbright's remarks enraged Paul Nitze, who was also in the room. The idea that covert action against communism could be wrong struck him as absurd. If this operation was immoral, he yelled at Fulbright, then what were they doing in this room?. The United States "had every right—indeed, an obligation—to excise communism from Latin America as if it was a spreading cancer," he said. William Bundy, who was also there, agreed with Nitze. "Damn it to hell," he thought to himself, "these are bridges we crossed long ago."

---

177  Wyden, 122-123, 146-147; Reeves, 79.
178  Schlesinger, 236.

The president asked the senior members sitting at the table for a yes or no vote. Every single one of them said yes. Latin America specialist Adolph Berle answered, "I'd say let her rip!" It seemed as though Fulbright was brought in to act as a foil just for this meeting. William Bundy saw the meeting as a bit of a "charade." He thought as soon as Kennedy asked for a vote that "this is not the right way to do it." He said yes and felt like everyone had to support the president.

Secretary of State Dean Rusk was irritated, because Kennedy had some men below the level of cabinet member sitting at the table as if they were his equals. He thought the invasion would fail, but he kept his opinion to himself. "I felt that my role was to penetrate weak points and raise searching questions about assumptions later taken for granted," he said. Rusk came to conclude that he "served President Kennedy very badly in this instance... I was too busy sitting on my little post of responsibility."[179]

Kennedy adjourned the meeting by saying, "Gentlemen, we better sleep on it." As everyone left the room, the president called Schlesinger over and asked for his opinion now. He said he was against it. Kennedy "nodded his head once or twice but said little," Schlesinger remembers, "my explanation seemed

---

179  Rasenberger, 158-160.

to me hurried and disorderly, so the next morning I went to the office at six-thirty and wrote down my views in time to put them on the President's desk before his day began."

Kennedy's aide feared disaster was coming and felt a huge personal regret "for having kept so silent during those crucial discussions in the Cabinet Room, though my feelings of guilt were tempered by the knowledge that a course of objection would have accomplished little save to gain me a name as a nuisance. " "It is one thing for a special assistant to talk frankly in private to the President at his request," he explained, "and another for a college professor, fresh to the government, to interpose his unassisted judgment in open meeting against that of such august figures as the Secretaries of State and Defense and the Joint Chiefs of Staff, each speaking with the full weight of his institutions behind him." In this formal setting, Schlesinger had been reduced to being a mere bureaucrat trapped in a box—a mechanism of the war state.

"Moreover, the advocates of the adventure had a rhetorical advantage. They could strike virile poses and talk of tangible things—fire power, air strikes, landing craft, and so on," Schlesinger later wrote, "to oppose the plan, one had to invoke intangibles—the moral position of the United States, the reputation of the President, the response of the United Nations, world public opinion, and other such odious concepts.... But just as the members of the White House staff who sat in the Cabinet Room failed in their job of protecting the President, so the representatives of the State Department failed in defending the diplomatic interests of the nation. I could not help feeling that the desire to prove to the CIA and Joint Chiefs that they were not soft-headed idealists but were really tough guys, too, influenced State's representatives at the cabinet table."[180]

The two commanders of the CIA operation, Jake Esterline and Colonel Hawkins, came to Richard Bissell's house. Despite all of the work they had put into the invasion plan, they told him that they wanted to resign. They didn't like the change in the landing site. They didn't think there would be enough people revolting in Cuba to make it work and didn't think there would be enough firepower from the sixteen old B-26 bombers to support the Cubans they had been training. It would be a "terrible disaster" they told Bissell. They could be sending men to their deaths for nothing.

Bissell listened to them, said it was too late to think of ending it, and appealed to their friendship. "He earnestly asked us not to abandon him at this late date,"

---

180  Schlesinger, 239-240.

Hawkins wrote later. They agreed to stay after Bissell promised to contact Kennedy and get more aircraft. If his two principal CIA invasion planners had left, eyebrows would have shot up. He managed to keep them on board.[181]

Allen Dulles believed that even though President Kennedy insisted that he did not want to directly involve the US military in the invasion, he would in the end if it came to that. "We felt that when the chips were down—when the crisis arose in reality—any action required for success would be authorized," he later wrote. "I have seen a good many operations which started out like the B of P", he explained, "insistence on complete secrecy—non-involvement of the U.S.—initial reluctance to authorize supporting actions. This limitation tends to disappear as the needs of the operation become clarified." If it didn't work, it would only be due to the president's lack of a "determination to succeed," Dulles argued. But Kennedy meant what he said.[182]

Kennedy gave the go-ahead for the invasion and called Bissell to give him the news. Then "almost as an afterthought," he asked him how many planes would be used. Bissell said sixteen. "I don't want it on that

---

181  Wyden, 159-160; Rasenberger, 175-176.
182  Grose, 522.

scale," the president said, "I want it minimal." Bissell didn't ask what that meant, but he was glad to hear that the operation was a go. He called Beerli and told him to use only six planes.

On April 15, 1961, the CIA invasion force set sail for Cuba. The B-26 bombers attacked the island and destroyed five of Castro's planes and damaged a dozen more of them, but half of his air force didn't receive a scratch. Bissell sent Tracy Barnes to tell Adlai Stevenson, the US ambassador to the United Nations, that the bombers were piloted by Castro defectors. Stevenson repeated the CIA cover story to the world as if it were true. The next day, Stevenson figured out that he had been lied to, and even worse that no one believed him. [183]

A flurry of phone calls ensued that reduced whatever slim odds the invasion had to succeed to zero. Stevenson called Secretary of State Dean Rusk in a rage of anger over the CIA. He had made a fool of himself, and by extension the whole country, by peddling the CIA cover story on national television to the world. Dean Rusk talked to Kennedy and McGeorge Bundy. Calls went back and forth between them. McGeorge Bundy called the CIA.

---

183  Wyden, 170, 186-188.

Allen Dulles wasn't there to pick up the phone. On the day of the CIA's biggest operation in its history, he was in Puerto Rico, where he gave a speech to a business group and where he had been lounging around a hotel for a week. In his absence, the deputy director, General Charles Cabell, now served as acting director. Cabell had a career in the air force before he moved into the CIA. There he served as a figurehead. At meetings, he would often fall asleep, probably hung over. He liked to travel on inspection tours all over the world, where he would be given briefing reports that, as Robert Amory put it, "you could get out of Section Four of the *New York Times*." Cabell knew very little of what was really going on in the CIA and that made him valuable to Dulles as a front man. His real purpose was to testify to Congress for the CIA when needed without really being able to say anything and impress everyone with his shiny medals.

After the invasion, David Phillips and others directly involved in the Bay of Pigs invasion would call Cabell "Old Rice and Beans." Cabell found out that the B-26 bombers were not fully loaded with supplies and weapons. So he ordered that they be loaded with bags of rice and beans to drop to the men on the beaches and keep them supplied. David Phillips questioned the idea. "I don't want to have to explain to an appropriations committee why we're flying nearly empty planes over Cuba," he replied. Some of the big bags almost landed on top of a few of the Cuban invaders. They almost died for Cabell.

General Cabell sat in the invasion operations room smoking a cigar. McGeorge Bundy reached him on the phone and told him that there would be no more air strikes unless "they could be conducted from a strip within the beachhead." Bundy didn't have time to talk because he was going to New York "to hold the hands of Ambassador Stevenson." If you have a problem call Secretary of State Dean Rusk who is "the proxy of the President" for now he said. [184]

General Cabell and Richard Bissell left the room to head to the State Department and talk to Rusk in person. Those left in the room were livid. Curse words flowed. Howard Hunt remembered he was seething from the "agonizing uncertainty." "I bet Cabell's just doing this to give him a chance to puff himself up over a meeting with Rusk," someone told him.

Bissell and Cabell reached Rusk. They told him the air strikes were critical to success. Rusk picked up a phone in front of them and called Kennedy. He gave the president their arguments and then told him that he thought the strikes were "important, but not critical... I'm still recommending, in view of what's going

---

184  Weiner, 201; Rasenberger, 65; Wyden, 196-197.

on in New York that we cancel." He moved the phone away from his mouth and said, "Well, the President agrees with me, but would you, General Cabell, like to speak to the President?"

"Well, you've put it to the President a second time, I don't think he's going to override your recommendation," Cabell said, "there's no point in my talking to the President."

Cabell came back to the operations room with the bad news. Jake Esterline thought about killing him. Men pleaded with him to go back to Rusk and try again. One person told Cabell he was the lowest form of scum he ever saw. He sat there smoking another cigar "taking it." [185]

As soon as the invasion fleet reached the shore of Cuba it ran into trouble. It took the Cubans extra critical time to form a beach head, because most of their landing crafts smashed against coral reefs. The operation disintegrated. The reputation of the CIA and the great Allen Dulles began to sink into the ocean.

Allen Dulles flew to Baltimore on a CIA plane. Richard Drain, who had been one of the CIA men who briefed General Gray and the Joint Chiefs of Staff on the invasion plans, picked him up and drove him back to Washington. He told the CIA director that the

---

[185] Wyden, 197-120, 203-204; Weiner, 203.

air strikes had been canceled, because "Stevenson was raising hell with the President" and now things are "all going to hell."

Dulles sat in silence as they drove for twenty-five minutes to his home in Georgetown. Drain was surprised that he didn't seem to be concerned. His boss asked him no questions. When they got to their destination, Dulles told him to come inside and have a few drinks with him.

They went into Dulles's private library. Drain expected the director to now grill him on the operation and to then get on the phone and do something. But he didn't, because he had something else on his mind.

"Dick, you served in Greece, didn't you?" Dulles asked him, "I have to go to the White House tomorrow to a reception for (Greek Prime Minister) Caramanlis. Can you refresh my memory about him?" Men were dying in Cuba and the director of the CIA was worrying about making the right impression at a cocktail party. Drain never forgot that night in Dulles's home.[186]

On the beaches of the Bay of Pigs, 114 men of the CIA Cuban brigade army died and 1,189 were taken prisoner. They fought for two days. On the last night, the brigade commander radioed, "Please don't desert us. Am out of tank and ammo. Tanks will hit me at

---

186  Wyden, 266-267.

dawn. I will not be evacuated. Will fight to the end if we have to." "We were screwed by Kennedy," Esterline said later, "they made me send these men to their slaughter. I will never forget this as long as I live."[187]

Fidel Castro rounded up the survivors and forced them to sit on hard benches in a sports stadium. He stood above them lecturing them for hours, humiliating them as cameras filmed the scene for television. Pepe Roman, the commander of the CIA brigade, said, "I was discouraged with everything. I hated the United States, and I felt that I had been betrayed. Every day it became worse and then I was getting madder and madder and I wanted to get a rifle and come against the U.S."

Castro sentenced them all to thirty years of hard labor, which could be overturned on payment. He valued Roman and the other brigade leaders at $500,000 a person and the entire collective army at sixty-two million dollars. Kennedy organized a ransom payment and they all returned to the United States.[188]

According to Jackie Kennedy, the night the Cuban brigade surrendered, her husband "came back over

---

[187] Walter Poole, *History of the Joint Chiefs of Staff: The Joint Chiefs of Staff and National Policy, Volume 8, 1961-1964* (Washington, DC: Defense Department, Office of the Chairman of the Joint Chiefs of Staff, Office of Joint History, 2011), 114; Weiner, 203; Rasenberger, 329.

[188] Rasenberger, 341-342, 357.

to the White House to his bedroom and he started to cry, just with me. You know, just for once—just put his head in his hand and sort of wept. And I've only seen him cry about three times." He was as upset as he was when she lost a child.[189]

Secretary of Defense Robert McNamara felt devastated by what happened. He later wrote that he accepted the plan "uncritically." He listened to the briefings. "I had even passed along to the President, without comment, an ambiguous assessment by the Joint Chiefs." The morning after the invasion failed, he went to the Oval Office and told Kennedy, "I know where I was when you made the decision to launch the invasion. I was in a room where, with one exception, all of your advisors—including me—recommended that you proceed. I am fully prepared to go on TV and say so."

Kennedy told him not to do that. "I made up my mind not to let him down again," McNamara remembers. McGeorge Bundy also offered to resign, but Kennedy kept him too. Bundy wrote a memo saying that one of the lessons to be learned is that "the President's advisers must speak up in council... The President and his advisers must second-guess even military plans... Those who are to offer serious advice

---

189 Kennedy and Beschloss, 186.

on major issues must themselves do the necessary work."[190]

Leaked stories soon appeared in the newspapers giving insider accounts of the doomed operation. Kennedy thought they were coming from the Joint Chiefs of Staff, because none of the stories ever cast them in a negative light. He convened his top cabinet members and said that the stories would stop. They were all to blame, but since he was the president he was the one who had the final responsibility and had to face it publicly. Kennedy held a press conference and declared, "There's an old saying that victory has a hundred fathers and defeat is an orphan."

The president told his closest aides in private that he blamed the CIA and the Joint Chiefs for the fiasco. "He could not understand how men like Dulles and Bissell, so intelligent and experienced, could have been so wrong," he told Schlesinger. He waited a few months and then fired Allen Dulles along with Bissell and Cabell. He appointed as CIA director John McCone, a Republican who had been chairman of the Atomic Energy Commission toward the end of Eisenhower's presidency. Richard Helms took Richard Bissell's place as head of CIA covert

---

190 Robert McNamara, *In Retrospect: The Tragedy and Lessons of Vietnam* (New York: Random House, 1995), 26-27; Goldstein, 41-42.

operations. Staying away from the Bay of Pigs operation paid off for him. But the Joint Chiefs who supposedly had so much military experience didn't adequately advise President Kennedy before the invasion either. They kept their jobs, but the President "would never be overawed by professional military advice again," Schlesinger wrote.[191]

Kennedy told Kenneth O'Donnell that he was suspicious. He wondered if the CIA and the military had assumed he would just drop his restrictions on the use of US military force once the invasion got going. "They couldn't believe that a new President like me wouldn't panic and try to save his own face. Well they had me figured all wrong," he told Dave Powers.[192]

McGeorge Bundy came to a different conclusion about the Joint Chiefs of Staff. He thought the Pentagon was "bureaucratically cautious about dissecting another agency's most cherished enterprise." If the chiefs had attacked Allen Dulles's and Richard Bissell's pet project, then they would not be able to rely on their support in the future if they were to need it.[193]

---

191  Schlesinger, 270-273.

192  Kenneth O'Donnell and John Powers, *"Johnny, We Hardly Knew Ye": Memories of John Fitzgerald Kennedy* (New York: Pocket Books, 1973), 316.

193  Goldstein, 42-43.

The Pentagon had simply kept as far away from the operation as it could. Curtis LeMay, the five-star general of the air force who served on the Joint Chiefs of Staff, didn't even see the basics of the invasion plans until the day before it began. He immediately thought it would fail and passed that opinion on to Undersecretary of Defense Roswell Gilpatric, who merely shrugged. Some in the military thought Kennedy was to blame for the disaster. General Lauris Norstad, the commander of NATO, thought Cuba made for the worst defeat for the United States "since the War of 1812."[194]

Why did the invasion happen? A simple explanation is that John F. Kennedy was a new president and the CIA and the military were all for it. However, as Kennedy told one person, "All my life I've known better than to depend on the experts. How could I have been so stupid to let them go ahead?" Kenneth O'Donnell thought that when he came into office the plan had become so advanced that it had "seemed almost impossible to cancel it." The president of Guatemala had told him that he wanted the Cubans out of his country by the end of April. Kennedy got reports that the

---

194 Warren Kozak, *LeMay: The Life and Wars of General Curtis LeMay* (New York: Regnery History, 2011), 329-330; Michael Beschloss, *The Crisis Years: Kennedy and Khrushchev, 1960-1963* (New York: HarperCollins Publishers, 1991), 129.

Soviets were about to give Cuba MIG fighter jets, so any attack had to happen before they arrived. Robert Kennedy thought that "if he hadn't gone ahead with it, everybody would have said it showed that he had no courage."[195]

As for Allen Dulles and Richard Bissell, Schlesinger came to conclude that it was a "proposal on which they had personally worked for a long time and in which their organization had a heavy vested interest. This cast them in the role less of analysts than of advocates, and it led them to accept progressive modifications so long as the expedition in some form remained; perhaps they unconsciously supposed that, once the operation began to unfold, it would not be permitted to fail." It would have been embarrassing to Dulles and Bissell if they had said that after all of this money and training they gave the Cuban exile brigade it was not enough to succeed in Cuba. Bissell was on a career path to become director of the CIA. Now both were out of government.[196]

The whole operation occurred as a culmination of the past ten years of the growth of the war state. It brought a state of affairs that led to disaster, by placing men like Dulles and Bissell in a position to get the

---

[195] Wyden, 310; O'Donnell and Powers, 312-313; Rasenberger, 131.

[196] Schlesinger, 227.

government to back such a crazed scheme. The war state had greatly increased the power of the executive branch of the government while shrinking the power of the actual individual who served as president. According to Supreme Court justice William Douglas, "this episode seared him. He had experienced the extreme power that these groups had, these various insidious influences of the CIA and the Pentagon on civilian policy, and I think it raised in his own mind the specter: Can Jack Kennedy, President of the United States, ever be strong enough to really rule these two powerful agencies? I think it had a profound effect... it shook him up!"[197]

Kennedy said that "before my term has ended we shall have to test a new whether a nation organized and governed much as ours can endure. The outcome is by no means certain." "The textbooks had talked of three coordinate branches of government: the executive, legislative, the judiciary," Schlesinger wrote, "but with an activist President it became apparent that there was a fourth branch: the Presidency itself. And, in pursuing purposes, the President was likely to encounter almost as much resistance from the executive branch as from the others. By 1961 the tension between the

---

197  Fletcher Prouty, *The Secret Team: The CIA and Its Allies in Control of the United States and the World* (California: Institute for Historical Review, 1990), 417-418.

permanent government and the presidential government was deep in our system." Schlesinger's "permanent government" is the war state bureaucracy with its allies in the military-industrial complex and the Congress.

This situation didn't begin until the presidency of Franklin Roosevelt. Roosevelt needed to create emergency agencies to fight the depression and mobilize the nation to fight World War II. He couldn't do what he wanted simply through the old Departments of Labor, Agriculture, Commerce, Sate, War, and Navy, so he bypassed them by creating new more powerful divisions of government. As a result, Schlesinger wrote, "Roosevelt left his successors a much bigger government, and in due course the iron law of organization began to transform what had served as brilliant expedients for him into dead weights for them."

"The permanent government soon developed its own cozy alliances with committees of Congress, its own ties to the press, its own national constituencies. It began to exude the feeling that Presidents come and go but it went on forever. The permanent government was, as such politically neutral; its essential commitment was to doing things as they had been done before," Schlesinger argued. In his view, "the Bay of Pigs was a crucial episode in this struggle. This disaster was a clear consequence of the surrender of presidential government to the permanent government."[198]

President Kennedy never would have dreamt up the Cuban invasion by himself. It was a policy that came from the war state bureaucracy, what Schlesinger called the "permanent government," without any prior authorization. Neither President Eisenhower nor President Kennedy asked for an invasion of Cuba. Richard Bissell made a bureaucratic maneuver by taking advantage of the transition period between the time Kennedy won the presidential election and the time he actually got in office to turn what had been a simple guerrilla sabotage operation against Castro into a full-scale invasion, with disastrous consequences. If a president does nothing but blindly approve the policies that come from the war state bureaucracy, then he functions as a mere figurehead with very little actual individual power.

At the height of the Cold War, this could be a dangerous thing for a president to do. To his credit, President Kennedy did not want to become responsible for another calamity much less the cause of one. He knew he had to do something to get a hold of the situation. According to McGeorge Bundy, Kennedy told him that "there must not be another Cuba." Robert

---

198  Schlesinger, 624-627.

Kennedy, in Bundy's view, believed that "someone must have done this to Jack. The President couldn't have possibly done this to himself. And, therefore, in a fairly determined way the Attorney General was going to find out just who had done it."[199]

According to Schlesinger, Kennedy's way of dealing with the problem of the "permanent government" was not to create more organizations, as Roosevelt did, but instead to use a few key aides that he trusted to reach directly into the bureaucracy to get his own initiatives carried out. "This was his preferred method," Schlesinger wrote, "hence his unceasing flow of suggestions, inquiries, phone calls directly to operating desks and so on. This approach enabled him to imbue government with a sense of his own desires and purposes." Several times, Kennedy created major new government initiatives by declaring new objectives in major speeches and then picking two or three key men to carry them out behind the scenes.[200]

After the Bay of Pigs, Kennedy realized that he had to get the war state under control. He asked Maxwell Taylor, who had served as chairman of the Joint Chiefs

---

[199] McGeorge Bundy Oral History Interview, JFK Library, 26-27,(see http://archive2.jfklibrary.org/JFKOH/Bundy,%20McGeorge/JFKOH-MGB-01/JFKOH-MGB-01-TR.pdf, accessed 10/10/12)

[200] Schlesinger, 627-633.

of Staff under Dwight Eisenhower, to come back into government to help him make changes. They created a committee to investigate the Bay of Pigs disaster. Robert Kennedy joined it, Taylor led it, and Allen Dulles sat on it. It concluded that pretty much everyone involved, from the president on down, shared responsibility for the failure.

Lyman Kirkpatrick Jr., the CIA inspector general, did an internal investigation for the agency. He later noted that "no one seriously studied" whether Castro could be overthrown. "If there was a resistance to Fidel Castro it was mostly in Miami," and "all intelligence reports coming from allied sources indicated quite clearly that he was thoroughly in command of Cuba and was supported by most of the people who remained on the island," he wrote. As for the president, Kirkpatrick felt that Kennedy "seemed to think this was going to be some sort of mass infiltration that would perhaps, through some mystique, become quickly invisible. It is not known whether the President examined in any depth the concept of the air raids or the attention they would attract." Kennedy did not seem to have a real grasp of the operation, but neither did anyone else it seems. "Why was nothing known about the reefs offshore? Because no leader was sufficiently qualified in amphibious operations," he concluded.[201]

When Allen Dulles showed up at General Taylor's Bay of Pigs committee, he came holding NSC 5412/2, which contained the legal authorization for the CIA to engage in covert operations. Over the course of a decade, most of these operations had been miserable failures and they culminated in the Bay of Pigs fiasco. Kennedy called for change. "I think, however, that rather than destroying everything and starting all over, we ought to take what's good in what we have, get rid of those things that are really beyond the competence of the CIA, then pull the thing together and make it more effective," Dulles told the committee.

One of the last witnesses General Taylor called was General Walter Bedell Smith, the former CIA director. He testified that "when you are at war, cold war if you like, you must have an amoral agency which can operate secretly. I think that so much publicity has been given to CIA that the covert work might have to be put under another roof." "It's time we take the bucket of slop and put another cover over it," he said. The Bay of Pigs operation politically destroyed the CIA. No president would ever trust it again, and it would

---

201 Wyden, 315-323; Peter Kornbluh, ed., *Bay of Pigs Declassified: The Secret CIA Report on the Invasion of Cuba* (New York: The New Press, 1998).

become publicly discredited by a series of congressional investigations in the 1970s.[202]

Under the advice of Attorney General Robert Kennedy and General Maxwell Taylor, the president decided to take the overall control of covert operations out of the hands of the CIA. He issued a series of presidential executive orders to do it. First, he issued NSAM-55 (NSAM stands for National Security Action Memorandum), which was addressed to the chairman of the Joint Chiefs of Staff and told him that from now on he was responsible for both "military and paramilitary" operations and put him in a position to be able to demand any information from the CIA or any other agency if that agency started to develop one. He then issued NSAM- 57 to prevent the CIA from ever again getting involved in any operation as large as the Bay of Pigs invasion.

This order stated that "Under this principle, the Department of Defense will normally receive responsibility for overt paramilitary operations. Where such an operation is to be wholly covert or disavowable, it may be assigned to CIA, provided that it is within the normal capabilities of the agency. Any large paramilitary operation wholly or partly covert which requires significant numbers of militarily trained personnel,

---

202  Weiner, 205-207.

amounts of military equipment which exceed normal CIA-controlled stocks and/or military experiences of a kind and level peculiar to the Armed Services is properly the primary responsibility of the Department of Defense with the CIA in a supporting role."[203]

Kennedy did not believe that the Joint Chiefs of Staff had properly advised him on the Bay of Pigs operation, so he made General Taylor his personal military adviser and representative to the Joint Chiefs of Staff. He then took covert operations against Castro out of the sole possession of the CIA by putting them under a new project titled Operation Mongoose. He appointed General Edward Lansdale, who had worked with the CIA in the Philippines and in Vietnam, in charge of it, and he placed his brother in a supervisory role over him and all covert operations.

Operation Mongoose consisted of 600 CIA officers operating mostly out of the Miami area. They had about five thousand agents wage covert guerilla operations against the Castro government, including assassination plots. Richard Helms thought they were mostly a bunch of "nutty schemes"—and they were. [204]

---

203 Documents 32, 34, United States State Department, *Foreign Relations of the United States, 1961-1963, Volume VIII, National Security Policy* (see, http://history.state.gov/historical-documents/frus1961-63v08/comp1, accessed 10/10/12)

204 Weiner, 214.

As a result of the Bay of Pigs disaster, President Kennedy did what came naturally to him and circled the wagons. Once, when flying on Air Force One, he pointed to a sleeping O'Donnell and said, "You see Kenny there? If I woke him up and asked him to jump out of this plane for me, he'd do it. You don't find that kind of loyalty easily." He told someone else once that if he cut off Jackie Kennedy's head and brought it into the Oval Office and handed it to his secretary Evelyn Lincoln, she would just go and get a box to put it in it without asking a single question.[205]

According to Theodore Sorensen, after the Bay of Pigs, Kennedy asked "RFK and me to give him the sort of candid, critical assessment he did not feel he had received on the planning of that inherently flawed operation." The two began to sit regularly in national security meetings as the president's personal representatives. When Kennedy made future decisions, he made sure that he got several options to consider instead of just one. He also made sure he got advice from people who were personally loyal to him to complement those that came from people who were there simply because they were the leader of a division of

---

205  Reeves, 104.

the war state bureaucracy and a part of the "permanent government."[206]

President Kennedy's dependence on a few key advisers brought a much more informal management style than Dwight Eisenhower used in the White House. Kennedy held few formal National Security Council meetings, which meant he had less contact with representatives from the military. One army officer detailed to the White House said that the Kennedy national security staff "really seems to be an agglomeration of six to a dozen hearty individuals picking up balls and running with them ad libitum as the President or McGeorge Bundy directs" which leads to a "helter-skelter intellectual parlor game." [207]

This way of doing business angered a lot people who got cut out of the loop. General Curtis LeMay found that even though he was a member of the Joint Chiefs of Staff, President Kennedy and his men rarely consulted with him. Kennedy used General Maxwell Taylor, the chairman of Joint Chiefs of Staff, and Secretary of Defense Robert McNamara as his main men for military affairs. LeMay couldn't stand McNamara, who, Lemay felt, had to have "control of everything and speak for everybody and most people just threw up

---

206 Ted Sorensen, *Counselor* (New York: Harper Perennial, 2008), 320.

207 Poole, 6.

their hands and gave up." As for Taylor, he would go to the White House for the Chiefs, but then LeMay felt "many, many times the chairman didn't fully brief the Joint Chiefs on what was going on."

General White of the air force remarked of Kennedy's men, "in common with many other military, both active and retired, I am profoundly apprehensive of the pipe-smoking, tree-full-of owls type of so called defense intellectuals who have been brought into this nation's capitol. I don't believe a lot of these often over-confident, sometimes arrogant young professors, mathematicians, and other theorists have sufficient worldliness or motivation to stand up to the kind of enemy we face."

Curtis LeMay did not think Kennedy had much respect for military advice and was wrong to blame the Joint Chiefs for any part of the Bay of Pigs invasion. "All these articles that you have seen," LeMay said, "that have been written by the great brains of the Kennedy administration, including Robert Kennedy, on the Bay of Pigs as to the bad military advice and the betrayal of the military to President Kennedy is just a bunch of hogwash, because it was not a military operation.... it was a civilian operation from start to finish." In LeMay's view, the Kennedy people were "cockroaches."

The way LeMay saw it, "everyone that came in with the Kennedy administration is the most egotistical people that I ever saw in my life. They had no faith in the military; they had no respect for the military at all. They felt that the Harvard Business School method of solving problems would solve any problem in the world. They were capable of doing it; they were better than all the rest of us; otherwise they wouldn't have gotten their superior education, as they saw it. And the fact that they had it entitled them to govern the rest of us, and we shouldn't question their decisions."

The general would hear of McNamara overwhelming people he would deal with using "what he called facts and figures and so forth that may or may not have been correct." "He could quote figures and statements and paragraphs and things of that sort and have all that right at his finger tips, which is a very impressive performance," LeMay said.

As for General Maxwell Taylor, LeMay thought he was more a political operative than a real military man who had a history of favoring the army over the air force and the navy. He was "Chief of Staff of the Army under Eisenhower and when General Twining was Chairman of the Joint Chiefs, and the Joint Chiefs didn't agree with Taylor then on what he was trying to do with the army" with his ideas of flexible response, LeMay said, "but that time when the argument got too hot and heavy, General Twining would just bundle all up and go over and sit down and talk to the President.

The President didn't agree with Taylor either, talking about President Eisenhower, so that was it. Taylor wasn't getting any place with his wild ideas, so he retired. He came back with the Kennedy administration as a civilian advisor, President's assistant as a civilian. And then he was put back in uniform, a retired officer as Chairman of the Joint Chiefs!"

LeMay thought it was really McNamara, though, who was making the decisions in the White House when it came to the military and not Taylor, because he thought that the secretary of defense didn't trust "Maxwell Taylor any more than the rest of us because he had the military background. He has absolutely no respect for the military at all—none. As a matter of fact he had little respect for anybody, completely ruthless and unprincipled people!"[208]

President Kennedy held a meeting with General Lemay and the other Joint Chiefs of Staff to clear the air with them on May 27, 1961. Drawing on a paper that General Taylor wrote he told them that they were responsible to give him "unalloyed advice." Taylor thought they took it as a lecture, because when Kennedy finished they just sat there in "stony silence."

---

208  Ibid, 300; Curtis LeMay Oral History Interview, LBJ Library, June 28, 1971, (see http://web2.millercenter.org/lbj/oralhistory/lemay_curtis_1971_0628.pdf#page=4&zoom=auto,0,851, accessed 03/03/2013)

From then on Kennedy remained respectful of them, but skeptical of their advice." They always give you their bullshit about instant reaction and their split-second timing, but it never works out. No wonder it's so hard to win a war," he told an aide.[209]

One other impact the Bay of Pigs disaster had on Kennedy was to move him to announce a goal of landing a man on the moon. It ultimately cost twenty billion dollars. President Eisenhower had resisted calls to expand the space program in order to keep government spending down. Now he thought Kennedy's announcement was "almost hysterical" and later complained to astronaut Frank Borman that the country's space program "was drastically revised and expanded just after the Bay of Pigs fiasco... It immediately took one single project or experiment out of a thoroughly planned and continuing program involving communication, meteorology, reconnaissance, and future military and scientific benefits and gave the highest priority— unfortunate in my opinion—to a race, in other words, a stunt."[210]

---

209 Steven Rearden, *Council of War: A History of the Joint Chiefs of Staff, 1942-1991* (Washington, DC: U.S. Department of Defense, National Defense University, Joint History Office, Office of the Director, 2012), 216.

210 Beschloss, 166.

President John Kennedy's challenges had only begun. He was set to hold a diplomatic summit with Soviet Premier Khrushchev in Vienna on June 4, 1961, which was only about two months after the Bay of Pigs. Would the Soviets see that disaster as a sign of weakness to take advantage of?

The Joint Chiefs were afraid that Khrushchev would see it that way. So they sent Kennedy a memo as he left for Europe:

"In your conversations with Premier Khrushchev... be assured that you speak from a position of decisive military superiority in any matter affecting the vital interests of the United States and our allies... It is the considered judgment of the Joint Chiefs of Staff that the military forces under your command... can achieve decisive military victory in any all-out test of strength with the Sino-Soviet Bloc to the extent that the United States will retain the dominant power position in the world. Thus, in your discussions, be assured that you may represent the national interest with confidence."[211]

---

211  Poole, 143.

# CHAPTER VI
## TARGETING EVERYTHING RED

How would you describe Nikita Khrushchev? In a photo, he looks like a fat man with a chubby face. He was a natural optimist and a survivor. He had risen from humble beginnings as a metalworker in a Ukrainian steel factory to become a commissar for the Soviet Communist Party during the violent Russian revolution. He then rose in the party to become Stalin's governor in the Ukraine, where he supported Stalin's purges as all commissars did. During World War II, he assisted in the defense of Stalingrad against the Nazis and after the war became one of Stalin's closest advisers.

As dictator, Stalin ruled at the dinner table. Every night he would gather his henchmen and over food and late-night drinking sessions make decisions for the fate of Russia. When he became displeased with one of his men, the target would often disappear never to be seen again. Toward the end of his life, his closest associates began to fear that he would launch another giant purge and kill them all. But then he had a stroke and died.

Khrushchev and Stalin's other cronies decided that they did not want to live in such personal danger again. Instead of one-man total dictatorship, they moved to create something akin to rule by committee. The Communist Party of the Soviet Union had an inner circle of about a dozen people called the Presidium. Stalin used it as an administrative arm to run the government, but his successors used it as the ruling body over Russia.

Its members came from the state bureaucracy and the Communist Party. They dedicated their lives to the state. The Presidium met weekly and kept its sessions secret. When the Presidium members approved a resolution, they made it a rule that they all had to back it without any sign of disagreement even if their decision came after an intense debate. In recent years, though, transcripts of many of their meetings have been released and we now have a better understanding of Soviet policy than was available to even the CIA during the time. We can now know the reasons behind things that were mysteries to American leaders when they happened, such as why Khrushchev sent nuclear missiles to Cuba and provoked the Cuban Missile Crisis.

One thing the Presidium members did after Stalin died was to quickly charge Lavrentiy Beria, his KGB head, with numerous crimes and have him executed. They all feared that Beria would turn himself into another Stalin and kill them, so they got him first. They then appointed Georgi Malenkov as premier, Khrushchev as the first secretary of the Communist Party, and Molotov as foreign minister. By 1954, after about two years of behind-the-scenes political jockeying, Malenkov resigned his position and Khrushchev became chairman of the Presidium, making him head of the Soviet state. He, in effect, became something akin to a dictator of Russia who had to answer to the Presidium committee.

Khrushchev became the leader of a deeply troubled empire. For one thing, it had an inefficient economy that can only be described as backward when compared with that of the United States and its Western European allies. Living standards inside the Soviet Union were low and were even worse in its Eastern European satellite states.

In 1953, the Soviets sent twenty thousand troops into East Berlin to stop a strike that had turned into a general uprising. To regain control of Berlin, they had to kill over five hundred people. In 1956, they had to send even more troops into Hungary and kill two thousand more people to quell another revolt. Every morning, many people in East Berlin went into West Berlin for work, but each day many of them voted against communism with their feet by not returning home. In fact, from June 1953 on about fifteen thousand people fled Soviet-dominated East Germany every month by going to West Berlin. Khrushchev knew he had to improve the living conditions inside the Soviet empire and do something to stop the flow of people leaving it, or it would disintegrate.[212]

He also knew that the military power of the United States made the Soviet Union look like a dwarf in comparison. Central to the power of both nations, though, was the atomic bomb. As a Cold War leader, Khrushchev had to come to grips with the meaning of nuclear weapons just as Presidents Truman and Eisenhower had.

On August 12, 1953, the Soviet Union exploded its first hydrogen bomb. Khrushchev watched a secret film of the test and came home disturbed and depressed. "When I was appointed First Secretary of the Central Committee and learned all the facts about nuclear power I could not sleep for several days," he

---

212  Aleksandr Fursenko and Timothy Naftali, *Khrushchev's Cold War* (New York: W.W. Norton & Company, 2006), pp. 15-21.

told a reporter. The film he saw showed houses blowing up dozens of miles from the bomb-detonation site. It raised the specter of world annihilation. A witness to the test said it "apparently transcended some kind of psychological barrier. The effect of the first atomic bomb explosion had not inspired such flesh-creeping terror," but this one was so powerful it made it too awful to comprehend. What had man wrought?

While Khrushchev watched President Eisenhower and his Secretary of State John Foster Dulles base their policies on building nuclear weapons and threatening to use them if war came, he developed thinking that mirrored theirs. He thought that if the Soviet Union developed its own nuclear arsenal, then the two sides would actually be forced to be reasonable with one another. "There are only two ways," he said, "either peaceful coexistence or the most destructive war in history. There is no third way." "Let these bombs get on the nerves of those who would like to unleash war," he boasted in a speech.

Nikita Khrushchev wanted to keep military spending in the Soviet Union under control, just as President Eisenhower tried to do in the United States. He decided to scrap Stalin's project of building a navy to try to compete with the West to focus on nuclear missiles. His country couldn't even produce enough food to feed its people. Khrushchev hoped that the money saved by building nuclear weapons instead of conventional weapons could be used to invest in the Soviet economy and raise the living standards of everyone in the entire Soviet empire. He saw Ike play nuclear poker in order to get cease-fire negotiations going to end the Korean War and to defend the islands of Matsu and Quemoy against China. Khrushchev would develop his own game of brinksmanship.[213]

The Soviet Union, however, was not as powerful as the American politicians, reporters, and national security bureaucrats linked to the military-industrial complex claimed it was. NSC-68, written and approved as the guiding national security document for the United States in 1950, argued that if the country did not vastly increase its defense spending, then in just a few years Russia would be on track to produce enough conventional and nuclear weapons that they would be able to completely run over Western Europe and defeat the United States in an atomic attack. During the Eisenhower administration, politicians, such Senator Henry Jackson of Washington, linked to Boeing and other defense contractors, claimed that the Soviet Union had produced so many bombers that a "bomber gap" existed, while the Gaither Report claimed that

---

213 Vladislav Zubok, *A Failed Empire: The Soviet Union in the Cold War from Stalin to Gorbachev* (Chapel Hill: The University of North Carolina Press, 2009), 127.

by 1960 Khrushchev would have the ability to launch a first-strike missile launch that would cripple the ability of the United States to retaliate. Such claims helped complete the transformation of the United States into a permanent war state by the end of the 1950s, but none of them were even close to reality.

Yes, in 1955, the Soviet Union had plenty of nuclear bombs and was more than capable of exploding them in tests, but it had no way to deliver any of them as a weapon against an American city. The American B-52 bomber could fly 7,343 miles when refueled, which was far enough to reach the Soviet Union, but the Russia M-4, called the Bison bomber by NATO, couldn't reach the United States, because its designers couldn't figure out an easy way to refuel it in the air. The M-4 could only fly five thousand miles, which was too short for it to reach either coast of the United States from the closest point of the Soviet Union.

What is more, the Soviet Union had only four of these M-4 bombers. When the Russians put on a major air show, they took the four bombers and had them fly around in wide circles to give the impression that there were dozens of them. Khrushchev was pleased when American newspapers reported on a supposed "bomber gap" thanks to the Bison bomber. They saw what they wanted to see.[214]

---

214 Fursenko and Naftali, 39-41.

Nor were Soviet scientists able to develop an intercontinental ballistic missile until August of 1957. They called it the R-7. It took the Russians five failed launches to finally get the rocket to succeed in a test flight with a dummy warhead. After that launch, they shot a rocket straight up into space and deployed the world's first satellite, Sputnik, into the earth's orbit. It was nothing but a round ball that made a beeping noise that ham operators all over the world could pick up on their sets, but it gave the world the impression that the Soviets were ahead in rocket science.

Sputnik helped provoke the panic about a "missile gap" in the United States. President Eisenhower tried to calm people, saying that there was no reason to fear just because the Soviets "put one small ball in the air," but few believed him, and those who benefited from the public anxiety added fuel to the fire. Lyndon Johnson said, "Soon they will be dropping bombs on us from space like kids dropping rocks onto cars from freeway overpasses." In a Presidium meeting, Khrushchev claimed that now Russia could negotiate with the United States, because "main-street Americans have begun to shake from fear for the first time in their lives."

In reality, the Soviet rocket program was pitiful. The R-7 could barely function as a viable weapon. It weighed three hundred tons and operated on liquid oxygen fuel. That made it so that when the rockets were fueled up they were in danger of exploding. American missiles used solid fuel, which enabled them to be launched on about ten minutes' notice. The Russians, though, couldn't keep their missiles fueled up all of the time. That meant it took them hours to prepare them for launch, making them very vulnerable to attack.

What is more, it cost over half a billion dollars to create one R-7 launch site. By 1960, the Soviets had two launching pads for the rockets and only four rockets that were operational. They targeted New York, Washington, Chicago, and Los Angeles as four "hostage cities" in case the United States launched a first strike. Whether they would have been able to get there or not was up to chance.

In 1959, the Soviet Union deployed in East Germany a dozen short-range primitive R-5M missiles, derived from Nazi World War II V-2 rocket technology and capable of striking targets in Western Europe and London, up to 750 miles away. The United States put similar Jupiter missiles in Italy and Turkey in response. By 1960, the Americans had plenty of missiles that could reach the Soviet Union from the United States, but the Soviets weren't able to go beyond the R-7 and develop a reliable intercontinental missile able to reach the United States until April of 1962.

The whole Soviet missile program became more expensive than Khrushchev expected, causing the share of his country's national income that went to military production to increase from 2.9 percent to 5.9 percent from 1958 to 1961.

Having a few missiles made the Soviet Union into a superpower, but their high costs caused Khrushchev much grief. "Missiles are not cucumbers," he complained, "one cannot eat them and one does not require more than a certain number in order to ward off an attack." Instead of a costly unlimited arms race, he hoped to come to some sort of agreement with the United States. The tougher he could be, he thought, the easier it would be to get what he wanted. "The purpose," he told his Presidium members, "is to give a rebuff, to steer to detente."[215]

What Khrushchev aimed to do was consolidate the Soviet empire's position in Eastern Europe and then demilitarize the Cold War. He knew that Russia could not compete with the United States in an arms race. "If we're forced into doing this," he told his son, "we'll lose our pants." But just as Eisenhower had critics in the American war state so did Khrushchev face critics in his government too. He heard reports of military men complaining of "Nikita's folly" for reducing the

---

[215] Zubok, 130-132; Fursenko and Naftali, 151-152, 194, 209, 244.

armed forces by 1.3 million men in three years in order to put a priority on nuclear weapons. He told the dictator of Egypt not to listen when military advisers ask for more money, because, if "you give them twice as much as they asked for and the very next day they will tell you that it is not enough."

Khrushchev also came under fire from his communist ally Mao Zedong of China, who thought both should maintain a hard line against the West. Mao wanted more action in Southeast Asia. Khrushchev went to China and met with him. "I tried to explain to him," he remembered, "that one or two missiles could turn all the divisions of China to dust. But he wouldn't even listen to my arguments and obviously regarded me as a coward." Mao personally insulted Khrushchev and then pissed him off when he started to shell Matsu and Quemoy. The Chinese leader thought it was funny. He told his underlings that "the islands are two batons that keep Khrushchev and Eisenhower dancing." China sent a note to the Presidium saying that if the United States used nuclear weapons against them, the Soviets should not bother coming to their defense, because there would be so many people left in China that it wouldn't matter. "We may lose more than three hundred million people. So what? War is war. The years will pass and we'll get to work producing more babies than ever before," Mao told Khrushchev.

This type of talk only convinced Khrushchev and the Presidium that the Chinese were an unstable ally. His son said, "He never liked war and was scared of it—after all he served on the front. When they showed war movies on television he turned them off—because even the best war movie is a lie." The Presidium had been planning to send Mao an atomic bomb with instructions on how to build more of them, but they now decided against the idea. China eventually tested its first atomic bomb in 1964 and a hydrogen bomb in 1967. Khrushchev saw Mao's bravado as either irresponsible boasting or some form of "Asiatic cunning." In reality, Mao's wild talk was probably his way of claiming to be the real leader of world communism. Khrushchev didn't like it and continued to focus his energy on coming to some sort of negotiated settlement with the West.

To consolidate the Soviet position in Eastern Europe, Khrushchev needed a deal on Berlin. Berlin lay inside East Germany. The United States and West Germany had free access to roads that went through East Germany and to West Berlin. People were fleeing from East Germany and the Soviet bloc by going to West Berlin and then on to West Germany. Khrushchev wanted the United States and West Germany to agree to give up their control of West Berlin and make Berlin into its own free city state. That would stop the road travel out of Berlin. If they wouldn't agree, then he planned to sign a treaty with East Germany that would enable it to take control of the roads going through it and stop the open access. He had to stop the flow of people out of the Soviet bloc and into the West via Berlin.

If he could get the West to agree to a settlement on Berlin, Khrushchev knew that not only would he be able to shore up the Soviet empire, but he would also silence his critics inside the Presidium and in the military. In fact, if he could personally negotiate with the leaders of the United States and its NATO allies, he would become the indispensable man in the Soviet Union. He decided to try to scare them and then get them to "sit at the negotiating table." He announced to the world that he was giving the West a six-month ultimatum—either they would come to an agreement or he would sign his own treaty with East Germany and shut down the roads himself.[216]

The ultimatum put him in a bit of a bind. He didn't want war. Yet the United States couldn't agree to anything under such a threat in fear that to do so would

---

[216] Fursenko and Naftali, 243; Zubok, 133-137; Michael Beschloss, *The Crisis Years: Kennedy and Khrushchev 1960-1963* (New York: HarperCollins Publishers, 1991), 42-43; Melvyn Leffler, *For the Soul of Mankind: The United States, The Soviet Union And The Cold War* (New York: Hill and Wang, 2007), 158.

make its NATO allies question how serious it was in Europe. So the Americans didn't respond and eventually Khrushchev simply announced that he was extending his deadline to give everyone more time. He then tried a new strategy of writing President Eisenhower directly and telling him that he would like to have some sort of meeting or summit to try to find out what they could agree on.

Eisenhower agreed and invited Khrushchev on a three-week tour of the United States ending with a meeting with him at Camp David. The trip had its odd moments. Khrushchev would be the first Soviet leader to visit the United States and neither did he nor anyone else in the Soviet Union know where or what Camp David was. He worried that it might be a prison camp. "One reason I was suspicious was that I remembered in the early years after the Revolution, when contacts were first being established with the bourgeois world, a Soviet delegation was invited to a meeting held someplace called the Prince's islands. It came out in the newspapers that it was to these islands that stray dogs were sent to die," he said, "I was afraid maybe this Camp David was the same sort of place, where people who were mistrusted could be kept in quarantine." Once he found out that it was simply a presidential retreat in the mountains of Maryland, he got excited.

"It shows how ignorant we were in some respects," he recalled. The US press didn't know much about him either. He brought his family with him and they didn't know the names of his children. Some reporters thought his wife was a relative of Molotov.

The Soviets had only one airplane that could fly across the ocean far enough to reach the United States, the specially designed turboprop TU-114. Engineers found microscopic cracks on its fuselage, but Khrushchev insisted that they use it anyway so that the world could see that the Soviet Union had first-class technology. Just to be safe, the Soviet merchant marine notified cargo ships in the Atlantic to be on alert in case the plane had to make an emergency landing in the ocean. A crack team of engineers went on the flight and listened to the fuselage for signs of trouble.

The twelve-hour flight was a misery for its passengers. Engine noise prevented them from sleeping. The plane stood fifty feet above the ground in order to hold its giant fuel tanks, so when it landed at Andrews Air Force Base, the Americans discovered that they didn't have a ladder tall enough to reach the plane. "Therefore," Khrushchev said, "we had to leave the plane not in the formal dignified way called for by protocol, but practically climbing down using our hands and our legs."

Once safe on the ground, Khrushchev decided to honor Abraham Lincoln by visiting his memorial. Then he went to the grave of Franklin Roosevelt and visited with Eleanor Roosevelt. He made a quick meeting with President Eisenhower and was pleased after Ike told him that he realized that the situation in Berlin was "abnormal." He found that crowds that lined the streets of New York and Washington, DC, just looked at him in silence. "I do not have horns," he told one audience.

He traveled to Los Angeles and got angry when he was denied a visit to Disneyland. "Is there some kind of cholera or launching pad out there?" he wanted to know. The mayor of Los Angeles challenged Khrushchev at a dinner party to build his anticommunist credentials. The Soviet leader stormed back to his hotel and threatened to fly back home. His trip handlers helped calm him down. He got drunk.

Nikita Khrushchev was impressed by the American economy. He had never seen anything like it. To one American, he confessed that the Soviet Union was like "a hungry person who had just awakened and wanted to eat... Therefore the Soviet Union was not trying now to develop the production of any sophisticated consumer goods; it was simply trying to satisfy basic needs." He marveled at how much more efficient American farms were when compared with those in Russia—"we provide each cow with a stall, each one is allotted with a fork and a knife.. What kind of idiocy is this!"

In the last few days of the trip, Khrushchev met with President Eisenhower at Camp David. The two had a polite conversation, but they didn't come to any concrete agreements. They agreed that the situation in Berlin couldn't last forever and that the two were both concerned about the cost of the arms race and hoped that disarmament deals could be made in the future. They agreed to meet again along with Harold Macmillan and Charles de Gaulle, the leaders of England and France, in Paris in a few months to talk more.

Khrushchev came away with the impression that Ike wanted a more peaceful world but was unable or unwilling to do anything about it. On one hand, he thought he was simply old and tired like "someone who had just fallen through a hole in the ice and had been dragged from the river with freezing water still dripping from him." But he also suspected that Eisenhower was not really in control of the government and thought that powerful militarist forces centered around Allen Dulles and Vice President Richard Nixon dominated him. He told the Presidium that the president was "under influence of various groups and ad hoc situations."[217]

---

217  Fursenko and Naftali, 227-239; Zubok, 140.

The Paris summit got scuttled after the Soviet Union shot down a CIA U-2 spy plane and captured the pilot, Gary Powers. The plane had violated Russia's air space by flying across its territory right on the eve of the summit. At first, Eisenhower tried to save the summit by claiming that he did not authorize the U-2 flight, but he quickly realized that this statement caused a problem. "To deny my part in the entire affair would have been a declaration that portions of the government of the United States were operating irresponsibly, in complete disregard of proper presidential control," Eisenhower wrote in his memoirs. The president retracted his statement that the flight was "unauthorized" and said that he had authorized the U-2 operations in general, but had not approved this specific flight.

Khrushchev demanded an apology. Ike denied him. In turn, the Soviet leader refused to meet with him and became convinced that CIA director Allen Dulles had deliberately sent the U-2 into Russia just to destroy the summit. Gary Powers told his KGB interrogators that this couldn't be true. "Whoever organized my flight, in my opinion," he said, "did not want to disrupt the summit. If they had known that this flight would break up the summit, they would not have done it."[218]

---

218 Fursenko and Naftali, 280-289.

Khrushchev was pleased when John Kennedy defeated Richard Nixon and became president. It wasn't so much that he liked Kennedy, but that he hated and feared Richard Nixon more. The KGB tried to analyze the election and informed Khrushchev that "Kennedy's position is quite contradictory." It claimed that Kennedy came from a liberal wing of the Democratic Party willing to accommodate with the Soviet Union in order to reduce Cold War tensions, but it made note of the fact that Kennedy accepted the "missile gap" analysis and would probably escalate the arms race before negotiating. The Russian foreign ministry saw the new president as someone "unlikely to possess the qualities of an outstanding person."

In Khrushchev's view, President Eisenhower was a man of peace who couldn't control militarist forces inside the US government. He hoped Kennedy would be a strong leader able to do so, but he was disturbed to see men like Dean Rusk, a former head of the Rockefeller Foundation, and Robert McNamara, who had been the president of Ford Motor Company, in Kennedy's cabinet. Khrushchev overestimated the influence of Rusk on Kennedy and mistakenly thought the car company was really an arms merchant. He didn't know what to make of Kennedy after the Bay of Pigs invasion of Cuba. He wondered if Kennedy was really behind it or if the botched CIA operation had been a setup by Allen Dulles to harden Cold War tensions like he thought the U-2 incident was.

Whatever the case, he made a public protest against the invasion and then sent a written note to the US ambassador to the Soviet Union, Llewellyn "Tommy" Thompson, telling him that he hoped "the differences which have arisen recently would be resolved and U.S. Soviet relations improved." Khrushchev wanted a summit meeting with President Kennedy in order to try to make a deal on Berlin, and Kennedy wanted one to display presidential leadership after the Bay of Pigs disaster. The two agreed to meet in Vienna, Austria.[219]

What were Kennedy's thoughts about the Soviet Union? Right after he became president, he held a meeting of his top advisers to "chart our future relations with the Soviet Union." At the meeting were Vice President Lyndon Johnson, Secretary of State Dean Rusk, National Security Adviser McGeorge Bundy, Ambassador Tommy Thompson, and the former US ambassadors to the Soviet Union George Kennan and Charles Bohlen.

Kennedy began the meeting by saying, "Now tell me about Russia" and then did a lot of listening. He wanted to make it clear that he was coming to this meeting with no preconceived notions of what to do. Dean Rusk was surprised that he "wanted to look

---

219  Ibid., 338-341; 348-349.

at everything from the beginning, the ground up." Thompson told the president that Khrushchev's "deepest desire is to gain time for the forthcoming triumphs of Soviet economic progress." He thought that amongst the Presidium members Khrushchev "is the most pragmatic lot of them and he is tending to make his country more normal... This is evident in their quarrel with the Chinese, and I think that is our one hope of the future." He thought the Soviet leader's "great long-run worries" were that China and West Germany would get the atomic bomb.

Rusk came away from the meeting thinking that Kennedy "had a mentality free from preconceived prejudices, inherited or otherwise... almost as though he had thrown aside the normal prejudices that beset human mentality." He didn't quite approve of this type of thinking when it came to Russia and hated the idea of Kennedy going to a summit to see the Soviet leader. Charles Bohlen thought that this talk was nothing like the anticommunist Cold War rhetoric he had heard from Kennedy on the campaign trail. "He saw Russia as a great and powerful country and we were a great and powerful country, and it seemed to him there must be some basis upon which the two countries could live without blowing each other up."[220]

---

220   Beschloss, 68-70.

During the two-hour meeting, Vice President Lyndon Johnson sat there hardly saying a word. The vice president often refused to give an opinion at such meetings, saying that he simply didn't have one. "We knew he wasn't being modest," Kennedy's aide Ted Sorensen later said, "LBJ was not a modest man. That was his way of registering an unsubtle complaint that he was not being kept sufficiently informed, even on legislative matters; and JFK resented it." As a result, "Lyndon rarely offered advice and was not frequently consulted by the President before major decisions were made," Sorensen wrote.[221]

Khrushchev and Kennedy communicated directly through personal letters and back-channel emissaries. The Soviet leader began the letter exchange right after Kennedy's election. Georgi Bolshakov, a KGB agent undercover as a Russian reporter in Washington, had made personal contact with Robert Kennedy. Bolshakov was a likable hard-drinking man who had become friends with many American reporters, including personal friends of the Kennedys such as Charles Bartlett and Frank Holeman, and the artist William Walton at whose house Kennedy stayed right before his inauguration. He told them his heroes were Khrushchev and Kennedy. He knew Khrushchev

---

221 Ted Sorensen, *Counselor* (New York: Harper Perennial, 2008), 245.

well because one of his closest friends in Russia was Khrushchev's son in-in-law Aleksei Adzhubei, the editor in chief of *Izvestia*. Robert Kennedy and Bolshakov met about once a month for a year and a half.

Robert Kennedy explained to his brother that Khrushchev "didn't want to go through their ambassador evidently." He didn't completely trust his bureaucracy and the Kennedy brothers did not trust theirs either. According to Robert Kennedy, "I unfortunately—stupidly, never—I didn't write many of the things down. I just delivered the messages verbally to my brother and he'd act on them. And I think sometimes he'd tell the State Department and sometimes perhaps he didn't." Bolshakov and the attorney general worked out some of the details of the summit together.

Ambassador Thompson warned Kennedy that Khrushchev was preparing to make new demands on Berlin. After meeting with the Soviet leader, he left convinced that he would sign a separate peace treaty with East Germany to close off Western access to Berlin. This would end Western occupation rights. Thompson reported to Kennedy that Khrushchev "realized this would bring period of great tension, but he was convinced would not lead to war. I told him.. it was my duty as ambassador to see that he was under no misunderstanding of our position and that if he signed separate treaty and force was used to interfere with our communications it would be met with force."

Thompson worried that both the Soviet Union and the United States did not believe that either one wanted to go to war, but that meant one side could push things too far so as to cause one. In his view, Kennedy had to convince "Khrushchev that we will fulfill our commitment to people of Berlin and on other that it is not our intention to saw off limb on which he has crawled." In the long run, though, he thought that "it would not be to our advantage to revert to all-out cold war or have Soviet Union swing over to Chinese policy. Time is on our side. I consider this more true in view of real possibility eventual split between Soviet Union and Red China."[222]

Khrushchev, though, wasn't interested in waiting for better days, but was preparing to create an immediate crisis over Berlin. "If I go to a cathedral and pray for peace, nobody listens. But if I go with two bombs, they will," he told a confidant. At his last Presidium meeting before his summit with Kennedy, he explained that he had decided that he had to play a hand of nuclear poker. "I attach a lot of significance to the meeting with Kennedy," he told his colleagues, "because we are approaching the moment when we must

---

222 Beschloss, 152-157; Richard Reeves, *President Kennedy: Profile of Power* (New York: Simon & Schuster, 1993), 136-138.

solve the German question. This is the key issue." The flood of people into West Berlin had reached a crisis point and the leaders of East Germany were demanding that he do something about it. Robert Kennedy had told Bolshakov that the president wanted a nuclear test-ban treaty and to work for peace in Southeast Asia, but when it came to Berlin he was only willing "to discuss it and not to seek any kind of agreement at this meeting." "He is a son of a bitch," Khrushchev said.

Khrushchev told the Presidium that West Germany will not start a war, but America might. He said that Kennedy himself was not the problem. He claimed that the Bay of Pigs and disappointing back-channel negotiations were proof that the president was not really in control. In Khrushchev's view, that meant that Kennedy was just like Eisenhower, meaning that he was a prisoner of the CIA and the Pentagon. "That's why we cannot vouch for America," he said, "its decisions are not based on logical principles; rather it is governed by different groups and sudden coincidental events. That's why America could easily start a war, even if it is fully aware—according to military circles—of the fact that the situation could grow worse. That's why certain forces could emerge and find a pretext to go to war against us."

His solution was to make a war ultimatum over Berlin in hopes that it would lead to negotiations.

Without a settlement, East Germany would disintegrate. The only way out was to force the Americans to deal. Khrushchev didn't think war would actually come, and didn't want one, but he claimed that "the risk that we are taking is justified; if we look at it in terms of a percentage, there is more than a 95% probability that there will be no war." He thought that the Western European countries would not go to war over Berlin, because if one came, "the main deployment of nuclear weapons will be in the territory of West Germany, France, and England. They are intelligent people, and they understand this," so they would prevent the United States from starting one. Their leaders suspected that his missiles couldn't yet destroy the United States, but they knew he could devastate Europe and England.[223]

Before President Kennedy met Khrushchev in Vienna, he first stopped in Paris and talked with Charles de Gaulle. The leader of France told him not to give an inch on Berlin. Yes, Khrushchev might talk tough and may threaten war, but it would be a bluff, de Gaulle advised him. He tried it with Eisenhower once before. "Russia does not want a war," he said. If it did, it would have started one already. He also told him not to take communism seriously. Lenin's

---

223   Beschloss, 176; Fursenko and Naftali, 354-357.

communism was different from Stalin's, and Stalin's was different from Khrushchev's, and in the end all that matters is the nation state. Like all ideologies, communism is just a shibboleth used to justify the power of the Soviet state. "Russia is real," but Europe will back you, de Gaulle said. So "stand fast" and "you can listen to your advisers before you make up your mind, but once you've made up your mind don't listen to anyone," he counseled Kennedy.[224]

Khrushchev and Kennedy met for several days in Vienna. They talked around their mutual desire for arms control and a need to work together to control the situation in Laos and Southeast Asia, but on the final day, Khrushchev delivered his American counterpart an ultimatum on Berlin. He told Kennedy that he wanted to come to an agreement with him on Berlin to make it a "free city," but if this were impossible, he would sign a treaty himself with East Germany and block all Western access to West Berlin.

"This is an area where every President of the United States since World War II.. has reaffirmed his faithfulness to his obligations," Kennedy responded, "if we were expelled from that area and if we accepted the loss of our rights no one would have any confidence in U.S. commitments and pledges... Western Europe

---

224 Reeves, 148-149.

is vital to our national security, and we have supported it in two wars. If we were to leave West Berlin, Europe would be abandoned as well. So when we are talking about West Berlin, we are also talking about Western Europe."

Khrushchev said he would give the West six months until December to stay in Berlin. Then its forces would have to go. He would let a token number of troops stay in West Berlin along with Soviet troops under UN supervision, but that's it. Kennedy said that meant "a face-to-face confrontation" would come. The Soviet premier then slammed his hand on the table and said, "I want peace, but if you want war, that is your problem."

Kennedy left the meeting saying, "If that is true, it's going to be a cold winter." Khrushchev later recalled that the president "looked not only anxious, but deeply upset... I would have liked very much for us to part in a different mood. But there was nothing I could do to help him." He liked him as a person, but politics is "a merciless business," he explained. According to Dean Rusk, "Kennedy was very upset... He wasn't prepared for the brutality of Khrushchev's presentation... Khrushchev was trying to act like a bully to this young President of the United States." Jackie Kennedy thought that Khrushchev "could be jolly," but at the summit, he displayed "just naked, brutal, ruthless power." The president told reporter James Reston, "I've got a terrible problem. If he thinks I'm inexperienced and have no guts, until we remove those ideas we won't get anywhere with him. So we have to act."[225]

Khrushchev gave a televised speech to the Russian people wearing the green uniform of a Soviet general to observe the twentieth anniversary of Hitler's invasion of Russia. In the speech, he declared that if anyone tested the Soviet will on Berlin, they would "share the fate of Hitler." He boasted that the Red Army would get anything it needed to defend the country if war came.

A few days later, the Soviet ambassador came to the White House and presented Kennedy with some post-summit gifts. They included a hand-carved model of an American whaler and a dog named Pushinka. With the dog came a note from Khrushchev saying that it was "a direct offspring of the well-known cosmos traveler Strelka." The president asked his wife, "How did this get here?" "I'm afraid I asked Khrushchev for it in Vienna. I was just running out of things to say," she explained.[226]

---

[225] Beschloss, 211-225; Fursenko and Naftali, 360-363; Caroline Kennedy and Michael Beschloss, *Historic Conversations on Life with John F. Kennedy* (New York: Hyperion, 2011), 209-210.

[226] Beschloss, 236-238.

Why did Khrushchev make war threats one day and then suddenly send gifts to the White House the next? The dynamics of the Cold War confrontation between the Soviet Union and the United States were generated by the existence of nuclear weapons. Simply having the weapons made them world superpowers capable of destroying the planet with their killing machines. Neither country ever desired war with the other. Instead, the two nations communicated with each other with threats, bluffs, and a respectful open hand all at once. It was a strange game of atomic diplomacy and as long as the two sides continued to play it, they risked creating a calamity no one wanted. The military-industrial complex profited from Cold War tensions and the war state derived its power from it. The Bay of Pigs disaster taught Kennedy that his job was to control it.

"We may drift to disaster over Berlin—a terrible diplomatic defeat or (out of sheer incompetence) a nuclear war," the prime minister of England wrote in his diary. Kennedy told one reporter that he thought there was now a one-in-five chance of nuclear war. "The only plan the United States had for the use of strategic weapons was a massive, total, comprehensive, obliterating attack upon the Soviet Union," National Security Adviser McGeorge Bundy told his boss, "an attack on the Warsaw Pact countries and Red China with no provision for separating them out.. An attack on everything red." The newspapers blared that a new Berlin crisis was on. Reporter Joseph Alsop wrote that Kennedy had to decide "whether the United States should risk something close to national suicide in order to avoid national surrender."[227]

The Joint Chiefs of Staff sent Secretary of Defense Robert McNamara a memo, asking him to forward it on to the President, which said that if it came to war the United States would "clearly" prevail if it attacked first. If the Soviets struck first then "the degree to which we are successful in prevailing is dependent upon the timeliness of our response." In summary it said, "Our strengths are adequate to deter enemy deliberate and rational resort to general war and, if general war eventuates, to permit the United States to survive as a viable nation despite serious losses, and ultimately to prevail and resume progress toward its national objectives."[228]

The president's Deputy National Security Adviser Walter Rostow wrote a memo saying that this crisis

---

[227] Reeves, 179; Alan Brinkley, *John F. Kennedy* (New York: Henry Holt & Company, 2012), 81.

[228] Walter Poole, *History of the Joint Chiefs of Staff: The Joint Chiefs of Staff and National Policy, Volume 8, 1961-1964* (Washington, DC: Defense Department, Office of the Chairman of the Joint Chiefs of Staff, Office of Joint History, 2011), 144.

could actually be an opportunity to defeat the Soviet empire. "We must begin now to present Khrushchev with the risk that if he heightens the Berlin crisis, we and the West Germans may take action that will cause East Germany to become unstuck," it read. He had the idea that we could "take and hold a piece of territory in East Germany that Khrushchev may not wish to lose (for example, Magdeburg)." If the United States wasn't willing to do that, then he thought that it must at least "be prepared to increase the risk of war on his side of the line as well as facing it on ours." In other words, Kennedy should keep putting pressure on the Soviet Union until it backed down no matter what it took. Perhaps he should send "some tactical nuclear weapons in Berlin."

If these actions led to nuclear war, that was fine for Rostow, because "we had better face it now than two years from now, in Southeast Asia as well as in Central Europe" while "Soviet missile capabilities are incomplete." Kennedy didn't respond to his ideas. Rostow thought he was a wimp, someone for whom nuclear war was his "greatest nightmare." According to the Undersecretary of the Air Force Townsend Hopes, Walter Rostow "proved to be the closest thing we had near the top of the U.S. government to a genuine, all-wool, anti-communist ideologue and true believer."[229]

Rostow was an ideas man, writing proposals nonstop. Kennedy liked him as a person but thought many of his memos were crazy, some of them he thought were so wacky that they were humorous. Most went into his trash basket. Rostow tended to come up with an ideological viewpoint and then marshal evidence to back it up even if it didn't correspond with reality. McGeorge Bundy, Rostow's boss, was more of a facilitator than an originator of ideas. He mainly organized the ideas of others in the national security bureaucracy and presented them to Kennedy.[230]

To figure out what to do, Bundy and Kennedy held a national security meeting and invited Dean Acheson, the former secretary of state during the Truman administration, to attend. He told them that he didn't think Khrushchev was creating the Berlin crisis out of desperation or weakness, but because "he sensed weakness and division in the West and intends to exploit it to the hilt." Before the meeting, he told a group of people that he thought the Bay of Pigs proved that Kennedy was a weak "gifted young amateur" who

---

229 David Milne, *America's Rasputin: Walt Rostow and the Vietnam War* (New York: Hill and Wang, 2008), 92-94, 169.
230 Kennedy, 315-316; Milne, 165.

might be an appeaser like his father was before World War II.

Acheson recommended that the United States embark on a new $800 million arms spending package similar to the one he helped engineer with NSC-68 back in 1950. He wanted a new buildup of nuclear weapons and conventional forces in Europe and for the president to get on TV and declare a state of national emergency. Some in the room disagreed. Tommy Thompson thought declaring a national emergency over this would make the country look "hysterical." However, Vice President Lyndon Johnson and Undersecretary of Defense Paul Nitze thought such a statement would mobilize the nation around the president and enable Kennedy to embark on a new round of massive defense spending increases that they wanted too.[231]

The Joint Chiefs of Staff held a meeting amongst themselves and looked over the situation. They compared the current Berlin Crisis to the Khrushchev's Berlin demand of 1958. They believed that somehow the United States had lost credibility since then. However, the balance of power had not changed much since that time. So they came to the conclusion that Eisenhower's firmness over Taiwan compared with

---

231   Reeves, 190-200; Beschloss, 242-244.

what they saw as Kennedy's weakness at the Bay of Pigs had provoked this current crisis.

They put together a position paper which said that they feared that the "Soviets may now believe they can force the issue on Berlin without undue risk of general war." Therefore, "military preparations should be such as to hold out no hope to the Soviets that they can... wage a localized non-nuclear war with profit, or escape mortal damage themselves." They decided to get their chairman to go to Robert McNamara and read him what they wrote.[232]

Kennedy wasn't sure what to do. He had the CIA brief former President Eisenhower and then gave him a call. Ike told him that declaring an emergency "would be the worst mistake possible" that he could make, because it would show Khrushchev that all he "has to do is needle us here and there to force us into such radical actions." It would turn the United States into a pitiful giant. Kennedy didn't need to do anything except convince Khrushchev that he would use nuclear weapons to defend Berlin. As for increasing defense spending, he thought that was a stupid idea too because the president had to ask himself "how long we can continue to spend ever greater sums of money... Any squeeze on the civilian economy with

---

232  Poole, 146-147.

ever-growing government control could finally lead to a managed economy with everything centralized and controlled by the government."

Kennedy cut Acheson and Lyndon Johnson out of the next few key discussions he had over Berlin and decided to go for a minor increase in defense spending, to call up reserves, and give a public speech announcing that he considered any move against West Berlin as a direct attack "upon us all." Once he had a consensus with his key cabinet advisers for these decisions, he then held a full national security meeting, with Johnson and Acheson in attendance. Acheson left the meeting telling people that "this nation is without leadership."[233]

Khrushchev backed down and erected a wall between West and East Berlin to stop the flow of people out of the Eastern Bloc. He told the East Germans that the wall represented an "iron ring" that would protect them "before concluding a peace treaty." Construction of the wall started on August 13, 1961, when East German police dug up roads along the sixty-seven mile border between East and West Germany and strung barbed wire between East and West Berlin. The East Germans reduced the number of access points between the two sides of the city to one—Checkpoint

---

233  Fursenko and Naftali, 371-372; Beschloss, 286.

Charlie—and then replaced the barbed wire with concrete. The police either arrested or shot on sight people who tried to cross over. According to Kennedy's aide Theodore Sorensen, they all thought the wall was "illegal, immoral and inhumane, but not a cause for war."[234]

In retreat, Khrushchev exploded the biggest thermonuclear bomb in the world—a fifty-megaton monstrosity called the Tsar Bomba. Then he exploded a thirty-megaton bomb. The bombs produced a blast radius of over thirty-five miles in diameter and were too big to put on a missile or even deliver by airplane, but they provided Khrushchev with a display of Soviet power to the world after folding on Berlin. The Tsar Bomba created the largest bomb detonation in human history. The crater it created can still be seen from space today.

The US military demanded that Kennedy resume atomic testing in response. He didn't want to, because scientists had discovered that nuclear tests had caused the radioactive particle strotium-90 to appear in supermarket milk bottles. After weeks of hemming and hawing, though, he complied. The Pentagon and politicians connected to the defense industry still talked as if the missile gap were real and demanded more

---

234   Fursenko and Naftali, 377-384.

defense spending. Kennedy had already approved the construction of one thousand intercontinental ballistic missiles. Joint Chiefs of Staff member General Curtis Lemay, who was the head of the air force, wanted three thousand, while General Thomas powers, who was in charge of the Strategic Air Command under him, wanted ten thousand. One thousand was considered a compromise, but it angered the Joint Chiefs of Staff.[235]

In the summer of 1961, the United States had over 200 Titan and Atlas missiles capable of reaching the Soviet Union and hundreds of solid-fuel Minutemen missiles in development. It also had 3,400 nuclear warheads on submarines and bombers. CIA analysts looking at U-2 photos dismissed the notion of a missile gap, but many remained unconvinced or simply wanted to believe in it anyway. Allen Dulles had given the lobbyists a hand by declaring that the U-2 proof shouldn't be considered "conclusive" because cloud cover over areas of the Soviet Union could be used to hide missiles.

Intelligence analysts were about to know without a doubt what the Russians actually had. After twelve failed launches, the CIA put into space its first spy satellite code-named Corona. It passed over Russia and

---

235 Reeves, 231.

found that their few intercontinental missiles were all at one launch facility, which made them vulnerable to a surprise attack. They also now had 200 bombers with questionable ability to reach the United States and seventy-eight missiles on about a dozen submarines that spent almost all of their time in port. The United States had more than an overwhelming nuclear strike advantage over the Soviet Union. Yes, there was a missile gap, but it was in favor of the United States.[236]

At a national security meeting on July 20, 1961, Joint Chiefs of Staff chairman Lyman Lemnitzer and General Hickey, the chairman of the "Net Evaluation Subcommittee," presented the president with a plan to launch a devastating first-strike nuclear attack against the Russians. By crunching the numbers, they calculated that even though at that moment the Soviet Union barely had the ability to respond to an American missile launch, the best time to carry out an American first strike against them would not come until "late 1963, preceded by a period of heightened tensions."

The Strategic Air Command called this a "counterforce" force strategy, because it required that the United States aims its nuclear missiles at Soviet nuclear weapons instead of cities to make a priority out of

---

236  Fursenko and Naftali, 371; Reeves, 228-229.

annihilating its nuclear weapons capability before it could get it off the ground. According to a Pentagon history of the Joint Chiefs of Staff, General Lemnitzer considered the creation of this plan "to be among the most important achievements of this era" with which "its existence created a new aura of confidence" for the military men who knew of it.

Kennedy asked what would happen if the United States launched a first strike before 1963. The CIA director, who was in attendance, answered that if he struck before the optimal time window "the attack would be much less effective since there would be considerably fewer missiles involved." The United States would have so many missiles that by late 1963 it would be able to lay the Soviet Union completely to waste and the Russians probably would only be able to get a few missiles off or bombs into the United States in response, if even that. Carl Kaysen, who helped with the plan, thought it had a 90 percent chance of wiping out all Soviet missiles before they could retaliate. In the aftermath of a successful first strike, Americans would have been able to simply sit in designated fallout shelters to protect themselves from the radioactive dust blowing across the ocean from Russia. By 1964, though, the Soviets would probably have enough operational missiles to make a successful first strike impossible. That is, unless the United States built the three thousand or ten thousand missiles the air force recommended instead of stopping at the one thousand that were slated to be constructed.

According to notes of the meeting, Kennedy then asked how long people would have to stay in fallout shelters if he gave their plan the go-ahead. One of the authors of the attack report "replied that no specific period of time could be cited due to the variables involved, but generally speaking, a period of two weeks should be expected." Scientists later argued that such an attack on the Soviet Union would have thrown so much soot and smoke into the atmosphere that it would have made the planet unlivable by creating a "nuclear winter" ice age, but these men had not considered that possibility. People would have come out of their shelters to a living hell. "The President directed that no member in attendance at the meeting disclose even the subject of the meeting," records a summary of the discussion given to Vice President Lyndon Johnson.

As the presentation continued, the president tapped his front teeth with the fingernail of his thumb and gripped his chair until his knuckles got white—a sign that he was angry. He had heard enough. Kennedy suddenly got up out of his chair and walked right out of the room in disgust. Dean Rusk followed behind him as he headed to the Oval Office. Kennedy muttered to his secretary of state, "And we call ourselves the human race."

Dean Rusk later said of this meeting that it was an "awesome experience" and that afterward the president realized that "a nuclear war must never be fought." "Under no circumstances would I have participated in an order to launch a first strike, with the possible exception of a massive conventional attack on Western Europe," Rusk wrote. But some at the very top of the war state bureaucracy felt that it was necessary to at least make a bolt out of the blue nuclear launch against Russia an option available to the president.[237]

Daniel Ellsberg, who was working as a consultant in the Pentagon at the time, helped do some of the staff work that was put together to create the nuclear attack plans. After the president's briefing, he was ordered by one of Kennedy's National Security Council staffers to get data from the Joint Chiefs of Staff on the number of estimated dead that would occur in such a strike. When he got the information, it amounted

---

[237] Reeves, 228-231; Kai Bird, *The Color of Truth: McGeorge Bundy and William Bundy: Brothers in Arms* (New York: Touchstone, 1998), 206; James Douglas, *JFK and the Unspeakable: Why He Died and Why It Matters* (New York: Touchstone, 2008), 236-237; James Galbraith, "Did the US Military Plan a First Strike for 1963?" *American Prospect*, Dec 19, 2001, accessed 12/10/2012 http://prospect.org/article/did-us-military-plan-nuclear-first-strike-1963; Poole, 27-28.

to 500 to 600 million people. He remembers to this day staring out of his window with the information in hand thinking, "This piece of paper, what this piece of paper represents, should not exist. It should never in the course of human history have come into existence."

Robert McNamara ordered Ellsberg to his office for a lunch meeting to talk about the attack plans. "I had written papers that had gone to him but had never met him before," Ellsberg wrote, "he impressed me strongly and positively that day with his conviction that under no circumstances must there be a first use of U.S. nuclear weapons," because McNamara said "it would be total war, total annihilation, for the Europeans!" Ellsberg felt strong loyalty to the secretary of defense, because he had "a sense that McNamara and his trusted lieutenants were men with my values and concerns trying to tame powerful and irrational institutional forces—largely, though not all, within the same building—that threatened to steer us toward nuclear disaster."[238]

Kennedy was uncomfortable with the arms race. He authorized a classified study group for the Arms Control and Disarmament Agency to come up with a plan to put a cap on missile production. The group,

---

238 Daniel Ellsberg, *Secrets: A Memoir of the Vietnam War and the Pentagon Papers* (New York: Penguin Books, 2002), 57-60.

called the Foster Panel, named after Kennedy's disarmament adviser William Foster, came up with the idea that having enough missiles to kill half of a country's population would be enough to deter them from starting a nuclear war. They saw no reason to build thousands upon thousands of nuclear weapons to deter the Soviets. Therefore, the panel recommended that President Kennedy propose to the Russians that each side build no more than one thousand total delivery vehicles, may they be bombers, land-based missiles and sea-based missiles put together, which was twice what the panel thought was really necessary.

Of course the air force commander of the Strategic Air Command alone already wanted ten thousand Minutemen land-based missiles and Kennedy had agreed to one thousand. Robert McNamara figured that it would only take four hundred such missiles to kill half of the people in the Soviet Union. Producing more only served to give more money to the military-industrial complex and to give the president a continued first-strike option. Nuclear parity between both sides would make war less likely, because it would serve to deter both from starting a war. Kennedy and McNamara explored the idea of building fewer weapons, but his secretary of defense told him if he tried it he would be "politically murdered" by the Joint Chiefs of Staff and their congressional allies. National

Security Advisor McGeorge Bundy told the president that the ideas of the Foster Panel were simply "too radical" to try to implement.[239]

President Kennedy had increased defense spending by 14 percent. He had McNamara brief congressmen and reporters off the record to reveal the country's predominant nuclear superiority over the Soviet Union, but it still wasn't enough for people. So he decided to reveal to the public the real facts about the balance of power between the Soviet Union and the United States in order to put a stop to the demands from congressmen allied with the military-industrial complex for even more arms spending.

He decided not to deliver a speech himself on the subject, because he thought that it might sound too warlike, so he had Deputy Defense Secretary Roswell Gilpatric deliver one revealing the nation's military strength. Gilpatric said that the United States currently had hundreds of bombers, six invulnerable Polaris submarines able to launch ninety-six missiles, dozens of intercontinental ballistic missiles, and a force so large that "the total number of our nuclear delivery vehicles, tactical as well as strategic is in the tens of thousands." "The destructive power which the United States could bring to bear even after a Soviet surprise

---

239 Bird, 215-216.

attack upon our forces would be as great as, perhaps greater than, the total undamaged force which the enemy can threaten to launch against the United States. In short we have a second strike capability which is at least as extensive as what the Soviets can deliver by striking first. Therefore, we are confident that the Soviets will not provoke a major nuclear conflict," he said. At a separate event, Robert McNamara revealed that "we have nuclear power several times that of the Soviet Union."

These statements humiliated Khrushchev. His entire domestic and foreign policy programs had been based on creating an illusion of nuclear strength. The Gilpatric speech made President Eisenhower furious. When he was president, he avoided boasting of the country's superior nuclear position in fear that doing so would increase Cold War tensions by causing the Soviets to increase their own arms spending or to make some desperate response. His secretary of state wrote him saying, "If what is now being said by the Administration had been said by the Democrats during the last two years as it should have been, then Khrushchev's present attitude might well be quite different from what it is." "Amen," Ike replied.[240]

---

240  Beschloss, 330-332; Reeves, 246-247.

Premier Khrushchev was in big trouble. His Berlin gambit had misfired. A high-ranking Soviet general who had begun to spy for the CIA informed the agency that people at the top of the Russian military were saying that "if Stalin were alive, he would have done everything quietly, but this fool is blurting out his threats and intentions and is forcing our possible enemies to increase their military strength." Soviet intelligence received murky information that suggested that the Americans had considered a first strike after the Vienna summit. Khrushchev's nuclear weapons program proved to be deficient. He had planned to produce enough weapons to deter the United States, use them to limit defense spending so that he could reinvest in the Soviet economy, and to placate his own defense ministers, and he faltered on every front. [241]

Nuclear weapons development in the Soviet Union proved to be too costly and too slow to match the Americans'. Khrushchev had been counting on the development of the R-9 and R-16 intercontinental missiles to become a deterrent against the United States. The R-9 had mechanical failures and the R-16 took hours to fuel and launch, while US missiles could be launched in minutes. The Russians deployed the first of a few dozen R-16s in the first few months of 1962,

---

241 Zubok, 141; Fursenko and Naftali, 424.

but the head of the rocket forces told Khrushchev that if they tried to use them "before we managed to move the R-16 and lift it into place, nothing would be left of us."[242]

Khrushchev couldn't speed up the development of his nuclear weapons program by devoting more money to it, because the Soviet economic programs proved to be an inefficient mess too. In hindsight, looking back from today, we can tell that the rate of Soviet economic growth actually peaked in the late 1950s and entered a downward spiral until it ultimately collapsed in the 1980s. This trend was only interrupted by an increase in oil prices in the 1970s, which helped Russia generate profits from the export of oil. In 1962, meat production ended up being only 40 percent of what the Soviets expected it to be. By the start of 1963, Khrushchev gave speeches preparing people for the reality that their standard of living was not going to go up as fast as he had promised, blaming it on the Cold War.[243]

In the aftermath of the erection of the Berlin Wall and Gilpatric's speech, Khrushchev became desperate and grasped for a way to create a quick settlement to end his Cold War struggle with the West. Even though the Berlin Wall had stabilized East Germany, he still

---

242 Fursenko and Naftali, 429.
243 Ibid, 513-514, 543.

wanted to get a treaty signed with the United States and NATO over Germany in order to get them to recognize the Soviet Union as an equal power. Perhaps if he could get Berlin declared an international city and replace both Soviet and NATO troops with some coalition of United Nations troops in it, they could end the Cold War. Then he hoped to join Kennedy in a test-ban treaty to begin a path to armaments control. His thoughts were scattered. He knew he wanted a deal and decided he had to do something to force one. His own leadership was at stake as a world leader, and probably the long-term viability of the Soviet Union as a world power was too. It simply could not keep up with the United States. He wanted to strike a bargain with the West and was prepared to make a Hail Mary pass to force Kennedy into one.

In a January 1962 speech to the Presidium, Khrushchev explained his theory of dealing with the United States. In this secret meeting, Khrushchev admitted to the men at the apex of Soviet state power that the United States is "not weaker than we are." "That is why he could play the same trump card against us that we were trying to use against him—the position of strength card," he said. The reason he could never get a deal over Berlin was that President Kennedy "himself, is a person of little authority in circles that decide and give direction to the policy of the United States of

America. He is of no authority to both Rockefeller and du Pont." In Khrushchev's view, Kennedy "is a young and capable man, it is necessary to give him his due, but he can neither stand up to the American public, nor can he lead it."

From its weaker strategic position, the Soviet Union, according to Khrushchev, had no choice now but to increase the tensions between it and the United States in order to prevent the Americans from taking advantage of the Soviets and to try to get some agreement with them. "We should increase the pressure," he explained, "we must not doze off, and while growing, we should let the opponent feel this growth. Don't pour the last drop to make the cup overflow; be just like a meniscus, which, according to the laws of surface tension in liquid, is generated in order that the liquid doesn't pour out past the rim. If we don't have a meniscus we let the enemy live peacefully," and then he may take actions against the Soviet bloc. But how could he accomplish this?[244]

"What about putting some of our hedgehogs down the Americans' trousers?" Khrushchev asked one of his generals. The United States had nuclear missiles in Turkey and Italy. The Soviet premier came up with the idea of putting missiles right next to the United States

---

244  Ibid., 413-414.

in Cuba. He ordered his military to come up with a plan to do it. Such a move could solve several problems at once. It would finally give the Russians the capability to strike at the United States with nuclear missiles, would prevent Kennedy from trying to invade Cuba again, and might serve as a bargaining chip that would force the president to finally deal on Berlin.

Khrushchev went to his vacation Dacha. "I paced back and forth brooding over what to do," he recalled. He decided to do it. "The Americans had surrounded our country with military bases and threatened us with nuclear weapons," he explained, "and now they would learn just what it feels like to have enemy missiles pointing at you; we'd be doing nothing more than giving them a little of their own medicine."

He outlined his new plan to the Presidium. "In addition to protecting Cuba," he said, "our missiles would equalize what the West likes to call the balance of power." After his presentation, a debate went on for a long time, with some there thinking it was an awful idea. Anastas Mikoyan, the deputy chairman of the Presidium, had earlier told Khrushchev that yes "we have to defend Cuba, but with this approach we risk provoking an attack on them and losing everything." The idea scared Foreign Minister Gromyko too.

Khrushchev ended the meeting and asked for a recess for a few days so that everyone could think about it.

The Soviet premier used the time to rally support for his proposal, code-named "Anadyr." At the next Presidium meeting, he asked for approval and got a unanimous vote for his operation. He told Aleksandr Alekseyev, the KGB's top agent in Cuba, to tell Castro about the plan. Khrushchev explained to him that the "missiles have one purpose to scare them, to restrain them... to give them back some of their medicine. The correlation of forces is unfavorable to us, and the only way to save Cuba is to put missiles there." They would keep the missiles secret until after the November congressional elections in the United States. Then he would go to the United Nations, reveal their existence to the world, talk to Kennedy, and then go to Cuba and sign a defense pact with Fidel Castro. The island dictator agreed. In one chess move, Khrushchev hoped to forever alter the dynamics of the Cold War and hopefully find a way to some sort of settlement from a new position of strength. "I am going to grab Kennedy by his balls," he boasted to Raul Castro.[245]

President Kennedy had an inkling that some sort of new crisis with the Soviet Union was going

---

245 Fursenko and Naftali, 431, 435-536; Zubok, 144-145.

to come. Khrushchev continued to talk about coming up with some new peace treaty for Germany and making Berlin an international city in letters to Kennedy. He also complained that the United States seemed unwilling to negotiate because of its policy of "position of strength." "The establishment of the military bases around the Soviet Union, the discontinuance of trade with it—all that was aimed at the isolation of the USSR and other socialist countries, at undermining their economy. Such policy has suffered a defeat," Khrushchev wrote, so the two sides need "to spare no effort to normalize relations, and first of all among major powers, and not to preserve the hotbeds of tension."

The Soviet leader warned Kennedy though that "if in the past Dulles threatened the Soviet Union relying on the atomic weapons monopoly, now there is no trace of such monopoly. The USSR and the US are equal. Therefore it would be senseless to threaten one or the other side with war. The USSR is threatening nobody, it does not want war, and all its efforts are aimed at excluding war. It is senseless to threaten war on the Soviet people which is seeking only the normalization of international situation and liquidation of the vestiges of the war. The one who tries to frighten the Soviet people and threaten them will get in response the same that he is threatening with and not in a lesser degree."[246]

American intelligence detected Soviet ships going to Cuba. Moscow announced that it was only sending advisers and technicians to help their ally. On August 29, 1961, U-2 planes took pictures of ground-to-air defensive SA-2 missiles being installed on the island. Ted Sorensen visited with Soviet ambassador Anatoli Dobrynin, who told him that "nothing will be undertaken before the American Congressional elections that could complicate the international situation or aggravate the tension in the relations between our two countries. This includes a German peace settlement and West Berlin... The Chairman does not wish to become involved in your internal political affairs."

A concerned President Kennedy told Robert Kennedy to invite Georgi Bolshakov to the White House for a quick talk. "I believe that the outlook for American-Soviet relations is good. The signing of a treaty on banning nuclear tests will be the next milestone along the road to their improvement," he told the Russian.

---

246   Documents 30 and 32, *Foreign Relations of the United States, 1961-1963, Volume VI, Kennedy-Khrushchev Exchanges*, U.S. Department of State, accessed 12/10/2012 http://history.state.gov/historicaldocuments/frus1961-63v06/comp1

After the meeting, Robert Kennedy went outside with Bolshakov and said, "Goddamn it, Georgie, doesn't Premier Khrushchev realize the President's position? Doesn't the Premier know that the President has enemies as well as friends? Believe me, my brother really means what he says about American-Soviet relations. But every step he takes to meet Premier Khrushchev halfway costs. If the Premier just took the trouble to be, for a moment at least, in the President's shoes he would understand him." Robert Kennedy then startled Bolshakov by telling him that he even feared for his brother's life—"in a gust of blind hate they may go to any length."[247]

As they were speaking, the Soviet Union was sending nuclear missiles to Cuba capable of striking the United States. People in the intelligence community and in the Kennedy administration knew it was possible, but almost everyone thought it couldn't happen. It was simply inconceivable to them that Khrushchev would create such a dangerous situation. The Soviet ambassador made statements saying that the Soviets were only placing defensive weapons in Cuba and Kennedy's people chose to believe him.

That is all but one person—John McCone, the director of the CIA. At a meeting with Robert Kennedy,

---

247  Reeves, 346-347.

McNamara, and Dean Rusk, he told them that "if I were Khrushchev I'd put offensive missiles in Cuba. Then I'd bang my shoe on the desk and say to the United States, how do you like looking down the end of a gun barrel for a change? Now, let's talk about Berlin and any other subject I choose." McCone understood the strategic balance of power between the United States and the Soviet Union and how it placed Khrushchev in a desperate situation. The Kennedy White House issued a statement to the Russians and the world saying that the administration was monitoring the island, that it had seen no evidence of "offensive ground-to-ground missiles" on it, and that "were it to be otherwise, the gravest issues would arise."

The Soviet premier complained to Kennedy about a U-2 plane that accidently flew over Soviet airspace. Days later, a U-2 got shot down over China. As a result, the Kennedy White House canceled further U-2 flights, including those over Cuba. The administration didn't trust the CIA. National Security Adviser McGeorge Bundy confronted James Reber, the CIA man who chaired the Committee on Overhead Reconnaissance, with the question, "Is there anyone involved in the planning of these missions who wants to start a war?"

McCone pleaded to resume the U-2 flights over Cuba. President Kennedy gave him the go-ahead. During the five-week break in the flights, the Soviets installed ninety-nine nuclear warheads in Cuba under their noses. There were now a total of forty-three thousand Soviet troops on the island. On October 14, a U-2 airplane piloted by Major Richard Heyser passed over the island and took 928 photos in six minutes. Twenty-four hours later, CIA analysts looked over the photos and saw the construction of R-12 medium-range missile sites capable of reaching Washington, DC. Once they were ready, the missiles would take three hours to arm and launch. Once armed and elevated, they could be put on a thirty-minute, fueled-up-and-ready-to-launch standby for up to a month. The Soviets were building six missile sites for R-12 missiles and three sites for R-14 missiles that had twice the range of the R-12 missiles.

On the morning of October 16, 1962, Richard Helms, the CIA's deputy director of plans, brought the photos to Robert Kennedy. "Kennedy got up from his desk and stood for a moment staring out the window," Helms remembered, "he turned to face me." "Shit! Damn it all to hell and back," the attorney general said. McGeorge Bundy had already given the president the news. He set a meeting for 11:50 a.m. to talk with his key advisers about what today is known as the Cuban Missile Crisis. They had been targeting the Soviet Union and everything red for years with nuclear annihilation. Now Khrushchev suddenly had them in the crosshairs. What would they do about it?[248]

---

248 Tim Wiener, *Legacy of Ashes: The History of the CIA* (New York: Random House, 2008), 220-228; for technical info on Soviet rockets see http://www.russianspaceweb.com/r12.html accessed 12/10/12.

# CHAPTER VII
## KHRUSHCHEV, KENNEDY, AND THE KILLING MACHINES

President John Kennedy learned from his Bay of Pigs experience that he had to manage things differently during a crisis. The decision making that went into the Bay of Pigs operation was uncoordinated. Most of his advisers gave it their approval with very little thought put into it, and as a group they never had a debate over it. Too many of them had a tendency to simply look after their own bureaucratic interests and not the interests of the country as a whole or even that of the presidency. They green-stamped a CIA operation to be agreeable.

With the Cuban Missile Crisis, Kennedy immediately decided to set up a special group of advisers to meet regularly to decide on what to do. Instead of merely representing their own bureaucracies, they were literally locked in a room together so that they were forced to work as a team. He chose the person he trusted beyond anyone else, his brother Robert Kennedy, to chair the meetings. The group was called the Executive Committee of the National Security Council or EXCOMM for short. The meetings were designed to create debates that would lead to consensus decision making everyone who attended would back. The president needed a united administration and a united government to navigate this crisis.

Kennedy realized that he needed to keep the meetings secret until they decided what to do. For one thing, he didn't want Khrushchev to know that he had discovered the missiles. He also knew that it would only be a matter of days before leaks from the military or the intelligence community reached the press or Congress. So time was of the essence. To maintain secrecy, Ted Sorensen wrote, "the President urged us in that first meeting to avoid large numbers of official limousines parked behind the White House, and to adhere—as he would—to our respective routine schedules, including even campaign speeches and social commitments."[249]

At the first meeting, a CIA photography expert told everyone in attendance that it did not appear that the

---

249 Ted Sorensen, *Counselor* (New York: Harper Perennial, 2008), 287.

missiles were in a position to be fired yet, but he predicted that in ten days they would have all of the missile launchers built and ready to be operational. The group then speculated on why Khrushchev had put missiles in Cuba.

Dean Rusk said it was because the Soviet premier "knows that we have a substantial nuclear superiority, but he also knows that we don't really live under fear of his nuclear weapons to the extent that he has to live under fear of ours. Also we have nuclear weapons nearby, in Turkey and places like that." He probably is going to try to "bargain Berlin and Cuba against each other" or "provoke us into a kind of action in Cuba which would give an umbrella for them to take action with respect to Berlin."

National Security Adviser McGeorge Bundy didn't think the missiles meant anything when it came to the balance of power between the United States and the Soviet Union. Yes, it helped the Russians gain the ability to hit the country with nuclear weapons at that moment, but they would have the capability to do that in two more years anyway. No one thought they were putting missiles in Cuba to start a war, so it didn't really matter from a strictly military point of view.

"Well, what is this then if it isn't a military problem?" Robert McNamara asked. The secretary of defense provided his own rhetorical answer—"this is a domestic political problem." What did he mean by that? The president isn't simply an elected representative of the republic known as the United States of America, but since World War II he has also dually served as the chief executive officer of a war state, with tentacles inside the national security bureaucracy and allies in Congress. Today the purpose of the war state is to protect the country from terrorists, but during the Cold War it was to contain and oppose communism. That made it Kennedy's job too. McNamara pointed out that as president he had promised in statements that if Cuba possessed nuclear weapons, he would act. So now he had to. A week later, President Kennedy privately told his brother that if they did nothing on Cuba "they would have moved to impeach."

On this first day of the crisis, everyone agreed that the missiles had to be destroyed and probably with air strikes. Maxwell Taylor, the chairman of the Joint Chiefs of Staff, said that they wouldn't be able to simply attack only the missiles, because they would also need to target all of the antiaircraft batteries on Cuba to protect the American planes carrying out the bombing missions. To do the attack right, they would have to do a complete bombing of Cuba. It would take a few days to prepare such an air strike, and at the same time he recommended giving the command to mobilize the army to invade the island—something that could be ordered seven days after the air strikes begin. Robert McNamara predicted that there would be two to three thousand casualties from the air attack, including Russian soldiers on the island. Khrushchev might invade West Berlin in response.

President Kennedy asked Taylor how effective the air strikes would be. Taylor said, "It'll never be a hundred percent, Mr. President, we know. We hope to take out a vast majority in the first strike. But this is not just one thing, one strike - one day, but continuous air attack for whenever necessary, whenever we discover a target."

Kennedy said that they were going to have to get the missiles out of Cuba and leaned toward ordering air strikes. Dean Rusk said that the question was whether they would launch a surprise attack against Cuba or else make public demands to have them removed first. McNamara thought that made more sense.

Vice President Lyndon Johnson said, "I think the question we face is whether we take it out or whether we talk about it. And, of course, either alternative is a very distressing one. But, of the two, I would take it out—assuming that the commanders felt that way."

As the meeting ended, Kennedy said that they had three options to think about—a limited air strike against the missiles, a general air strike against Cuba, or an invasion of Cuba. Bundy said he would work on a political track for them to consider instead of military action.[250]

In the afternoon, the group reconvened and Robert McNamara presented the option of setting up a naval blockade of Cuba to prevent any new weapons from coming in. "And then an ultimatum," he said, "a statement to the world, particularly to Khrushchev, that we have located these offensive weapons. We're maintaining constant surveillance over them. If there is ever any indication that they're to be launched against this country, we will respond not only against Cuba, but we will respond directly against the Soviet Union with a full nuclear strike." After the ultimatum, they could see if Khrushchev backed down and if he didn't, they would still have the option of attacking Cuba. The drawback to this plan, though, was that by the time it took to see how the Soviets reacted to a blockade, they could have the missiles in Cuba fully operational.

The next morning, Wednesday, October 17, 1962, the Joint Chiefs themselves met and informed the EXCOMM group that they were against a blockade and opposed to any air strikes that were limited only to the missiles. If they instituted a blockade, they saw it as a complement to air strikes and probably invasion.

---

250  Ernest May and Philip Zelikow (eds.), *The Kennedy Tapes: Inside the White House During the Cuban Missile Crisis* (New York: W. W. Norton & Company, 2002), 32-52, 100.

Kennedy invited Dean Acheson to attend the Wednesday EXCOMM meeting. The former secretary of state said that the president should immediately order a bombing raid on Cuba. When Kennedy asked what Acheson thought Khrushchev would do in response, he said that the Soviet Union would probably bomb NATO missiles in Turkey. Then the United States would have to bomb missiles inside the Soviet Union. Asked what would happen next, Acheson said, "By then, we hope cooler heads will prevail."

Robert Kennedy said that if they suddenly bombed Cuba, it would be like "Pearl Harbor in reverse." This remark angered Acheson, who said he thought that if they didn't, it would be like Munich. He left the meeting in a huff. The EXCOMM group had become split between the options of air strike and blockade accompanied by an ultimatum.

Kennedy and his advisers realized that they had a problem. If they simply launched a surprise attack against the missiles, they would face complaints from their European allies, who would see the attack as a wild overreaction since they had gotten used to living under the threat of the Soviet missiles that were capable of reaching them. Such an attack would risk dragging them into World War III without any attempt at diplomacy or even with consulting them first. It could fracture the NATO alliance, thereby isolating the United States from the rest of the world.[251]

Despite the risks to NATO, the Joint Chiefs of Staff wanted to attack Cuba, with most of them seeing air strikes as a prelude to a full invasion of the island. By Thursday night, more of the EXCOMM members were now leaning toward implementing the blockade option. Some still wanted air strikes. McGeorge Bundy thought it might be best to do nothing. He argued that in the long run, the missiles wouldn't matter and that anything they might do would invite a Russian move on Berlin that would divide NATO.

On Friday, October 19, 1962, President Kennedy had a tense morning meeting with the Joint Chiefs of Staff, who continued to push for military action. Maxwell Taylor opened the meeting by telling Kennedy that the chiefs understood the international political problems that a surprise attack could cause, but after they talked it over they "were united" on destroying the missiles and the best way to do it was "with the benefit of surprise."

President Kennedy then spoke, saying, "Let me say just a little, first, about what the problem is from my

---

251  Kenneth O'Donnell and David Powers, *"Johnny, We Hardly Knew Ye": Memories of John Fitzgerald Kennedy* (New York: Pocket Books, 1973), 373; Richard Reeves, *President Kennedy: Profile of Power* (New York: Simon & Schuster, 1993), 378-379; May and Zelikow, 73-74.

point of view. First I think we ought to think of why the Russians did this. Well, actually, it was a rather dangerous but rather useful play of theirs. If we do nothing, they have a missile base there with all the pressure that brings to bear on the United States and damage to our prestige. If we attack Cuba, the missiles, or Cuba, in any way then it gives them a clear line to take Berlin... We will have been regarded as—they think we've got this fixation about Cuba anyway—we would be regarded as the trigger-happy Americans who lost Berlin. We would have no support among our allies."

Kennedy thought that if he ordered them to attack Cuba, "there's bound to be a reprisal from the Soviet Union, there always is—of their just going in and taking Berlin by force at some point. Which leaves me only one alternative, which is to fire nuclear weapons—which is a hell of an alternative—and begin a nuclear exchange, with all this happening."

The risks of a blockade, in Kennedy's view, were that the Soviets would respond by blockading Berlin "and say we started it. And there'll be some question about the attitude of the Europeans." Therefore, "I don't think we've got any satisfactory alternatives," he said, "and that's what has made this thing be a dilemma for three days. Otherwise, our answer would be quite easy."

General Taylor said, "We recognize all these things," but they had to act, because "if we don't respond here in Cuba, we think the credibility of our response in Berlin is endangered." He then turned the meeting over to air force General Curtis LeMay, who acted as a spokesman for those who wanted swift military action. He tried to argue against a blockade, telling Kennedy that "if we do this blockade that's proposed and political action, the first thing that's going to happen is your missiles are going to disappear into the woods." The president responded by asking if that could be the case now.

LeMay said it's possible, but "if they were going to hide any of them, then I would think they would have hid them all." As for Berlin, the general tried to answer Kennedy's worries about it by saying that he didn't think the Soviets would do anything if they attacked Cuba. He argued that exactly the opposite is what they had to worry about—"if we don't do anything to Cuba, then they're going to push on Berlin and push real hard because they've got us on the run. If we take military action against Cuba, then I think that the.."

Kennedy cut him off, asking, "What do you think their reprisal would be?"

"I don't think they are going to make any reprisal if we tell them that the Berlin situation is just like it's always been," LeMay answered, "so I see no other solution. This blockade and political action I see leading into war. I don't see any other solution for it. It will lead right into war. This is almost as bad as the appeasement at Munich."

Admiral George Anderson of the navy then told Kennedy that he agreed "that the course of action recommended to you by the Chiefs from the military point of view is the right one. I think it's the best from the political point of view." He then told the president that he could fully carry out a blockade if so ordered, but he thought it wouldn't stop the Russians from turning Cuba into a missile base.

President Kennedy explained to the Joint Chiefs of Staff that he didn't see how the Russians could accept an attack on Cuba "any more than we can let these go on without doing something. They can't let us just take out, after all their statements, take out their missiles, kill a lot of Russians and not do anything. It's quite obvious that what they... I would think they would do, is try to get Berlin. But that may be a risk we have to take."

General LeMay continued to insist that he thought Khrushchev wouldn't do anything. Perhaps LeMay thought that if they suddenly wiped out Cuba, the Soviets simply wouldn't be able to respond out of fear of facing a devastating first strike from the United

States. Or perhaps he simply had no fear himself of nuclear war against the Russians, thinking he could win one if things came to that. He could tell his arguments were not getting him what he wanted with Kennedy so he gave the president a subtle threat.

"There's one factor that I didn't mention that's not quite in our field, which is the political factor," LeMay warned Kennedy. "I think that a blockade and political talk would be considered by a lot of our friends and neutrals as being a pretty weak response to this. And I'm sure a lot of our own citizens would feel that way, too. In other words, you're in a pretty bad fix at the present time."

"What did you say?" Kennedy said.

"You're in a pretty bad fix," LeMay replied.

Kennedy said, "You're in there with me—personally," with a forced chuckle.

General Taylor then interrupted the conversation and told the president that they were examining all options and were making plans for implementing a blockade and any other contingencies. He warned the president, though, that if they only did a blockade they would have to run surveillance flights over Cuba and "we just don't see how they can do that without taking losses and getting into some form of air warfare over this island." LeMay and Taylor then both agreed that Tuesday morning, October 23, would be the optimal time for them to begin air strikes. After that they could mobilize the army and invade Cuba within eleven days if he gave the word.

"I appreciate your views," Kennedy said, "I'm sure we all understand how rather unsatisfactory our alternatives are. The argument for the blockade was that what we want to do is avoid, if we can nuclear war by escalation or imbalance." The president clearly didn't want any military action against Cuba to spiral into general war nor did he want to simply wipe out the missiles on Cuba and then end up launching a nuclear first strike against the Soviet Union in response to them moving on Berlin. The imbalance of forces was on the side of the United States. That meant that if the missiles on Cuba were removed or destroyed, then the country would have a window of opportunity to launch a nuclear first strike against the Soviet Union through the end of 1963. He didn't want the crisis to lead to a situation where he would be pressured to start a nuclear war. Kennedy was not going to become a prisoner of the war state.

After the president ended the meeting and left the room, the military brass continued to talk amongst themselves while unbeknownst to them a tape recorder continued to run. General David Shoup, the commander of the Marine Corps, a bit taken aback by the way Lemay talked to the President said, "Well what do you guys? You, you pulled the rug right out from under him."

"Jesus Christ. What the hell do you mean?" LeMay asked.

"I just agree with that answer, general," Shoup corrected himself, "I just agree with you. I just agree with you a hundred percent. I just agree with you a hundred percent. That's the only goddamn... He finally got around to the word escalation. I heard him say escalation. That's the only goddamn thing that's in the whole trick. When he says escalation that's it. It's been here in Laos; it's been in every goddamn one of these crises. When he says escalation that's it."

"That's right," LeMay said.

"You're screwed, screwed, screwed. And if some goddamn thing, some way, he could say, either do this son of a bitch and do it right and quit friggin around. That was my conclusion. Don't frig around and go take a missile out," Shoup said.

General Wheeler, the army chief of staff, broke in to say that "it was very apparent to me, though, from his earlier remarks, that the political action of a blockade is really what he's—"

"—That's right. His speech about Berlin was the real" point of Kennedy's talk with them, Shoup said.

After the meeting, Kennedy told Kenny O'Donnell, "Can you imagine LeMay saying a thing like that?

These brass hats have one great advantage in their favor. If we listen to them, and do what they want us to do, none of us will be alive later to tell them that they were wrong."

National Security Adviser McGeorge Bundy, though, told Kennedy that he had now changed his mind. Instead of doing nothing because of the danger to Berlin, he now thought they should go along with the chiefs and launch a surprise air strike. Kennedy told Sorensen that he was "a bit disgusted" with Bundy's shift in opinion. The president had to leave Washington the next morning to keep appearances on an already scheduled campaign trip to Ohio and Illinois. As he left, he told his brother and Ted Sorensen to "pull the group together" and get a consensus for air strikes. The president cut the trip short and came back Saturday morning.[252]

The EXCOMM debate between air strikes and blockade grew more heated. Robert McNamara emerged as the leading proponent of the blockade option while General Maxwell Taylor continued to argue for a military attack on Cuba. McGeorge Bundy agreed. Taylor said this would be their last chance to

---

252 May and Zelikow, 109-123; O'Donnell and Powers, 368-369; Gordon Goldstein, *Lessons in Disaster: McGeorge Bundy and the Path to War In Vietnam* (New York: Henry Holt & Company, 2008), 74.

end Castro and "did not share Secretary McNamara's fear that if we used nuclear weapons in Cuba, nuclear weapons would be used against us." He claimed that if they did not destroy the missiles "we would have to live with them with all the consequent problems for the defense of the United States." The Soviets also had some bombers sitting lined up in the open on an air strip in Cuba. General Taylor said "that if we do not destroy the missiles and the bombers, we will have to change our entire military way of dealing with external threats." That was too much to contemplate.

Ted Sorenson disagreed. Dean Rusk said that "a sudden air strike had no support in the law or morality, and, therefore, must be ruled out." President Kennedy ended the day coming down in favor of announcing a blockade with a demand to Khrushchev to remove the missiles. They would prepare for air strikes in case he didn't comply.

After Kennedy's decision, General Taylor went to the Pentagon and told the Joint Chiefs of Staff that "this was not one of our better days." He informed them that the president told him, "I know you and your colleagues are unhappy with the decision, but I trust that you will support me in this decision." Taylor told them that he told the president that of course they would. General Wheeler responded by saying, "I never thought I'd live to see the day when I would want to go to war."[253]

According to Kenny O'Donnell, "that afternoon, as he prepared to deliver his ultimatum to Khrushchev, President Kennedy betrayed the only sign of nervousness that we saw him show during the entire thirteen day period of the missile crisis. He telephoned Jackie at Glen Ora, where she was spending the weekend with Caroline and John, and asked her to come back to the White House with the children that evening so that he and his family could be together if there was a sudden emergency. The intelligence officials had pointed out to us that if the Russians learned of President Kennedy's discovery of the missiles and his plan to demand their removal, Khrushchev might try to beat him to the punch by ordering a surprise nuclear attack on Washington." The Soviets were going to eventually realize that they were in a use them or lose them situation in Cuba.

In the evening, President Kennedy took a swim in the White House pool. Dave Powers remembers that he "talked about the crisis situation and about the danger of a nuclear world war." "Dave, if we were only thinking of ourselves it would be easy, but I keep

---

[253] May and Zelikow, 124-137; also see http://whitehousetapes.net/clip/john-kennedy-curtis-lemay-youre-pretty-bad-fix accessed 12/16/12.

thinking about the children whose lives would be wiped out," Kennedy said.[254]

When Kennedy woke up Monday, October 22, 1962, he knew he would end the day giving a televised address to the world that would act as an ultimatum to the Russians. He spent the morning talking with General Walter Sweeney, the air force commander in charge of the operations against Cuba. He confirmed that he could not offer with one hundred percent assurance that he would be able to wipe out all of the missiles. Robert Kennedy said they were going to do the blockade and ultimatum and then "play for the breaks." They were not sure what would happen after the president delivered his speech.

President Kennedy met with David Ormsby-Gore, the British ambassador to the United States, who had been a close friend of his going back to the time when he was a young adult and his father served as the American ambassador to England. Ormsby-Gore was the first foreigner that Kennedy talked to about the crisis and he knew he would relay what was happening to Prime Minister Macmillan. The president explained the crisis to him in detail and the ambassador said he favored the blockade option, using the same logic that Kennedy himself had given the Joint

---

254  O'Donnell and Powers, 375-376.

Chiefs of Staff. Kennedy told him that the nuclear arms race had helped bring on the crisis. "A world in which there are large quantities of nuclear weapons is an impossible world to handle. We really must try to get on with disarmament if we get through this crisis, because this is really too much," he said.

Kennedy then phoned Eisenhower and got his backing and met with twenty senators and members of the House of Representatives in the Cabinet Room before he gave his address on television. CIA director John McCone gave them a full briefing on what the CIA had discovered in Cuba and then the president and secretary of defense explained to them their course of action. Some of the congressmen wanted to invade Cuba.

Senator Richard Russell, who chaired the Senate Armed Services Committee, said that he thought they should attack Cuba, because "we've got to take a chance somewhere, sometime, if we're going to retain our position as a great world power." If they don't respond, then they "might as well pull our arms in from Europe and save fifteen to twenty-five billion dollars a year and just prepare to defend this continent." Kennedy was taken aback when Senator Fulbright, who had opposed the Bay of Pigs invasion, also spoke in favor of attacking Cuba. Russell thought that the big decision is "coming someday, Mr. President. Will it ever be under more auspicious circumstances?"

Robert Kennedy later wrote that as for President Kennedy it was "the most difficult meeting. I did not attend, but I know from seeing him afterward that it was a tremendous strain." The president was upset, but later he talked about it with his brother and "was more philosophical, pointing out that Congressional leaders' reaction to what we should do, although more militant than his, was much the same as our first reaction when we first heard about the missiles the previous Tuesday."[255]

At the moment that the president was meeting with the congressmen, Khrushchev was dictating a military order to the Soviet commander in Cuba authorizing him to use short-range Luna cruise missiles (called Froggers by NATO), capable of delivering two-kiloton atomic bombs to targets thirty-one miles away to defend the island. The Soviets had enough of these missiles in Cuba to destroy a US naval carrier and invasion force. He had found out that President Kennedy was going to get on TV and deliver a speech about Cuba.

---

255 May and Zelikow, 138-140, 163-183; Charles Kenney, *John F. Kennedy: The Presidential Portfolio: History as told through the collection of the John F. Kennedy Library and Museum, Volume 2* (USA: Public Affairs, 2009), 209.

Khrushchev held an emergency Presidium meeting and told everyone that he didn't know if the Americans were about to announce the start of an attack on Cuba or what. He explained to the Presidium members that "we didn't want to unleash a war. All we wanted to do was to threaten them, to restrain them with regard to Cuba." But now, "the tragedy is that they can attack, and we shall respond. This may end in a big war," he said.

Anastas Mikoyan told Khrushchev that they needed to make sure they kept control of the missiles and did not hand them over to Castro. He said that he wasn't sure if they should use nuclear weapons at all to save Cuba. The Soviet defense minister, Rodion Malinovsky, tried to calm everyone by claiming that "the forces the Americans have in the Caribbean are not enough to seize the island." He talked Khrushchev out of sending the authorization order to the forces in Cuba to use tactical nuclear weapons in fear that the Americans might intercept it and then "be given a pretext to use the atomic weapon." He said to wait until they knew exactly what Kennedy said in his speech.

For an hour, the Soviets waited. Then a man from the foreign ministry came in to the Presidium room and handed Khrushchev a translation of Kennedy's speech. The Soviet leader quickly read over it and said, "It seems to me that by its tone this is not a war against Cuba but some kind of ultimatum." Kennedy announced that he was blockading the island to prevent the Soviets from sending any more missiles to it and demanded that all of the missiles they had already sent there be withdrawn. Everyone in the room let out their breath. It was around two in the morning in Moscow. The group decided to break up the meeting, go to sleep, and figure out what to do the next day.[256]

They decided to try to get the world behind them by publicly claiming that there were no missiles in Cuba. Privately, though, they tried to tell Kennedy that they were not trying to start a war. Khrushchev sent a letter to the president saying that "regardless of the weapon's class it has been delivered to defend against aggression." He then ranted against Kennedy's ultimatum, writing, "Consider what you are saying! And you want to persuade me to agree to this! What would it mean to agree to these demands? It would mean guiding oneself in one's relations with other countries not by reason, but by submitting to arbitrariness. You are no longer appealing to reason, but wish to intimidate us." Khrushchev said he would not stop sending ships to Cuba and claimed that "the violation of the freedom to use international waters and international air space is

---

256 Aleksandr Fursenko and Timothy Naftali, *Khrushchev's Cold War* (New York: W.W. Norton & Company, 2006), 468-475.

an act of aggression which pushes mankind toward the abyss of a world nuclear-missile war."[257]

Without Kennedy's authorization, the Strategic Air Command went to Defense Condition 2. All 1,400 of its bombers went on alert along with its ICBM missiles and nuclear submarines. Bombers fully loaded with nuclear bombs flew continuously in the air on standby for attack orders. John McCone reported to EXCOMM that some of the Soviet medium-range missiles in Cuba were now operational. The Joint Chiefs told them that if they are going to launch air strikes on Cuba, they needed to do so within a few days or else too many of the missiles would be in a launch position to be able to stop them. They remained fixated on the date of Tuesday, October 30, for air strikes. A decision would need to be made the day before. Kennedy came to conclude that he had two ways to remove the missiles: "one is to negotiate them out—in other words, trade them out. Or the other is to go in and take them out." It did not seem that the blockade itself would force the Russians to comply.[258]

The Soviets' public diplomacy fell apart when Adlai Stevenson, the American ambassador to the United

---

257 Document 63, *Foreign Relations of the United States, 1961-1963, Volume VI, Kennedy-Khrushchev Exchanges*, U.S. Department of State, accessed 12/10/2012 http://history.state.gov/historicaldocuments/frus1961-63v06/comp1 ; Fursenko and Naftali, 466-467.

258 May and Zelikow, 283, 288.

Nations, displayed to the world on television the photographic U-2 proof of Soviet missiles in Cuba. Khrushchev searched for a way to back down and save face at the same time.

The Joint Chiefs of Staff began to worry that time was working to the Soviet's advantage. In frustration General Lemay told the other chiefs, "we're spending $50 billion, if we can't take care of Cuba we should go home." They sent a position paper to Robert McNamara stating that if the Russians "hide behind the endless arguments of naive neutrals, then we have lost control and may well have lost our objective... The longer we talk, the more diffuse become the inevitable arguments, the weaker becomes whatever may be the final agreement. And when this happens, as it has in the past, we will have lent credence to the impression that we may be a strong country, be we are a country unwilling to use its strength. We have the strategic advantage in our general war capabilities; we have the tactical advantages of moral rightness, of boldness, of strength, of initiative, and of course control of this situation. This is no time to run scared."[259]

---

[259] Walter Poole, *History of the Joint Chiefs of Staff: The Joint Chiefs of Staff and National Policy, Volume 8, 1961-1964* (Washington, DC: Defense Department, Office of the Chairman of the Joint Chiefs of Staff, Office of Joint History, 2011), 179; 184.

On Friday, October 26, Khrushchev sent Kennedy a private letter saying that if he were to pledge not to invade Cuba, then Cuba would no longer need the missiles, so he would remove them. He pleaded with the president, writing, "We and you ought not now to pull on the ends of the rope in which you have tied the knots of war, because the more the two of us pull, the tighter this knot will be tied. And a moment may come when that knot will be tied so tight that even he who tied will not have the strength to untie it, and then it will be necessary to cut that knot."

One piece of bad news the EXCOMM group got earlier that day was that surveillance flights had detected short-range Luna missiles in Cuba probably armed with nuclear weapons. They were positioned in such a way that CIA director John McCone said "you couldn't shoot these up." McCone had a CIA analyst place on an easel new pictures showing these weapons and then pointed them out to President Kennedy. The missiles sat on small trucks that could be moved all over the island and hidden under trees. This is what made it impossible for McCone to guarantee that they could all be destroyed. The missiles weren't accurate. They had a range of up to thirty miles and could miss their target by a mile, which made it so they were good for delivering only one thing—small atomic weapons.

However, since they had such a short range, they could not be used to attack Florida or the continental United States. They could be used, though, to destroy American forces stationed in Guantanamo Bay or to defend against an amphibious invasion fleet. "Invading is going to be a much more serious undertaking than most people realize," McCone told Kennedy.

"Of course, if you had control of the air, could you chew those up?" Kennedy asked.

"Oh you could chew them up. But you know how it is. It's damn hard to knock out these field pieces. That was the experience we had in World War II and then Korea," McCone answered.

McCone thought the new missiles "would lead me to moving quickly on an air strike." The longer they waited, the more defensives they would build up. However, by the end of the day, Khrushchev's letter made them finally start to feel optimistic about the crisis. They received it late in the evening, so they decided to meet in the morning and figure out how to respond to it.[260]

The next day, though, within minutes after convening, Kennedy and his advisers received another

---

[260] Ibid., 290, 297-299; Philip Zelikow and Ernest May (eds.), *The Presidential Recordings John F. Kennedy: The Great Crises, Volume 3* (New York: W.W. Norton & Company, 2001), 323-330; David Coleman, *The Fourteenth Day* (New York: W.W. Norton & Company, 2012), 137-138.

message from Khrushchev—this one delivered publicly to the world. Now he wanted the president to take his nuclear missiles out of Turkey in return for the removal of his missiles in Cuba. Robert McNamara said, "How can we negotiate with somebody who changes his deal before we even get a chance to reply, and announces publicly the deal before we receive it?" They didn't know what to make of it. Were these hardliners talking to them now? Some of the EXCOMM members wondered if Khrushchev was still in control.[261]

Yes, he was. He simply felt more confident a day after he sent his first letter and wanted to salvage something out of the crisis. He read an article by influential newspaper columnist and Kennedy friend Walter Lippmann which suggested a deal for removing the missiles in both Cuba and Turkey would be a logical way out of the crisis. Khrushchev decided to run with it. He told the Presidium, "If we did this we could win." Kennedy hadn't yet responded to his first letter, so he thought maybe he was scared and just maybe the Lippmann idea came from the president himself. [262]

Kennedy and his advisers decided to ignore the Turkey deal and simply focus on the first letter they

---

261   May and Zelikow, *The Kennedy Tapes*, 314.
262   Fursenko and Naftali, 488.

received from Khrushchev. While Ted Sorensen drafted a response to it, they received news that a U-2 plane had been shot down over Cuba. Other lower-level surveillance flights needed by the chiefs to prepare for air strikes had also been shot at. According to the military rules of engagement, the air force had the right to retaliate against any attacks against their planes. Kennedy told them to hold off until they see what happens with the next exchange of letters and cancelled the next round of surveillance flights.

The EXCOMM group then received news that a U-2 plane on a routine air-sampling mission to look for evidence that the Soviets were testing nuclear weapons accidently flew into Soviet air space, causing the Russians to scramble jets to intercept it. Luckily, the plane got out of the area before they could reach it. Kennedy shook his head saying, "There's always one son-of-a bitch who doesn't get the message."[263]

At the same time all of this was happening, the Joint Chiefs of Staff, absent Maxwell Taylor, who was in the EXCOMM meeting, held their own meeting and wrote the president a recommendation to begin attacking Cuba the next day and no later than Monday, October 29, and to prepare to invade the island. They weren't simply talking to and advising the president and his

---

263  Sorensen, 300-301.

advisers, but now they were putting their recommendations for war into writing. Curtis LeMay thought that they now had "the Russian bear by the balls." This was their chance. "Now that we have gotten him in a trap, let's take his legs off right up to his testicles. On second thoughts, let's take off his testicles too," he told the other Chiefs.[264]

There were signs that the crisis was on the verge of spiraling out of control. The Joint Chiefs would demand a decision within forty-eight hours. Fidel Castro had become convinced that the United States was going to attack and sent Khrushchev a letter suggesting that he launch the nuclear missiles. The American U-2 plane that had been shot down over Cuba had been destroyed by a SAM missile commander without any prior authorization.

Even if Kennedy did not give the order to attack Cuba on Monday, he likely would have felt forced to give the Joint Chiefs of Staff permission to begin striking at SAM and antiaircraft sites that shot at surveillance planes. That could spiral into war. If that led to an amphibious assault on the island, the invasion forces could have been destroyed by the Luna missiles,

---

264 Zelikow and May, *The Presidential Recordings*, 399; Michael Dobbs, *One Minute to Midnight: Kennedy, Khrushchev, and Castro on the Brink of Nuclear War* (New York: Vintage Books, 2008), 22.

which would have brought the deaths of tens of thousands of Americans and a probable total nuclear war. The Chiefs wanted to take that gamble. The EXCOMM meetings had been going on for a long time and the pressure was beginning to show.

The advisers themselves spoke more of war. Robert McNamara now grasped for ways to try to prevent an invasion of Cuba from spiraling into total war and no longer talked of a diplomatic resolution. You can hear voices such as his that once sounded confident on the first day of the crisis sound stressed on tape recordings of the meetings. Pressure was building outside the room from the Joint Chiefs of Staff, their friends, and those of like mind to do something.

Days had gone by with no end to the crisis. Vice President Lyndon Johnson told the group, "I think you're going to have a big problem right here, internally, in a few more hours in this country. This ought to start the wires in now from all over the country, the states of the Union, saying where have you been? What are you doing? The President made a fine speech. What else have you done?"

"What, you mean about more action?" Dean Rusk asked.

"They want to know what we're doing. They see that there's some ships coming through the quarantine. There's a great feeling of insecurity. I told you the other day, before these fellows [congressional leaders] came in here. They're reflecting it. They're going to be saying I told you so. Tomorrow or the next day."[265]

Time was running out. According to Ted Sorensen, "toward the end of the crisis, the President shared with me his concern that Dean Rusk had overworked himself to the point of mental and physical exhaustion. If the crisis had lasted thirty-one days instead of thirteen, who knows what could have happened?"[266]

After Saturday's EXCOMM meeting, President Kennedy had a few of his advisers stay behind and he took them into the Oval Office. They included Robert Kennedy, Dean Rusk, Robert McNamara, McGeorge Bundy, Ted Sorensen, George Ball, Roswell Gilpatric, and Tommy Thompson. He told them that Soviet ambassador Dobrynin was waiting for Robert Kennedy for a private meeting. His brother was going to give him a stern oral message to settle the crisis. Dean Rusk said he had an idea. Tell the Soviets time was running out for a deal, the United States will pledge not to invade Cuba if they take the missiles back to Russia and in return the president will quietly remove the missiles from Turkey a few months later. There can be no

---

265  Ibid., 470.

266  Fursenko and Naftali, 487-489; Sorensen, 288.

public acknowledgment of the Turkey part of the deal. Most likely, the Kennedys had Rusk present this idea to the men in the room as if it was his own. Whatever the case, they agreed that it was worth a try.[267]

When Robert Kennedy met with the Soviet ambassador, he told him to tell Khrushchev of the deal. He then warned him that the president and his advisers needed an answer before Monday. The attorney general told him that the Joint Chiefs of Staff were aiming to launch air strikes and begin an invasion within a few days. The Soviets had to deal now or never. He did not think his brother would be able to hold off the military much longer. Time was running out. Dobrynin thought Robert Kennedy was close to crying.

The Soviet ambassador typed up a report of the meeting for Khrushchev, but he didn't have a reliable communications link with Moscow. So he called Western Union and gave it to a teenager who arrived on a bicycle. He watched the kid ride away thinking that if he stopped to see his girlfriend instead of delivering his message, he might not see tomorrow.[268]

When Khrushchev woke up the next morning, he read Dobrynin's message and brought it to the Presidium. They all agreed that the crisis had to end.

---

267  May and Zelikow, *The Kennedy Tapes*, 388-389.
268  Sorensen, 302; Reeves, 420.

On Sunday morning at 9:00 a.m. Washington, DC, time, Radio Moscow made a broadcast saying that in the interests of peace the Soviets were going to dismantle the missiles in Cuba, crate them, and return them to the Soviet Union. Khrushchev backed down.

President Kennedy and his advisers were euphoric, but the Joint Chiefs of Staff sent a memo to the president stating: "The JCS interpret the Khrushchev statement, in conjunction with the buildup, to be efforts to delay direct action by the United States while preparing the ground for diplomatic blackmail." They asked for permission to launch a complete air strike against Cuba the next day unless the United States received "irrefutable evidence" that the missiles were being dismantled and then to invade Cuba seven days later. Joint Chiefs of Staff chairman General Taylor sent a copy of the memo to Robert McNamara with a note on it saying that he disagreed with the other chiefs although he put his signature on it.[269]

President Kennedy had the Joint Chiefs come to the Cabinet Room. "I want to tell you how much I admire you and how much I benefit from your advice," he told them, "and your counsel and your behavior during this very, very difficult period." "We have been

---

[269] May and Zelikow, 404; http://www.gwu.edu/~nsarchiv/NSAEBB/NSAEBB397/docs/doc%2017%20JCS%20recs%20on%20OPLANs.pdf, accessed 3/20/2013.

had," Admiral George Anderson yelled at him. General LeMay pounded the table with his fist and said, "It's the greatest defeat in our history, Mr. President... We should invade today!" Robert McNamara looked at Kennedy and saw that "he was absolutely shocked. He was stuttering in reply."[270]

In the following days, some of the chiefs still grumbled for an invasion. In response, President Kennedy got McNamara to ask them what effect the Luna(FROG) missiles would have on the over 120,000 American soldiers the United States would use to invade Cuba in plans for an operation similar in size to that of the D-Day invasion during World War II. They sent Kennedy a memo saying "that since there are nuclear capable delivery systems in Cuba, we must accept the possibility that the enemy may use nuclear weapons to repel invasion. However, if the Cuban leaders took this foolhardy step, we would respond at once in overwhelming nuclear force against military targets."

"Assuming atomic weapons are not used, our medical plans are drawn to accommodate up to 18,500 casualties in the first ten days of operation," the memo continues, "this figure is based on casualty experience from past operations of this type. However, I must

---

270   Michael Beschloss, *The Crisis Years: Kennedy and Khrushchev 1960-1963* (New York: HarperCollins Publishers, 1991), 544.

caution against its being accepted as an accurate prediction of reality, as the nature of the resistance may range from passive to fanatic and we would expect it to be on the passive side, while remaining prepared for the sterner reaction. If atomic weapons were used, there is no experience factor upon which to base an estimate of casualties. Certainly, we might expect to lose very heavily at the onset if caught by surprise, but our retaliation would be rapid and devastating and thus would bring a sudden close the period of heavy losses."[271]

"One thing this experience shows," President Kennedy later told Arthur Schlesinger Jr., "is the value of sea power and air power; an invasion would have been a mistake—a wrong use of our power. But the military are mad. They wanted to do this. It's lucky for us that we have McNamara there." He also thought that it was "these constant desires to change the balance of power in the world, that is what it seems to me, introduces the dangerous element."[272]

---

271  *Cuban Missile Crisis 50 Years Later,* The National Security Archive, http://www.gwu.edu/~nsarchiv/NSAEBB/NSAEBB397/#_edn13, http://www.gwu.edu/~nsarchiv/NSAEBB/NSAEBB397/docs/doc%2022%2011-2-62%20memo%20to%20JFK%20re%20invasion%20plans.pdf, accessed 3/20/2103.

272  Arthur Schlesinger Jr., *A Thousand Days: John F Kennedy in the White House* (New York: Fawcett Premier, 1965), 760, 812.

The Soviets quickly crated up the ballistic missiles and warheads in Cuba and shipped them to Russia. However, they didn't send back until the end of the year any of the Luna missiles, which they defined as defensive missiles since they could not reach the United States. They had planned to turn them over to Fidel Castro, but his behavior during the crisis convinced Khrushchev that in time he would take all of the nuclear warheads back.

American surveillance planes took pictures of them on a dock, but the Joint Chiefs of Staff had no way to tell if any remained in Cuba or not. The continued presence of the Luna missiles in the first few months after the resolution of the Cuban Missile Crisis and possible continued presence afterward drove the Joint Chiefs of Staff up the wall. From November 1962 to February 1963 they raised the issue several times in meetings with President Kennedy, seeing them as a threat against their base at Guantanamo and claiming that they could be exported to any government in Latin America that happened to turn communist. They asked for low-level flights over Cuba to see if they were still there, but Kennedy turned them down. The president and his advisers, had already made a decision in a meeting in November to just forget about the Lunas, because as McNamara put it, they "clearly aren't offensive weapons in the way in which we meant the term." They didn't want to go to the brink of nuclear war again over them. Everyone realized how close they came, so McGeorge Bundy said, they were "not that important."[273]

Anastas Mikoyan thought that the Cuban Missile Crisis had ended "surprisingly well." According to Oleg Troyanovsky, who served as foreign policy assistant to Khrushchev, the Cuban Missile Crisis "had a tremendous educational value for both sides and both leaders," because it "made them realize, not in theory, but in practical terms, that nuclear annihilation was a real possibility and, consequently, that brinksmanship had to be ruled out." One top Communist Party leader in the Ukraine wrote in his diary, "We stood on the brink of war. In a word, we created a situation of untenable military tension, and then tried to extricate ourselves out of it."[274]

The Cuban Missile Crisis made for a turning point in the Cold War confrontation between the Soviet Union and the United States. Nuclear weapons could not be used to win a war in any rational sense. They

---

273 David Coleman, 144-145, 164-169; Notes Taken From Transcripts of the Joint Chiefs of Staff, October-November, 1962, Dealings With Cuban Missile Crisis; http://www.gwu.edu/~nsarchiv/nsa/cuba_mis_cri/621000%20Notes%20Taken%20from%20Transcripts.pdf, accessed, 5/13/2013.

274 Vladislav Zubok, *A Failed Empire: The Soviet Union in the Cold War from Stalin to Gorbachev* (Chapel Hill: The University of North Carolina Press, 2009), 149-150.

could only be used to threaten and bluff. President Eisenhower had done so to end the Korean War and to prevent China from attacking the islands of Quemoy and Matsu off Taiwan. Khrushchev had issued several ultimatums over Berlin and backed down every time. Kennedy threatened to go to war to defend Berlin. Now the Soviet leader folded once again under the threat of war to end the Cuban Missiles Crisis when events almost spiraled out of control.

After the Cuban Missile Crisis, the Soviet Union could not bluff at a hand of nuclear poker and fold again without destroying its reputation as a world power. Khrushchev's strategy of trying to create tensions to provoke negotiations with the United States had not only failed repeatedly, but now it was too risky to try ever again. He had to stop the bluffs to keep the threat real. If the two sides kept playing the brinksmanship game, they would eventually have to go through with it.

Instead, Khrushchev decided to try to make mutual concessions with President Kennedy for the good of both sides. The president's behavior during the crisis showed that he could stand up to the military and could now perhaps be someone he could make deals with. Khrushchev told the US ambassador in Moscow, "We may not love each other, but we have to live together and may even have to embrace each other, if the world is to survive."

The Soviet leader announced that he would no longer make public threats over Berlin, and in effect both sides from then on accepted the status quo in Berlin and the division of Germany. He told the British ambassador that he hoped to sign a test-ban treaty with Kennedy that could lead to disarmament, get the Chinese a seat at the United Nations, which he thought would only happen in a matter of time anyway, and get NATO and the Soviet Warsaw Pact to bury the hatchet with a nonaggression treaty. He told the Presidium that the Cuban Missiles Crisis gave the Americans a newfound respect of Soviet power, and from then on, instead of using pressure tactics against Kennedy, he would seek out compromises.[275]

As for President Kennedy, his aide Arthur Schlesinger Jr. wrote, "His feelings underwent a qualitative change after Cuba: a world in which nations threatened each other with nuclear weapons now seemed to him not just an irrational but an intolerable and impossible world. Cuba thus made vivid the sense that all humanity had a common interest in the prevention of nuclear war—an interest far above those national and ideological interests which had seemed ultimate."[276]

---

275  Fursenko and Naftali, 488-509.
276  Schlesinger, 815.

The use of the atomic bombs on Japan marked the final bombing mission of World War II and made for the first shot of the Cold War. It created the East-versus-West dynamics of the Cold War. The secretary of war at the time of its invention, Henry Stimson, told president Harry Truman that if the United States and the Soviet Union did not come to some agreement to control nuclear weapons after World War II, then a costly arms race would begin between the countries and lead to a dangerous world confrontation. No such agreement was made and that meant that the Cold War made some situation like the Cuban Missile Crisis practically inevitable.

The weapons could only be used to threaten, and eventually enough threats were made that the world came to the edge of nuclear destruction. The peaceful resolution of the crisis now made for a period of calm that both Kennedy and Khrushchev took advantage of to try to prevent anything like it from happening again. The game of nuclear poker had to stop. That meant taking steps toward controlling the killing machines. The two world leaders moved to detente.

Looking back on the time, Marcus Raskin, who served on the national security staff as an assistant to McGeorge Bundy, said, "After the Cuban Missile Crisis, it became clear to him [Kennedy] that there had to be a way out of the arms race. He really was frightened, truly frightened of it in ways he understood before, but not in an existential way. I would argue that it was at that moment when very serious discussions began going on internally within the administration."[277]

But, of course, there were those who disagreed. Kennedy told Norman Cousins, the editor of the *Saturday Review* magazine, "One of the ironic things about this entire situation is that Mr. Khrushchev and I occupy approximately the same political positions inside our governments. He would like to prevent a nuclear war but is under severe pressure from his hardline crowd, which interprets every move in that direction as appeasement. I've got similar problems. The hardliners in the Soviet Union and the United States feed on one another, each using the actions of the other to justify his own position." The war state derived its power from global tensions and conflict.[278]

Marcus Raskin remembers that on December 4, 1962, Jerome Wiesner, Kennedy's science adviser, sent a memo to the president claiming that the nuclear "defense build-up was an unmitigated disaster for the national security of the United States, that it forced the Soviets to follow the United States in the arms

---

[277] James Douglas, *JFK and the Unspeakable: Why He Died and Why It Matters* (New York: Simon & Schuster, 2008), 325.

[278] Arthur Schlesinger Jr., *Robert Kennedy and His Times* (New York: Ballantine Books, 1978), 643.

race, thereby making the United States less secure." Much of this memo remains classified, but a part of it that we can read today says, "The size and rate of build-up of the recommended force levels could easily be interpreted by the Soviets as an attempt on our part to achieve such a posture. The distinction between a creditable first strike capability and a strong second strike counterforce capability is very difficult for an enemy with inferior forces to judge."[279]

The next day, President Kennedy held a meeting with Secretary of Defense Robert McNamara, General Maxwell Taylor, and a few top civilian advisers to discuss the defense budget for 1963. He had Wiesner attend the meeting and give his opinion that the defense buildup was actually an "unprofitable" waste of money and counterproductive to the nation's security. Kennedy then told them that he was now considering cutting the Pentagon's funding for nuclear weapons and possibly even freezing further production of them. He made clear that he would never give the order for a first strike and if he wasn't going to do that, then, he wondered, what did they need to build so many missiles for?

Kennedy told them, "If the purpose of our strategic buildup is to deter the Russians, number one; number

---

[279] Douglas, 325.

two, to attack them if it looks like they are about to attack us or be able to lessen the impact they would have on us in an attack...if our point really then is to deter them...I mean with the Polaris submarines, with the planes we have, the navy's strategic force, and with the missiles we have, we have an awful lot of megatonnage to put on the Soviets sufficient to deter them from ever using nuclear weapons. Otherwise what good are they? You can't use them as a first weapon yourself, they are only good for deterring... If we fail to deter them and they attack us, then it's just—just destroy them out of—just to fulfill your part of the contract, we just drop it on their cities and destroy them and ruin the Russians. I don't see quite why we're building as many as we're building."

General Taylor responded by telling Kennedy, "I recommend staying with the program essentially as it is. There are too many imponderables for us to back away and go back to a very small force." The Russians were building more missile sites that the military wanted to target, they may build antimissile defenses and harden their targets, he argued.

"They can't harden their cities... I mean we're trying to just think: What is it that will deter them? De Gaulle thinks what he's got is going to be a big deterrent. And even what they had in Cuba alone would have been a substantial deterrent to me," Kennedy said.

Taylor explained that building this force wasn't simply to "destroy the cities, but ideally to destroy their military forces." As long as the Joint Chiefs had the potential to destroy all of the Soviet nuclear weapons and bombers, they could prevent them from retaliating from an American first-strike attack. "But everybody agrees that can't be done," Kennedy said.

"We can now. We can now," General Taylor responded.

"Well, yeah," said President Kennedy, "but, by '63, can you do that?"

[The recording source for this conversation is censored for twenty-seven seconds at this point for "national security" reasons] Kennedy responded to something General Taylor said (probably about using nuclear weapons in a first strike, because in a memo sent to McNamara he wrote that counterforce targeting was feasible only in a pre-emptive strike), by saying, "That's right, that's right. How could anybody accept that as a political goal? What political goal would that be unless you were faced with a most devastating attack?"

"I can't imagine Mister President, but we still approach the problem this way," Taylor said, "by that time frame we ought to have a dual capability: the ability to blunt importantly their ability to destroy us. And with our means today, if we have a surprise attack, we can indeed reduce that very substantially. Now it's still not good with ten million people lost, but nonetheless we don't think we should give up that possibility."

The Pentagon's counterforce first-strike plans estimated that in the worst-case scenario, the Russians would only be able to retaliate against a surprise attack through the end of 1963 with a few bombs left that would kill up to ten to twenty million people in the United States, and most likely they wouldn't be able to get any of their weapons off at all. If Kennedy reduced the number of weapons the United States was producing, he would cut down the time frame left for a viable first-strike option, something that people in the Pentagon wanted to maintain for as long as possible.

Robert McNamara told Kennedy that if they didn't build all of the requested missiles, then he'd come under political attack from the military and its allies in the Congress. "If we don't buy them then two claims will be made which we can't rebut," the secretary of defense said, "one, that we're changing the basic military strategy of this country to exclude procurement of weapons necessary to destroy the nuclear capability of the Soviet Union. This will be the charge that will be made. It will come out in the open because the air force feels very strongly on this already. We've cut them down substantially." General LeMay had wanted three thousand Minuteman missiles while the air force commander of the Strategic Air Command had wanted up to ten thousand of them and Kennedy had promised to build a thousand as a compromise.

"The second charge," McNamara said, "will be made that we will end up, and we are following a program that will lead us to a position, where the Soviets have more megatonnage and more warheads than we do. And I think those two charges, which I don't believe we can rebut, will seriously weaken our position within this country and with our allies."

Robert McNamara warned Kennedy that "there was created a myth in this country that did a great harm to the nation. And it was created by, I would say, emotionally guided but nonetheless patriotic individuals in the Pentagon. There are still people of that kind at the Pentagon. I wouldn't give them any foundation for creating another myth—and they are beginning to say the same sort of things sir—I'm not saying he [General LeMay] encourages this emotional bias, but he is saying that the program I am presenting is endangering the national security and he believes it." He isn't the only one, so we need to keep "our policy maintaining nuclear superiority, now maybe we can change that someday, but we can't change that today," he said.

John Kennedy had campaigned on a Cold War platform that blamed President Eisenhower for creating a mythical "missile gap" to become president. He now wanted to make changes and had become disturbed by the number of nuclear missiles the country was building, but he accepted McNamara's advice and approved the military budget without making any cuts to it.[280]

To General Curtis LeMay's way of thinking, there were dangers in the budget as it already was. "It became apparent to me that McNamara's goal was to try to build a strategic force that was equal to the Russian force. Sort of dragged his feet until the Russians built up to what we were equal. These men believed that if we were equal in strength then there wouldn't be any war. Well this is an indication of how impractical these type of people are," LeMay later said, "even if by some miracle you could design these two forces where they could be equal, will everyone think they are equal? You can't control men's minds. Then, if by some miracle you can design these two forces, how long are they going to stay equal? One is an open society; the other a closed society. When is the closed society going to

---

[280] Poole, 43; David Coleman, "Camelot's Nuclear Conscience," Bulletin of Atomic Scientists, May/June 2006, access 12/16/12 http://faculty.virginia.edu/nuclear/vault/readings/Bulletin%20-%20Camelot%27s%20Nuclear%20Conscience.pdf; John F. Kennedy Meeting Records December 1962, Tape 65, Part 2, 50 minutes into tape, accessed 12/16/12 http://millercenter.org/scripps/archive/presidentialrecordings/kennedy/1962/12_1962

come up with a breakthrough on some weapon system that will give them a tremendous advantage that you don't know anything about?" He thought that they mistakenly thought "1,000 Minutemen missiles would be enough for this."[281]

Even though President Kennedy's thinking about nuclear weapons had evolved and now diverged from that of the Joint Chiefs of Staff, he was boxed in, because the permanent government of the war state sets limits to what a president can and cannot do. Kennedy had just toyed with the idea of cutting the military budget and freezing further construction of the nation's arsenal of nuclear weapons and had basically been told by his secretary of defense that if he tried to do it, he would be ruined. McNamara wasn't trying to pressure him; he was looking out for him. The military-industrial complex is the most powerful lobby in the country.

Thwarted in making major changes to the military budget, President Kennedy moved toward detente with the Soviet Union in the Spring of 1963 in his own way. He came to the realization that a true turning point in the Cold War was at hand, but it could easily come and go. According to McGeorge Bundy, "I think

---

281  Curtis LeMay, Oral History Interview, 3/1/1976, LBJ Library, http://web2.millercenter.org/lbj/oralhistory/lemay_curtis_1971_0628.pdf, accessed 3/20/213.

his sense of perspective on this was cautious but very determined in the sense that the more he measured the situation after Cuba the clearer he was that a kind of corner had been turned and that it was certainly part of his job to keep that corner turned and to move along." In the first few months of 1963, Bundy said, "There was an extraordinary quiet" from the Soviet Union "and the President noticed, as we all did, that life was normal in Berlin for the first time, that there was no pressure for a conference or a peace treaty, that the whole noise level changed." [282]

Then on April 3, Robert Kennedy received a personal message from Khrushchev. "It was full of poison," he told his brother, with old arguments against a test-ban treaty, and about Berlin and Cuba. "It was as if a person had come down from Mars and written this," he said. The Kennedy brothers correctly realized that Khrushchev personally wanted to move to detente too but was under some sort of pressure of his own.

They discussed sending Robert Kennedy to Moscow to meet personally with him, but Dean Rusk and McGeorge Bundy told them it would be a huge political mistake. Instead, they sent Averell Harriman, who

---

[282] McGeorge Bundy, oral history interview, March, 1964, JFK Library, http://archive2.jfklibrary.org/JFKOH/Bundy,%20McGeorge/JFKOH-MGB-01/JFKOH-MGB-01-TR.pdf, accessed 3/20/2013.

had served as the US ambassador to the Soviet Union during World War II, and the journalist Norman Cousins, who had met with Khrushchev before to deliver a personal message on their behalf. "As soon as I heard that Harriman was going I knew you were serious," someone in the Soviet embassy told Arthur Schlesinger.[283]

According to Ted Sorensen, Norman Cousins reported back that "Khrushchev faced a critical choice at the next Soviet Central Committee meeting later in June. Under pressure from the Chinese because of his withdrawal of missiles from Cuba the previous year, he had either to denounce the United States as an imperialist warmonger who had failed to respond to his policy of peaceful coexistence or show some concrete change in response to his statesmanship. The United States, argued Cousins, should therefore speak first, demonstrating our peaceful intentions."

President Kennedy decided to do something only an individual president can do. He bypassed the permanent government bureaucracy and reached out to the Soviet Union himself by giving a major speech on detente without its input. As Sorensen wrote, "In foreign policy, much more than domestic policy—where Congressional legislation and appropriations are

---

[283] Schlesinger, *A Thousand Days*, 824; Fursenko and Naftali, 516-517.

the key—a president's words are policy." McGeorge Bundy told Sorensen that Kennedy wanted him to write a draft for the speech. The national security adviser got a few of his aides and Arthur Schlesinger to join in the work. They were to keep the text secret until the moment Kennedy was to deliver it, because, as Sorensen put it, "the President knew that the unprecedented message of the speech would set off alarm bells in more bellicose quarters in Washington, possibly producing leaks and political attacks in advance of his talk." Not even Secretary of Defense Robert McNamara or Secretary of State Dean Rusk knew the speech was being prepared.[284]

When Arthur Schlesinger looked at Sorensen's draft, he saw that "it was affirmative in tone, elevated in language, wise and subtle in analysis. Its central substantive proposal was a moratorium on atmospheric testing; but its effect was to redefine the whole national attitude toward the Cold War. It was a brilliant and faithful reproduction of the president's views and we read it with mounting admiration and excitement."[285]

The speech was titled "A Strategy of Peace." President Kennedy delivered it as a commencement address at American University on June 10, 1963. He

---

284  Sorensen, p. 312, 326.
285  Schlesinger, *A Thousand Days*, p. 822.

said that he had "chosen this time and place to discuss a topic on which ignorance too often abounds and truth is too rarely perceived—yet it is the most important topic on earth: world peace."

John Kennedy called for a redefinition of the country's role in the world and a turn away from the imperial premises of NSC-68. "What kind of peace do I mean?" he said. "What kind of a peace do we seek? Not a Pax Americana enforced on the world by American weapons of war. Not the peace of the grave or the security of the slave. I am talking about genuine peace, the kind of peace that makes life on earth worth living, the kind that enables men and nations to grow and to hope and to build a better life for their children—not merely peace for Americans but peace for all men and women—not merely peace in our time but peace for all time."

"I speak of peace because of the new face of war. Total war makes no sense in an age when great powers can maintain large and relatively invulnerable nuclear forces and refuse to surrender without resort to those forces. It makes no sense in an age when a single nuclear weapon contains almost ten times the explosive force delivered by all of the allied air forces in the Second World War," he continued.

President John Kennedy knew what he was saying was a huge departure from some of the speeches and statements he had made in the past. He didn't invent the tough anticommunist rhetoric which served as the ideological basis for the permanent war state after World War II, but to become president he used it and as president at times he had to deploy it. But now he wanted to move the country in a new direction that required a new way of thinking.

"Some say that it is useless to speak of world peace or world law or world disarmament—and that it will be useless until the leaders of the Soviet Union adopt a more enlightened attitude. I hope they do. I believe we can help them do it," he said, "but I also believe that we must reexamine our own attitudes—as individuals and as a nation—for our attitude is as essential as theirs. And every graduate of this school, every thoughtful citizen who despairs of war and wishes to bring peace, should begin by looking inward—by examining his own attitude toward the possibilities of peace, toward the Soviet Union, toward the course of the Cold War and toward freedom and peace here at home."

Kennedy asked that "first: let us examine our attitude toward peace itself. Too many of us think it is impossible. Too many think it is unreal. But that is a dangerous, defeatist belief. It leads to the conclusion that war is inevitable—that mankind is doomed—that we are gripped by forces we cannot control." "Our problems are manmade," he explained, "therefore, they can be solved by man. And man can be as big as he wants."

To make this new vision practical, President Kennedy said that Americans must not think of some "absolute, infinite concept of universal peace and good will of which some fantasies and fanatics dream," but "focus instead on a more practical and attainable peace—based not on a sudden revolution of human nature but on a gradual evolution in human institutions—on a series of concrete actions and effective agreements which are in the interest of all concerned."

According to Kennedy, this did not require that Americans had to "love his neighbor," but simply agree to "live together in mutual tolerance." So "second: let us reexamine our attitude toward the Soviet Union," he said, "no government or social system is so evil that its people must be considered lacking in virtue. As Americans, we find communism profoundly repugnant as a negation of personal freedom and dignity. But we can still hail the Russian people for their many achievements—in science and space, in economic and industrial growth, in culture and in acts of courage."

Kennedy explained that the Cold War had created a situation in which both sides "are both caught up in a vicious and dangerous cycle, in which suspicion on one side breeds suspicion on the other, and new weapons beget counter-weapons. In short, both the United States and its allies, and the Soviet Union and its allies, have a mutually deep interest in a just and genuine peace and in halting the arms race. Agreements to this end are in the interests of the Soviet Union as well as ours—and even the most hostile nations can be relied upon to accept and keep those treaty obligations, and only those treaty obligations, which are in their own interest."

To move forward, Kennedy said the nation had to "reexamine our attitude toward the Cold War" and "must deal with the world as it is, and not as it might have been had the history of the last eighteen years been different." To move toward peace and a mutual understanding or detente with the Soviet Union, the president announced that he would not simply declare a sudden total peace with the Russians, but instead take individual steps toward peace by making agreements that are in the best interests of both powers.

Therefore, he said he had made "two important decisions in this regard." Kennedy announced that "high-level discussions will shortly begin in Moscow looking toward early agreement on a comprehensive test ban treaty." Secondly, he said "to make clear our good faith and solemn convictions on the matter I now declare that the United States does not propose to conduct nuclear tests in the atmosphere so long as other states do not do so. We will not be the first to resume."[286]

Kennedy's address had an immediate impact on Khrushchev. The Soviet premier told British Labour leader Harold Wilson that it was "the best speech by any President since Roosevelt." Soviet newspapers reproduced the full text of the speech. Russians cut out parts of it and carried them in their wallets. The British ambassador to Moscow reported that "for the first time" the Presidium believed that Kennedy "was someone who was genuinely working for a detente and with whom they could do business." It represented a way out of the Cold War.[287]

Khrushchev held a Presidium meeting and told its members that the era of brinksmanship and threats was now over. "Let's change the tactic," he said, "we will not get an agreement from the Americans on Berlin" so let's just drop it. They can make some economic deals with West Germany and work on what they can do together with the Americans. On July 2, 1963, Khrushchev announced that he was prepared

---

[286] John. F. Kennedy, "American University Commencement Address," accessed 12/16/12 http://www.americanrhetoric.com/speeches/jfkamericanuniversityaddress.html

[287] Beschloss, 600-601.

to sign a partial test-ban treaty. Kennedy immediately dispatched Averell Harriman to Moscow.[288]

Two weeks later, Harriman arrived in Moscow with a five-man delegation and a British team led by England's minister of science, Lord Hailsham. Before Harriman even got on his airplane, the Soviets and Americans had agreed to set up a telephone "hot line" to send instant messages between the White House and the Kremlin. Technicians in Washington tested it by sending the message "the quick brown fox jumps over the lazy dog" to their counterparts in Moscow.

In his briefcase, Harriman had dozens of potential proposals for cooperation drawn up by the State Department. One of them called for the Soviets to abandon their promise to defend China with nuclear weapons in exchange for "a secret undertaking to support Chiang's efforts to return to the mainland." Another paper proposed a "Soviet or possibly joint U.S.-U.S.S.R. use of military force" against China to prevent it from developing an atomic bomb. They could both order bombers over Chinese nuclear facilities and drop bombs on them together, it argued.

When Harriman met with Khrushchev, the Soviet leader said, "Why don't we have a test ban? Why don't we sign it now and let the experts work out the details?"

---

[288] Fursenko and Naftali, 525-526.

Harriman presented him with a blank piece of paper and said, "Here Mr. Khrushchev, you sign first and I'll sign underneath."

Kennedy had told Harriman that he did not want just daily summaries of the negotiations, but constant updates "so we can appraise it ourselves." Kennedy personally involved himself in the negotiations. As they went on, a member of the American delegation would periodically leave the room, get on the phone with the president, and come back with instructions. This greatly impressed the Russians.

The night the treaty was signed, British Prime Minister Harold Macmillan wrote in his diary that he had "prayed hard for this, night after night." He went and told his wife the news with tears in his eyes. He sent President Kennedy a cable: "I found myself unable to express my real feelings on the telephone tonight... I do understand the high degree of courage and faith which you have shown."

Harriman told Khrushchev that an American amateur track team was in Moscow scheduled to compete. The Soviet leader said he had never seen a track meet before. They both went to Lenin Stadium together and sat in the officials' box. As the American and Soviet teams went on to the field arm in arm, Harriman and Khrushchev stood up and received a standing ovation from the crowd. Averell Harriman looked at Nikita Khrushchev and saw that he was crying.[289]

The test-ban treaty helped to deepen the split between the Soviet Union and China. Ray Cline, the CIA's directorate of intelligence, called Kennedy and told him that the Chinese had issued a statement calling the treaty "a dirty fraud" in which the "people of the Socialist camp, including the people of China, have been sold out by the Soviet Union through the policy pursued by the Soviet government in allying itself with the United States to oppose China." Cline told Kennedy that "we feel this name calling reveals a gulf that is not going to be easily bridged."[290]

President Kennedy did not stop with the test-ban treaty. Through Secretary of Defense Robert McNamara he changed the military's nuclear weapons strategy from a first strike counterforce strategy to one of "assured destruction." In a draft presidential memo McNamara defined "assured destruction" as the ability to absorb a Soviet attack and have enough weapons left to inflict unacceptable losses in retaliation. This led to what became known as "mutually assured destruction" - a nuclear war that would mean

---

289 Beschloss, 602, 619-624.

290 Meeting Tape 102.2, John F. Kennedy Library and Museum, access 12/16/12 http://whitehousetapes.net/clips/1963_0731_sinosoviet/

suicide for anyone who started one. From then on Robert McNamara used this as a benchmark for the size of America's nuclear arsenal.

General Thomas Powers of SAC had wanted 10,000 missiles, because he wanted to maintain the huge numbers advantage in missiles against the Soviets going forward to insure their destruction in a preemptive strike. According to a Pentagon history of the Joint Chiefs of Staff air force leaders were "dismayed" by McNamara's changes, because "having struggled to gain a decisive advantage over the Soviet Union, they saw their efforts coming to naught." As one general put it, McNamara and the President "did not understand what had been created and handed to them. SAC was about at its peak. We had, not supremacy, but complete nuclear superiority over the Soviets."

In 1962 the Joint Chiefs believed that they had the ability to launch what they termed a "coercive" nuclear attack against the Soviets that would destroy all of their missiles and, in the words of a Pentagon historian, "threaten such a great destruction of population (after most of the Soviet arsenal had been expended) that the Soviets would be willing to end hostilities on US terms." The Kennedy White House was now going to erode this ability away. General Curtis Lemay voiced "serious reservations" about this "apparent shift in basic US military strategy." The other service chiefs though did not complain, probably because their budgets were in competition with Lemay's.

Robert McNamara argued that in order to maintain a first-strike counterforce capability they would have to increase defense spending by an additional eighty-four billion dollars. This would provoke the Russians into accelerating their own build up and force the United States to outspend them on a three to one basis in order to maintain the advantage. It would create a mad arms race.[291]

President Kennedy took another controversial move by authorizing the sale of surplus wheat to the Soviet Union. This decision angered Vice President Lyndon Johnson, who warned Kennedy during a National Security Council meeting that "there aren't going to be many people who are going to stand up there and say you are right and at the same time I think this criticism will smear your image" and "there will be a lot of wild statements made about it." Johnson said he should have consulted with him first before he made this move, which he claimed was "potentially dangerous, very dangerous" for the president and seemed to suggest that this trouble was what he got for not

---

291  Steven Rearden, *Council of War: A History of the Joint Chiefs of Staff, 1942-1991* (Washington, DC: U.S. Department of Defense, National Defense University, Joint History Office, Office of the Director, 2012), 250; Poole, 32, 45-47.

keeping him in the loop. A few days later, Kennedy told Arthur Schlesinger that "the Vice President thinks that this is the worst foreign policy mistake we have made in this administration."[292]

Such criticisms did not stop President Kennedy from trying to make more deals with the Soviets. In an address to the United Nations on September 20, 1963, he announced that he would like to make a bold change to the American space program and work with the Soviets on a joint mission to the moon. "Why should the United States and the Soviet Union, in preparing for such expeditions, become involved in immense duplications of research, construction, and expenditure? Surely we should explore whether the scientists and astronauts of our two countries—indeed of all the world—cannot work together in the conquest of space, sending someday in this decade to the moon not the representatives of a single nation, but the representatives of all of our countries," he said.

Why did the president make this proposal? Kennedy said that cooperation in the space program "will require a new approach to the Cold War—a desire not to bury one's adversary, but to compete in a host of peaceful

---

[292] John F. Kennedy Meetings Recordings, October 1963, Tape 114a-49.1, accessed 12/16/12 http://millercenter.org/scripps/archive/presidentialrecordings/kennedy/1963/10_1963 ; Schlesinger, *Robert Kennedy and His Times*, p. 644.

arenas, in ideas, in production, and ultimately in service to all mankind." That was exactly the point. [293]

Accordingly, on November 12, 1963, Kennedy issued NSAM-271, titled "Cooperation with the USSR on Outer Space Matters." It ordered the head of the National Aeronautics and Space Administration to personally carry out implementation of his speech at the United Nations and consult with the State Department and any Soviet counterparts to come up with "specific proposals" for "cooperation between the United States and the USSR in outer space, including cooperation in lunar landing programs"[294]

This order represented a radical step toward ending the arms race. You see, it wasn't simply the number of nuclear warheads that made for the arms race, but the thrust and targeting technology behind the missiles that delivered them. These same rockets were used to launch satellites and space capsules into space. They would be used to send men to the moon. The technology behind

---

293 John F. Kennedy, "Address Before the 18th General Assembly of the United Nations, September 20, 1963," accessed 12/16/12 http://www.jfklibrary.org/Research/Ready-Reference/JFK-Speeches/Address-Before-the-18th-General-Assembly-of-the-United-Nations-September-20-1963.aspx

294 National Security Action Memorandum Number 271, accessed 12/16/12 http://www.jfklibrary.org/Asset-Viewer/qVncp893wEmJFplIn1AlHA.aspx

them was considered a closely guarded secret by military men on both sides of the Cold War.

Khrushchev's rocket scientists told him that it would be best to ignore Kennedy's proposal. They feared that the Americans would steal their technology. The Soviet leader told them he agreed, but then a few weeks later he changed his mind toward accepting it. "He thought that if the Americans wanted to get our technology and create defenses against it, they would do that anyway. Maybe we could get (technology) in the bargain that would be better for us, my father thought," Sergei Khrushchev said later.[295]

To make the test-ban treaty real, the Senate had to pass it. The day after the Soviet Union signed it, Secretary of State Dean Rusk told President Kennedy that he should wait before he sent it to the Senate, because "I think that some of the senators might feel that if you take it to the country straight away, that this consultation process is very much interfered with."

Kennedy told him that he thought he was wrong. "We should hit the country while the country's hot," the president said. "That's the only thing that makes any impression to these god damned senators... They'll move as the country moves. So, I think, we've got to go to the country

---

295  Frank Sietzen, "Soviets Planned to Accept JFK's Joint Lunar Mission Offer," accessed 12/16/12 http://www.spacedaily.com/news/russia-97h.html

while there's maximum interest." He had his press secretary announce that the president was going to give an immediate address to the nation that night.

Kennedy then called former president Harry Truman. "I want to congratulate you," Truman said, "it's a wonderful thing. My goodness life, maybe we can prevent a total war with it."

"I speak to you tonight in a spirit of hope," Kennedy began his televised address, "for the first time in many years, the path of peace may be open. No one can be certain what the future will bring. No one can say whether the time has come for an easing of the struggle. But history and our own conscience will judge us harsher if we do not now make every effort to test our hopes by action, and this is the place to begin... According to the ancient Chinese proverb, 'A journey of a thousand miles must begin with a single step.'"

In his closing remarks, President Kennedy said, "My fellow Americans, let us take that first step. Let us, if we can, step back from the shadows of war and seek out the way of peace. And if that journey is a thousand miles, or even more, let history record that we, in this land, at this time, took the first step."[296]

---

296 Reeves, 550; John F. Kennedy, "Address to the Nation on the Nuclear Test Ban Treaty, July 26, 1963," accessed 12/16/12 http://www.jfklibrary.org/Asset-Viewer/ZNOo49DpRUa-kMetjWmSyg.aspx

On September 23, 1963, the Senate passed the test-ban treaty by a vote of 80-19. On November 22, 1963, President Kennedy was shot to death in Dallas, Texas. He was a man of courage who spent the last few months of his life moving the country and the world in a direction to end the Cold War.

It was late at night when news of the shooting in Dallas reached Moscow. Nikita Khrushchev had just finished his evening reading and was heading up the stairs to his bedroom when he heard the government phone ring. He was almost never disturbed at this late hour, so he probably knew something bad had happened. He got the news. Then he gathered his family and a few close aides around the dining room table. Oleg Troyanovsky remembers that Khrushchev took President Kennedy's murder as a "personal blow" and spent the rest of the night in a state of shock.

The next day, he went to the US embassy in Moscow and signed a book of condolences. Some Americans there noted that he appeared to have been crying before he got there. He dispatched Anastas Mikoyan to Washington, DC, to attend John Kennedy's funeral. When Jackie Kennedy saw him in the funeral line, she noticed that he was trembling all over. She told him, "My husband's dead. Now peace is up to you."[297]

---

297 William Taubman, *Khrushchev: The Man and His Era* (New York: W.W. Norton & Company, 2003), 604; Beschloss, pp. 681-682.

On her last night in the White House, she got out a piece of stationery and wrote a message for Khrushchev. She tried to give Mikoyan "a message for you that day—but as it was such a terrible day for me, I do not know if my words came out as I meant them to," she wrote. She wanted him to know that "the danger which troubled my husband was that war might be started not so much by the big men as by the little ones. While big men know the needs for self-control and restraint—little men are sometimes moved more by fear and pride. If only in the future the big men can continue to make the little ones sit down and talk, before they start to fight."[298]

What would Kennedy have done if he had lived? A few months after his assassination, Jackie Kennedy told an interviewer that he was planning to go to a summit for peace in Moscow, remove J. Edgar Hoover from the FBI, replace Dean Rusk in the State Department, and get control of the government's policy in Vietnam, which he told her was "hopeless." Of course none of these things happened after he died.[299]

---

[298] Document 120, *Foreign Relations of the United States, 1961-1963, Volume VI, Kennedy-Khrushchev Exchanges*, U.S. Department of State, accessed 12/10/2012 http://history.state.gov/historicaldocuments/frus1961-63v06/d120

[299] Caroline Kennedy and Michael Beschloss, *Jacqueline Kennedy: Historic Conversations on Life with John F. Kennedy* (New York: Hyperion, 2011), 309, 343.

President Kennedy inherited a small US commitment in South Vietnam from the Eisenhower administration and sent over 15,000 more advisers there. He had put the country on his backburner and devoted his energy to other things. But then toward the end of his presidency the situation in Vietnam deteriorated. "With the easing of tension in his relationship with Khrushchev, the biggest most pressing problem during most of his time in the White House, Kennedy was able to give more of his attention in the last three months of his life to the discouraging situation in Vietnam," Kenny O'Donnell wrote.[300]

As Kennedy left the White House to leave for Dallas, he told national security aide Michael Forrestal, "When you get back, after the first of the year, I want you to organize an in-depth study of every possible opinion we've got in Vietnam, including how to get out of there. We have to review this whole thing from the bottom to the top."[301]

But the top down review never happened and Lyndon Johnson became president of the United States on November 22, 1963. Just a month later, at a White House Christmas Eve party, he went up to a few members of the Joint Chiefs of Staff and told them,

---

300  O'Donnell and Powers, 442.

301  Reeves, 66.

"Just let me get elected, and then you can have your war." He gave them a war, but not exactly the one they wanted. McGeorge Bundy served as national security adviser to both Presidents Kennedy and Johnson. In his view, "Kennedy didn't want to be dumb" and "Johnson didn't want to be a coward." President Kennedy "decided sometime in 1961 that he was not going to send in combat troops to South Vietnam. He was not going to do it because it was not going to work," he said. But President Johnson sent them. Over fifty-eight thousand Americans and two million Vietnamese would die in the next twelve years in Vietnam. [302]

As for Nikita Khrushchev, on October 12, 1964, his fellow Presidium members called him to a meeting and told him they were removing him from power. "Obviously it will now be as you wish," he told them, "what can I say—I got what I deserved. I'm ready for anything... We face a lot of problems, and at my age, it isn't easy to cope with them all. We've got to promote younger people. Some people today lack courage and integrity.. But that's not the issue now. Someday, history will tell the whole profound truth about what is happening today." He came to the meeting riding in a limo and left driving a Volga sedan.

---

[302] Stanley Karnow, *Vietnam: A History* (New York: Penguin Books, 1991), 342; Goldstein, 3, 67.

Later in the evening, Khrushchev told Mikoyan, "Could anyone have dreamed of telling Stalin that he didn't suit us anymore and suggesting that he retire? Not even a wet spot would have remained where he had been standing. Now everything's different... That's my contribution."[303]

---

303 Fursenko and Naftali, 536-538; Beschloss, 698-700.

# CHAPTER VIII
## CONCLUSION - A TWENTY-FIRST CENTURY EMPIRE OF DEBT

**A**s for the United States, after the Berlin Wall and Soviet Union both collapsed, the nation emerged out of the Cold War as the world's only superpower. But it really began its journey to this position during World War II. Before Charles de Gaulle became prime minister of France, he organized the Free French Forces during the war to oppose the Nazi occupation of his country. In 1944, he traveled to the United States to get assistance. Before the war, France, Germany, Great Britain, Russia, Japan, Italy, and the United States were all great world powers. The war put Russia and the United States on top.

When de Gaulle went for help, he traveled to Washington, DC, and met with President Franklin Roosevelt. He then went to New York City and stayed in the Waldorf Astoria. He looked out of the window of his room and marveled at the size of the city and the cars below. He sat down and began to pen a letter to send home. "This country has not built automobiles for three years and look at all the cars... what a capital they represent.. and what a powerful country," he wrote. He saw that the United States was now the most powerful country in the world and predicted that it would be that way for decades. Its industrial might and agricultural production were matched by no one. "She will be the wealthiest and best-equipped country after the war is over," he concluded, and "is already trying to rule the world."[304]

Before World War II, most of the globe was divided up into colonies controlled by one of seven great powers. Europe was devastated by the war, and England soon reached near bankruptcy and gave up its empire. The world became divided into a bipolar international power structure dominated by the United States and the Soviet Union, both of which emerged after the war as the world's two superpowers. The two nations did not plan to create new empires before the war. What happened is that the destruction of Europe created a huge power gap in the international political

---

304  Fredrick Logevall, *Embers of War: The Fall of an Empire and the Making of America's Vietnam* (New York: Random House, 2012), 60.

system. The United States and the Soviet Union filled that vacuum.

Franklin Roosevelt and Joseph Stalin both saw this situation coming. Both wanted to make sure that after the war ended another war like it would never happen again. That meant making sure that Germany would never get in a position again to start another one. Both leaders wanted to create a postwar order that ensured their respective nation's security. For Roosevelt, this meant trying to create a liberal internationalist world order built upon free trade and a diplomatic order centered at the United Nations, with headquarters in New York City and led by the United States. For Stalin, it meant turning Eastern Europe into a series of buffer states between it and Germany.

Harry Truman became president after Roosevelt died and dropped two atomic bombs on Japan to end the war in the Pacific without informing the Soviets ahead of time. The mere existence of the atomic bomb posed an existential threat against the Soviet Union and practically ensured that it would take some sort of defensive measures to protect itself. With the dropping of the atomic bomb, a Cold War between the Soviets and the United States seemed likely and without any international cooperation to control the new weapons, it became a certainty. Men like Secretary of War Henry Stimson saw it coming.

Once the war ended, both the United States and Soviet Union spent the next several years consolidating their respective positions. Stalin created a Warsaw Pact empire in the nations it occupied in Eastern Europe, while the United States became fearful that the devastation and economic collapse that existed throughout Europe immediately after World War II could serve as a breeding ground for communism. American leaders saw the Great Depression bring fascism to Italy and Germany and could easily imagine how similar economic hardships could cause Western Europe to go red unless they did something about it.

Out of such worries sprang the Truman Doctrine, the Marshall Plan, and covert operations funding anticommunist political parties in Greece and Italy. George Kennan's containment policy laid out the rationale for these policies and explained their purpose—basically to consolidate the position of the United States and its "free world" allies in Western Europe and prevent the Soviet Union from spreading its empire.

The United States came out of the war from a position of great power over the Soviet Union. While the United States had the atomic bomb, it would take the Russians several years to develop one. Stalin tried to blockade Berlin from June 1948 to May 1949 in an attempt to starve out West Berlin and prevent the United States from revitalizing West Germany, but he failed.

This defeat essentially marked the successful containment of the Soviet Union after which the Russians failed to expand their empire in any meaningful way. In fact, they had trouble holding on to what they had and eventually lost everything in 1989.

Although the United States successfully contained the Soviet Union in 1949, the Cold War went on for fifty more years and morphed from a Cold War in Europe designed to contain Soviet expansion into a global Cold War to manage the world. In 1949, the Soviet Union successfully exploded an atomic bomb—an act that changed the face of war forever. The fact that the two nations had atomic bombs made it so that conventional war between great powers was now obsolete. That meant the Cold War became a series of "limited" wars in places such as Korea, Vietnam, and Afghanistan, and an imperial "covert" war for control of various "third world" nations throughout the world.

The Central Intelligence Agency became the mechanism for the United States to hold imperial influence over other nations. The Constitution of the United States did not give the country a legal basis for interfering in the affairs of other countries, so the federal government created the CIA, with hands-off congressional oversight, to engage in this type of behavior. World order and plausible deniability became new watchwords of the day. The leaders of the CIA not only used their powers to defend the global interests of the US government but also to back the private corporate interests that they themselves were associated with, using what were all too often the flimsiest of pretexts. It was indeed "capitalism's invisible empire."

Without any explanation to the American people, the United States made the move from a policy of containment to one of global empire during the Truman administration. This decision was codified in NSC-68, which claimed that no nation on the planet could be neutral in the bipolar, East-versus-West world. Therefore, NSC-68 saw part of the world in the hands of the Soviet Union and communism and the rest of it under the leadership of the United States. This was a policy of empire, because it meant that any nation that tried to maintain an independent line from that of the United States but was not under the control of the Soviet Union became a target for CIA operations, ranging from propaganda activities and the bribery of officials to "covert" wars.

NSC-68 claimed that it was necessary to oppose the Soviet Union and dominate the world "to create conditions under which our free and democratic system can live and prosper." What is noteworthy for us today is that NSC-68 declared that "even if there were no Soviet Union we would face the great problem of free society, accentuated many fold in this industrial age, of reconciling order, security, the need for participation, with the requirement of freedom. We would face the fact that in a shrinking world, the absence of order among nations is becoming less and less tolerable." Today the Soviet Union does not exist, and the watchword of "order" still guides the policies of the United States of America. The word "order," in fact, has been the dominating desire for all empires throughout human history. The spirit of NSC-68 lives on today more than the spirit of 1776. At the beginning of the twenty-first century, the United States simply replaced a battle against communism with a "war on terror" to provide the ideological underpinning for imperial policies.[305]

NSC-68 also gave approval for endless deficit spending and a wild permanent increase in military spending. Before World War II, the United States never had a large permanent standing army or arms industry. Nor did hardly anyone pay any income taxes. In all wars previous to World War II, the nation demobilized. NSC-68 declared that the nation could never return to a peacetime footing ever again and should instead always be ready for instant war. It also called for deficit spending to finance armaments production and to try to grow the economy. As a result, a giant military-industrial complex grew in power and influence in the United

---

[305] Ernest May, *American Cold War Strategy: Interpreting NSC 68* (Boston: Bedford Books, 1993), 26, 52.

States and the nation itself became a war state. Today's economic malaise is one of its legacies.

In order to justify this unprecedented course for the United States, NSC-68 claimed that the country was in mortal danger from a growing Soviet threat. It argued that in just a few years the Soviet Union would be in a position to overrun Western Europe with conventional forces and obliterate the United States in a surprise atomic attack unless Congress and the president approved new massive defense expenditures. None of these projections about the potential Soviet power had anything to do with reality and most of it was simply made up out of thin air.

Thanks to exaggerations in news stories and pure propaganda, Americans lived in the 1950s in a state of terror over nuclear war when the Soviet Union didn't even have the capability to launch a missile that was able to reach the United States until the 1960s. Nor did it have a viable bomber force. In the 1950s, air force General Curtis LeMay said he had the ability to order SAC bombers to attack the Soviet Union and destroy all of its war-making capabilities "without losing a man to their defenses." Americans were completely safe, but they lived in constant fear.

By the time John Kennedy became president, the Joint Chiefs of Staff, in fact, believed they had such a strategic advantage over the Soviets that they had a window of opportunity to launch a devastating first-strike nuclear missile attack that could "win" a nuclear war against Russia until it would close in 1964. A Pentagon study of the arms race concluded that the Russian "strategic situation" even up to "1962 might have been judged little short of desperate." Nikita Khrushchev knew he was in a weak position. When his engineers told him that they could finally build a bomber that could "bomb the United States and then land in Mexico," he asked, "What do you think Mexico is—our mother-in-law? You think we can go calling anytime we want?"[306]

NSC-68 served as a seminal document in the making of US foreign policy. It essentially changed America's role in the world forever by justifying its transformation into a permanent big-government war state and imperial power. Still, it remained secret from the American people until it became declassified in the 1970s. When the Russians saw it, they could barely believe its exaggerations.

Georgi Kornienko, who served in the Soviet Union's foreign ministry as part of a small committee that made intelligence estimates for the KGB and Soviet leaders, remembers that when he got a copy of it and

---

306 Gareth Porter, *Perils of Dominance: Imbalance of Power and the Road to War In Vietnam* (Berkeley: University of California Press, 2005), 6-7.

showed it to the leaders of the Russian armed forces, "they termed it deliberately false and risible." "They could not believe that such an estimate was seriously adhered to by their counterparts from the U.S. Joint Chiefs of Staff to whom there is reference in the document," he wrote.[307]

But such wild estimates served a key purpose for the forces behind NSC-68. Men such as Dean Acheson and Paul Nitze aimed for a giant increase in defense spending and for a new role for the United States to play in the world and made the arguments they needed to make to get what they wanted. Americans had to be scared of the Soviet Union and the rest of the world to accept the transformation of their country into a war state. Acheson and Nitze worked the bureaucracy and succeeded in turning their ideas into official policy with the stamp of Harry Truman's presidential approval.

All of these things represented giant changes in the American experience. Some people at the time tried to understand what was happening. In 1956, the sociologist C. Wright Mills wrote about a "power elite" that was now ascendant over the country. He claimed that this elite was made up of corporate and political leaders, and a military establishment all tied into

---

307  May, 126-127.

the federal government that rendered the influence of voters—what he called "the masses"—essentially meaningless when it comes to the big decisions.

By the end of the 1950s, the transformation of the United States into a war state that began after World War II and was codified in NSC-68 was complete. The United States was formed as a continental democratic republic, but emerged out of the war as a war state with a world empire. As a result power that had once been in the hands of the states and congress flowed into the executive branch of the government. The defense industry generated more profits and the bureaucrats tied to the war state gained more power and influence inside the federal government. Corporate and state power became centralized together in an iron triangle of influence. In 1961, President Dwight Eisenhower gave a farewell address to the nation in which he warned of the power of the "military-industrial complex."

All of this happened behind the scenes during the administrations of Harry Truman and Dwight Eisenhower. Both men were made uncomfortable by the growth of the military-industrial complex and the power elite. Both men tried to contain their influence by blocking increases in defense spending, but both men failed in stopping the growth of the war state. Ironically, while the war state caused the powers of the executive branch of the government to grow exponentially, it diminished the power of the individual person holding the office of president.

By the time John Kennedy became president, a powerful "permanent government" bureaucracy staffed by members of what C. Wright Mills called the power elite and tied to the war state held sway inside the federal government. The disaster of the Bay of Pigs made Kennedy painfully aware of it and caused him to distrust it. The war state bureaucrats tried to repeatedly get President Kennedy to authorize sending combat troops to Vietnam and failed (the full story of Vietnam deserves to be told in a book of its own). It successfully pressured him into increasing defense spending. Yet, when it tried to get him to invade Cuba and potentially start a nuclear war during the Cuban Missile Crisis, he balked. He then went above its head by bypassing normal State Department channels to directly take steps with Nikita Khrushchev to move toward a detente in the Cold War.

Lyndon Johnson eventually gave the war state what it wanted and sent hundreds of thousands of American combat troops to Vietnam. But despite this new operation in the Cold War, which brought yet another giant increase in defense spending in the United States and the death of over fifty-eight thousand American soldiers, relations between the Soviet Union and the

United States did not turn for the worse during the Johnson administration. The time of Kennedy and Khrushchev marked a milestone in the history of the Cold War.

Both the United States and the Soviet Union had used nuclear bluffs against one another. President Eisenhower and Secretary of State John Foster Dulles used a strategy of what they called "nuclear brinksmanship" to try to control defense spending, bring an end to the Korean War, and prevent China from invading Taiwan. President Kennedy threatened to go to war to defend Berlin while Nikita Khrushchev believed that the weak strategic position of the Soviet Union forced him to increase nuclear tensions to try to get the United States to negotiate. He eventually became desperate and sent nuclear missiles into Cuba.

The Cuban Missile Crisis brought the world to the brink of nuclear war. After the crisis, Nikita Khrushchev decided to abandon his policies of threat and bluff and sought to cooperate with the United States, while President Kennedy simultaneously decided to try to move toward a detente with the Soviet Union in order to end the arms race and create a more stable international order. Even though their work was not completed—Kennedy was assassinated, and Khrushchev was removed from power the following year—their period of cooperation proved to be a turning point in the Cold War.

After the Cuban Missile Crisis and Kennedy's June 1963 "A Strategy of Peace" speech at American University, the Soviet Union and the United States never again directly threatened each other with war. Both silently acknowledged each other's sphere of influence. The Soviet Union dropped the Berlin issue. By the 1970s, the two countries reached a parity of around two thousand nuclear missiles a piece, and President Richard Nixon and Premier Leonid Brezhnev engaged in a new round of detente and arms-control agreements. Rhetoric got hot again in the Carter and Reagan years, but there was a big difference between their tough talk and the nuclear brinkmanship seen at the height of the Cold War.

When two powers have nuclear weapons, they make conventional warfare obsolete and make it so that nuclear war can bring world destruction. The only thing nuclear weapons can then be used for is to communicate threats. But once so many threats are made and so many hands of nuclear poker are folded, the game can't go on anymore without risking world destruction. Kennedy and Khrushchev reached that point after the Cuban Missile Crisis. They could no longer play another bluff. This made detente the only logical course of action for them even if it had opposition inside their own governments. The war state and the military-industrial complex simply derive their power and profits from international tensions.

The Soviet Union also had its own military-industrial complex even though its defense industry wasn't in private hands and didn't enrich people like the American military-industrial complex did and still does. At one point, Dmitri Ustinov, who served as the Soviet defense minister, decided that he didn't need any more nuclear missiles. One of the heads of Russian weapons production asked him to order a dozen more rockets anyway. "What will I do with them?" Ustinov asked. "But if you don't order them, how will I feed the workers?" the weapons producer responded. Ustinov put in the order.

According to Russian defense adviser Vitali Tsygichko, in the Soviet Union "everything was militarized." "The whole country worked with weapons. We just had to keep feeding the machine. We couldn't stop it," he said. Both the Soviet Union and the United States became addicted to war production. The military-industrial complexes in both countries became the most powerful interest groups in their respective governments. For a politician to doubt the wisdom of the war state meant to risk seeing the defense lobby send a flood of money to an election opponent and use the press to smear him.[308]

The true power of the war state, though, lay in the permanent government bureaucracies, especially

---

308 Nicholas Thompson, *The Hawk and The Dove: Paul Nitze, George Kennan, and the History of the Cold War* (New York: Henry Holt & Company, 2009), 261.

inside the Central Intelligence Agency and the Joint Chiefs of Staff. Their power, in turn, rested on the widespread public acceptance of the ideology of the war state—that the United States was in mortal danger from the Soviet Union and the spread of communism and therefore dependent upon the war state and the experts who ran it for its survival. When Kennedy gave his June 1963 "A Strategy of Peace" address and asked Americans to question the Cold War, he put this ideology at risk. It was an act no American president had done before or has done ever since.

His message in that speech has a resonance for you and me today. In this speech, President Kennedy said that the American people needed to "reexamine our attitude to the Soviet Union" and to "reexamine our attitude toward the Cold War" in order to control the arms race and reduce the risk of nuclear war. He asked people to understand that they had to "deal with the world as it is, and not as it might have been." This was a call to go beyond seeing the world in black-and-white terms of pure good and evil.

Today, as a country, we face a similar challenge. The United States is on a path to national bankruptcy thanks to the continued growth of the big-government war state. In almost every single year of my lifetime, more and more debt has been piled on top of the government's deficit. Outside social security and interest on the debt, defense spending makes up the largest portion of the federal budget. The United States spends more on the military than the countries with the next thirteen largest defense budgets combined. China is the second-largest defense spender in the world, and we spend more than six times on defense than it does.[309]

When one counts the interest on the debt from past wars and total defense expenditures, the US government spent almost 40 percent of its 2012 budget on the military. This budget includes spending on unnecessary new wonder weapons that don't even have any use in the types of wars of insurgency that the country is currently fighting. They might be useless in real war, but they are needed to generate more profits for defense contractors such as Lockheed Martin and Boeing, so the congressmen they fund demand them.[310]

Today the military-industrial complex is more powerful than ever and the war state has become a bloated fiscal nightmare intent to engage in seemingly endless

---

309 Peter Peterson Foundation, "Should Defense Spending Cuts Be Part Of Any Deficit Reduction Package?," October 23, 2012, accessed 12/17/12 http://pgpf.org/issues-in-brief/defense-spending-cuts-deficit-reduction-10232012.aspx

310 U.S. Government Printing Office, "Analytical Perspectives, Budget of the United States Government, Fiscal Year 2012," accessed 12/ 17/12 http://www.gpo.gov/fdsys/search/pagedetails.action?packageId=BUDGET-2012-PER

and unwinnable wars until the end of time—all on the basis of supposed threats that are even bigger exaggerations than the Soviet threat was ever portrayed to be during the Cold War. The problem is that if defense spending is not brought under control, eventually the size of the federal debt and the budget deficit will grow so large that the value of the US dollar will decline. It has already started.

If this continues, inflation will eventually explode on the American people worse than it did in the 1970s in the aftermath of the Vietnam War. The cost of oil that Americans will pay at the gas pump will go up and their standard of living will decline. A moment will come when Americans will have to decide whether they want to accept the costs of empire or not. This is simple mathematics and the iron law of economics. We are literally draining away our national wealth for the military-industrial complex.

Do you think I am being alarmist? I am not the only one saying this. The Council on Foreign Relations journal *Foreign Affairs*, which acts as a mouthpiece for the American foreign policy establishment, dissected the problem in a lead article in 2009. It noted that projections of the Congressional Budget Office show that "the international economic position of the United States is likely to deteriorate enormously as a result, with the current account deficit rising from a previous record of six percent of GDP to over 15 percent (more than $5 trillion annually) by 2030 and net debt climbing from $3.5 trillion today to $50 trillion (the equivalent of 140 percent of GDP and more than 700 percent of exports) by 2030." Countries that reach such high debt levels end up going through devastating economic crisis as interest rates spike and foreign creditors flee out of fear that the debts have grown so big that they will never get paid.

To stave off this coming crisis, the United States, *Foreign Affairs* argued, has to take measures "including containing the cost of medical care, reforming social security, and enacting new taxes on consumption" to raise government revenue and to force Americans into buying fewer imports in order to narrow the trade deficit. Implicit in the article is the fact that the standard of living for the average American will go down. Reducing defense spending isn't even considered. This is the cost of maintaining the military budget and the empire.

An alternative approach to the world is not even being contemplated in US foreign policy circles. In fact, this same issue of *Foreign Affairs* contains another article advocating the development of new nuclear weapons, because "it is becoming possible for the United States to conduct nuclear strikes that inflict relatively few casualties." This is the mind-set of the American power elite.[311]

As Dwight Eisenhower warned, though, the growth of the war state distorts the private economy of the United States and if it causes living standards to fall too much, it will also result in a loss of freedom. Private enterprise and individual initiative will then be snuffed out by the growth in size of centralized power. In that situation, the masses will get welfare crumbs from the government while a few private corporations connected to the federal government will make profits solely from those connections and not from the normal supply-and-demand dictates of the free market.

But there are alternatives to this future rooted in the principles of the Founding Fathers, who created the Constitution of the United States. To those who know very little history, the growth of the war state seems inevitable, but it was not. Men like senator Robert Taft saw choices. They argued that the United States did not have to go on a wild orgy of defense spending increases to defend itself. He said that all it had to do was maintain a limited nuclear deterrent to protect its position and those of its allies from the Soviet threat. He was right, but he was not only ignored but mocked

---

311 *Foreign Affairs*, November/December 2009.

by those who stood to benefit from the growth of the war state.

His message, though, is also a message for us today. The United States does not have to act as a pitiful giant scared of its own shadow. It does not have to try to control the world and try to engage in nation-building exercises to force people to become more like us. It can accept the world as it is. In reality, it is the only prudent thing to do, because it is impossible anyway for the United States to control a dynamic and changing world. Nation building does not work. A step back from such behaviors would enable it to defend its borders on the cheap and its allies with the might of its military.

President Kennedy asked people to rethink their relationship to the Cold War. Today you and I must rethink our country's relationship with the world and our own relationship with the federal government. We have to decide what kind of country we want to live in and want our children to live in.

Yes, the war state gives us individual psychic benefits. Only a half a percent of the American population today serves in the armed forces overseas. For the rest of us, the war state enables us to think we live in the most powerful country known to man and to live through the troops by cheering the wars and battles we see on TV. But we have to ask: Is this really wise for the world and for us? And is it worth it? Is it worth draining our wealth to watch this and to benefit a few dozen private corporations that make up the military-industrial complex and act as virtual parasites on the rest of the economy? Is it worth paying higher taxes, experiencing more inflation, and seeing freedom inside the United States curtailed to maintain a faltering empire of debt?

The promoters of the war state answer by claiming that it is all necessary for your own safety. But is it? In my view, our choice today is not one of safety or defense, because it really doesn't take much to defend the United States of America. Instead, our choice is between reducing military spending and creating a rational foreign policy or going bankrupt in order to maintain the power of the war state and its imperial policies that don't work and harm the national economy.

But I wrote this book for you not to provide all of the answers for today, but to understand how the country got to where it is in the here and now. Only by knowing history can we together understand the world we live in. The American experience was not always what it is now. There was a time when almost no one paid any income tax and Americans did not live in fear of the rest of the world. They walked tall and other people looked up to the United States as a bastion of freedom and saw it as the future.

Things are much darker at the moment. The world we live in today began after World War II with the creation of a permanent military-industrial complex and the transformation of the United States into a war state by the end of the 1950s. It changed the nation's relationship with the rest of the world and the American people's relationship with their own government. It helped to create a new power elite tied to a permanent government bureaucracy that made the real decisions of importance for the American people and fed them fear propaganda to get them to accept their decisions without question.

This is a history that very few people know anything about. I wrote this book in the hopes that others would come to know it. I hope you have gotten a lot out of it. If you have felt that your time reading this book has been well spent and that the history and facts in it are important for others to know too, then please tell them about it. Perhaps you might want to recommend this book to your friends or share it with them. Even though the permanent government bureaucracy inside the executive branch of the federal government has become more and more powerful, the United States of America still has a constitutional form of government and will continue to have one as long as the people stay active. The people must be armed with the knowledge to make wise decisions. They must know their history to understand the origins of our present predicament. We must all do our part.

# ABOUT THE AUTHOR

Michael Swanson lives in rural Virginia. He received a Masters Degree in history from the University of Virginia and then dropped out of the college's Ph.D. program to enter the business world. He ran a hedge fund from 2003 until 2006 and runs the website wallstreetwindow.com.

He came back to the doing of history with this book. It covers the critical years from 1945 to 1963 in which the military-industrial complex became a permanent fixture in the American experience and the power elite connected to it ascended into the bureaucracies of the federal government. He is currently working on a follow up book that will focus on other aspects of this history in even greater detail.

If you would like to be the first to know when Mike's next book is released via email go to www.writermichaelswanson.com and sign up to his update list. Your email address will never be shared with anyone else and you can unsubscribe at anytime.

Word of mouth is crucial for any author to succeed. If you enjoyed this book, please consider leaving a review at Amazon or your favorite book seller, even if it's only a line or two; it would make all of the difference and be very much appreciated.

CPSIA information can be obtained at www.ICGtesting.com
Printed in the USA
LVOW10s2046040316

477812LV00041B/1927/P